MAHARAJAS IN THE MAKING

MAHARAJAS IN THE MAKING

Life at the Eton of India 1935–40

John Hill

The Book Guild Ltd
Sussex, England

First published in Great Britain in 2001 by
The Book Guild Ltd
25 High Street
Lewes, East Sussex
BN7 2LU

Typesetting in Times by
IML Typographers, Chester, Cheshire

Printed in Great Britain by
Antony Rowe Ltd, Chippenham, Wiltshire

A catalogue record for this book is available from
The British Library.

ISBN 1 85776 531 1

CONTENTS

To Margaret, Michael, Timothy and Nicholas

1

Introduction to India

Brilliant patches of scarlet and maroon bougainvillaea against the dead white walls of the villas that rose up the hillsides fringing the lovely bay of Tangier were my first glimpses of oriental splendour.

It was October 1935, and I was on my way to take up an appointment to teach English and other subjects at Aitchison College, Lahore, in the Punjab in the old India. Aitchison College was one of the five 'Chiefs' Colleges' in India which had been founded for the sons of the Indian princes.

They had been established by the Government of India, with financial assistance and general support from the princes, to 'fit the young chiefs and nobles of India physically, morally and intellectually for the responsibilities that lay before them' so that instead of being 'solitary suns in petty firmaments' they might be developed into 'co-ordinate atoms in a larger whole'. Some of the princes' firmaments were far from petty but I suppose that this rather turgid phraseology meant that, after the proposed education, the princes would be more in harmony with the administrative, social, fiscal, economic and political standards of British India, which, in general, were ahead of those of the Indian states.

The first to be set up, in 1870, was the Rajkumars' College, Rajkot, in the heart of the Kathiawar peninsula in Western India. This area contained a large number of Indian states, in general not of major importance and varying from the conservatively backward to the enlightened. The second was Mayo College set up in 1872 at Ajmere in the centre of Rajasthan then called Rajputana. Rajputana means the country of the sons of kings and Rajasthan

1

means the country of kings. As these names imply, it was the heartland of Indian chivalry and age-old traditions. Some of the latter were admirable, some the opposite. Daly College at Indore in Central India was founded in 1886. There was also the Rajkumars' College at Raipur in Central India.

Aitchison College dated from 1888 and was ranked with Mayo College and Daly College as one of the top three. It thought it was the best and did not object to being called 'the Eton of India'. The Punjab was probably the most important province in the old India and the pivot of British power and influence. The Punjab was in general less conservative than the regions in which the other Chiefs' Colleges were placed. Aitchison College reflected this in its educational policy and school life and so was more up-to-date than the others. This was shown by the day boys coming to school in Rolls Royces and Buicks rather than on the backs of elephants as some had done at Ajmere not long before. I was looking forward to my new career with a keen anticipation, which was not to be disappointed.

I had been to a county grammar school at Kimbolton in a very quiet, rural area of the then Huntingdonshire (after World War II it was one of the few schools admitted to the Headmasters' Conference). I took an honours degree in English with French as subsidiary subject at King's College, University of London. My fourth year was spent at the Institute of Education, University of London, doing a course in teachers' training. I had worked hard for my first term, as acceptance into the honours school for English was competitive, based on one's first term's work and examination results. Having achieved my objective, I did very little more work. I boxed for the University and played cricket for my college. I was chairman of the University hostel where I lodged. As a result I got only third class honours. My professor was kind enough to give me a good testimonial, saying that I would have done better if other activities had not taken up so much of my time. I also got a good testimonial from my tutor at the Institute of Education.

The depression in Britain in the 1930s made it difficult to get jobs even in teaching, which was not very well paid. In any case, I had a burning desire to see something of the world; India, in

2

particular, fascinated me. I had overlooked the advertisement in the *Times Educational Supplement* but a friend pointed it out to me and I applied. It was my first application for a job and, to my surprise and delight, I was accepted, subject to a medical examination.

The P&O vessel on which I was travelling was a microcosm of British Indian society. On board were civil servants of most departments and varying seniority; Army officers of all ranks; returning Indian students and merchants; a few minor princes; executives of various British firms in India, usually referred to as 'box-wallahs' by analogy with the Indian hawkers who took their wares round in boxes; wives and families of civil servants accompanied by the annual 'fishing fleet' of younger female relatives and friends coming to India for the cold season, where with so many eligible bachelors to every girl, they could have a good chance of marriage; finally a sprinkling of attractive Anglo-Indian women of the demi-monde. I enjoyed myself a lot on the voyage, but also commenced my study of Urdu (or Hindustani) from a Hugo's Hindustani primer.

We touched at Gibraltar with its pony-drawn *tongas* from India and its policemen with English bobbies' helmets. Port Said saw the *gali gali* men with the standard but extremely slick conjuring tricks. We passed several Italian liners with their rails crowded with Mussolini's soldiers going to the conquest of Ethiopia. At Aden I had my first sight and smell of camels.

The Gateway to India, and Bombay, lived up to all I had read but soon it was time for the long journey to Lahore on the famous 'Frontier Mail'. Through the squalid industrial slums surrounding Bombay, through the rocks and jungles of Central India, skirting the deserts of Rajasthan and crossing the wide plains of the Punjab we ground and roared our way; through heat and dust, night and day, a shuddering, thundering juggernaut, a thin self-contained column of modern communication across the ageless, little-changing face of Mother India; this old face scorched and crinkled by the heat of deserts, swept by the force of flood, rent asunder by violent earthquakes — yet since the coming of the railway and the British raj bound together for the first time into some semblance of unity.

To a newcomer the diversity of the teeming population, the ever-changing kaleidoscope of the multicoloured crowds that thronged all the stations we passed through, the strident calls of hawkers and the pungent, acrid smell were a source of constant fascination.

It was interesting to watch the transition of climate, vegetation and human types from Bombay to the Punjab. The further north we went the less lush and green became the countryside and the more virile and martial the people. We finally drew into the great fortress-station of Lahore in the evening of the second day after leaving Bombay.

I was to be a housemaster from the outset and would live in my house. For the first few days I stayed with the Principal until my set of rooms – bedroom with attached bathroom and dressing room, lounge and dining room and outside kitchen – were ready. The night before I was to move into my rooms the Principal made it known through his bearer that I would require servants in the morning. As soon as I was up next day I saw about forty men squatting outside with timeless patience waiting for my appearance. They were probably all good servants. One had been Winston Churchill's bearer. Nearly all the servants of Europeans in the Punjab were Muslims. I chose two after quickly deciding that I could not live up to the 'image' expected by Winston Churchill's former bearer. They were Maula Baksh, 'the Gift of God', six feet two of astringent, whipcord, hawk-faced Muslim orthodoxy to be my bearer, and Ibn Ali, a shorter, stockier Punjabi Muslim with a ferocious squint, to be my cook. Maula Baksh was a Rohillah whose homeland was a strip of territory called Rohillakhand along the boundary between Uttar Pradesh and Madhya Pradesh. The Rohillas had originally been an Afghan tribe who had come raiding down into India some centuries ago. They had found the living so much easier than in their harsh motherland that they had stayed on. As the generations passed they had acquired the language, culture and polish of their neighbours but had always retained the underlying virility of their ancestors. This made them exceedingly good types in general and excellent servants. The servants in India in those days were so uniformly good and faithful that once a European had picked his

4

servants they remained with him, apart from unusual circumstances, for the whole of his service. Maula Baksh stayed with me as servant, adviser on language, custom and etiquette and general guide, philosopher and friend until I left for Malaya with the Indian Army.

Ibn Ali turned out to be an excellent cook. After some time I found that I had had no curries. When I enquired about this, he drew himself up to his full height, such as it was, and said with great dignity, 'Sahib, I am a master of the French and not the Indian school of cookery.' He then produced a treasured heirloom. This was an old book wrapped up as reverently as the Holy Quran in a silk handkerchief. On one page were recipes in French, complete with illustrations, and on the opposite page was an Urdu translation. When I insisted that he make curries and pillaus he naturally turned out delicious dishes. One thing I could never have though, was bacon for breakfast, or, of course, any pork dish.

After acquiring servants the next thing to do was to acquire furniture. The general practice in India was for quarters to be supplied rent-free but no furniture was supplied. It was possible to furnish a house throughout with lovely walnut furniture made in Kashmir for four or five hundred rupees but at that time I did not have the necessary capital to spare and so like most other young men in Lahore I hired furniture from one of the numerous contractors specialising in this line. Whilst I was making the arrangements in his shop I was amused to hear him say to someone at the other end of the telephone in the most strident voice, '*Commode hai, bath-tub hai lekin piss-part koi naihin.*' 'There is a commode, a bathtub but no chamber pot.'

The furniture was certainly not a work of art but it was reasonable looking and strong and the total monthly hire amounted to about a pound. This seemed quite cheap but I realised afterwards that I had hired furniture for five years, for which I had paid more than it would have cost to buy a houseful of better furniture. When I had settled in, I was taken round to fulfil the prescribed social formalities, which consisted of writing one's name in the books kept by the Governor, the Chief Justice and a few other V.I.P.s, and leaving a series of cards at other houses – nearly all in little white boxes by the garden gate on which were inscribed the name of the

5

occupants followed by the, to me, enigmatic inscription 'NOT AT HOME'. It appeared that the object of the exercise was to drop the cards without coming into contact with the person on whom one was calling. If by chance one was so maladroit as to meet face to face it was apparently a social gaffe.

In due course I received a series of invitations to dinners, cocktail parties and other social functions. I soon perceived that the British in India, by a process akin to social osmosis, had adopted a caste system similar to that of the Hindus and that the staff of Aitchison College was of the highest caste. Not long afterwards I realised that the social station to which the society of Lahore considered the Almighty had called me was somewhat out of keeping with my salary – at the minimum of the scale. However, so cheap was the cost of living in India in those days that there was little real embarrassment. I found that I was able to live in some respects at a standard I have never subsequently reached, even if I could not save any money.

The Principal of Aitchison College was Barry, an Englishman who had come to the College from the well-known Bishop Cotton School at Simla. He was an able and energetic man. I came to realise that he was rather an autocratic careerist who had been spoilt by the considerable power that he exercised and by the adulation that even admirable Indians seem to think it necessary to give to their superiors. These two factors affected many Britishers in India. I was not inclined to be a yes-man and eventually our relations deteriorated.

The Headmaster, Dhani Ram Kapila, was a Punjabi Hindu of great physical and mental sturdiness. I remember unthinkingly trying to compliment him by saying that his physique was as good as a European's and instantly realising how tactless I had been. Later when Barry went on leave he acted as Principal. This was the first time that an Indian had done so and created quite a sensation in the College. He performed his duties admirably.

The First Assistant and housemaster of the other senior house, John Gwynn, was a Welshman who wore thick spectacles. One of his duties was to organise the games every evening, which he did with keenness and efficiency. He was the type of cricketer to whom the game owes so much – making up in dedication, determination and service to the game what he lacked in natural brilliance. He was a difficult man to dislodge who occasionally made some big scores and took wickets with an extraordinary left arm action delivered off the wrong foot.

I was rather embarrassed to find that I came next in seniority after Gwynn and above well-qualified and experienced Indians of more than twice my age. However, they seemed to accept it and it seemed so inevitable in India that I did so also. However, I decided to treat them without any assumptions of superiority. I eventually learnt that this simple courtesy had earned me the nickname of 'The Saint' amongst them. This also was embarrassing.

The most senior Indian after Dhani Ram was Gajindra Singh. He was a mild, bespectacled Sikh. Unusually for Sikhs, and the staff of College, he took part in no sport or games. Although a colourless character he seemed to be well respected by the boys.

On the other hand the Sikhs and Muslims who composed the rest of the senior Indian staff were mostly colourful characters. Syed Zulfiqar Ali Shah Bokhari was a sensitive intelligent Muslim from an ancient family, originally, as his name implies, of Bokhara in Central Asia, where a considerable proportion of the Northern Indian Muslims originated. He was a very good fast bowler and forcing bat, a fine tennis player, a good swimmer and water polo player; a lively, pleasant, witty companion and an efficient and loyal colleague.

Khan Anwar Sikander Khan was a Muslim who taught Urdu and Persian. He was a quiet scholarly type, who played no games, but was one of nature's gentlemen.

Harnam Singh Bal was a massive Jat Sikh with shoulders as wide as a barn door. In spite of his size he was a good, agile hockey player. As a batsman he put up the dourest defence I have ever seen. Hardly anything ever got past him. If he could not stop the ball with his bat he would stop it with some part of his body on the theory that there was always a chance that he would not be l.b.w. He would watch the ball like a hawk, stonewalling and brooding over his bat for long periods but occasionally coming to life with a thundering cover drive or tremendous six.

Bakshi Sahib was a Sikh who was rather a figure of fun amongst the boys. (A bakshi is a paymaster at an Indian prince's court and like all Indians he kept this hereditary title or nomenclature of calling.) Every movement he made seemed to be crab-like – even on the hockey field or the tennis court. He played tennis with an excruciating style and with invariable strange sidling movements. Such was his tenacity that he was very difficult to beat.

Shahbaz Khan was a great bull of a man who held the shot-put record for the north of India. He was immensely strong and the pivot of the College water polo team – a game which seems to me to require more strength and endurance than any other I know. Because of the climate it was a very popular game in India.

Chaudhri Ata Ullah was a Muslim of Moghul origin and a great authority on the vast subject of Indian history from the earliest times. He seemed very shy and nervous but when drawn out could talk brilliantly on Indian history, legend and folklore.

Mohamed Akram was a typical open, friendly Punjabi Muslim whose father had been Trade Commissioner in Leh in Ladakh and who held the All-India mile record.

I was lucky to have such colleagues and I learnt what I could from them of the language and traditions of the north of India.

We had three European ladies as matrons and a southern Indian Christian lady, who taught some of the youngest children. The rest of the teaching staff were 13 northern Indians, mostly Muslims and Sikhs but with a few Hindus. As there were only about 180 boys at the College it was an extremely good teacher-pupil ratio.

There was still, even for such relatively Europeanised Indians as the teaching staff of the College, complete seclusion of their wives. It was not the correct thing to mention their wives in conversation and, although I suppose they were nearly all married as that was considered a religious and social duty by most Indians of all types, I was never sure of this. Teaching was not only far more interesting than it would have been in an English school but it was also far easier. Indian students, even the sons of princes and great landowners, most of whom would never have to achieve qualifications to earn their living, seemed to be imbued with a love of learning and an industry unknown in English schoolboys. There was also a difference in behaviour. As in the Indian Army, disciplinary trouble was unknown.

In addition to my year's post-graduate training at the Institute of Education, University of London, I had received some personal advice from specialists in teaching English as a foreign language, after it was known that I was to be appointed to Aitchison College. I soon realised that to be really proficient in teaching English as a foreign language, one has to have a reasonable knowledge of the principles of the mother tongue of one's students. Not only does this assist in the main problems of syntax but also in the more detailed aspects of idiomatic equivalents. Above all it is a great psychological asset.

I decided that I must get a good teacher as soon as possible. There was a large circle of professional teachers of Urdu in Lahore known as *munshis*. They had more or less uniform tariffs. Graduated rewards were given by Government and even some commercial firms to their European servants who passed the language examinations at the various levels. It was compulsory to pass at certain levels. Most officers agreed to give their rewards to their *munshis* if they passed. As most of the *munshis* were on a panel from which some members of the examining board were chosen in rotation, it was fairly obvious what occurred.

I was too frugal and too proud to agree to such an arrangement and I did not employ a normal *munshi*. I was advised to study under the *maulvi* attached to the College Mosque. Work started at seven o'clock in the hot weather. There was no official routine after lunch (at which time Maulvi Mahmud Hassan put in his appearance) until evening games and prep. He wore the *shalwar*, the very wide and very baggy white trousers of the orthodox Muslim. In the hot weather a thin *kurta*, or long Indian style shirt worn outside the *shalwar* surmounted this. In the cold weather he wore a neat grey *achkan*, the Indian frock coat buttoned to the neck. He wore on his head the red *Turki topi* (or fez) without which no *maulvi* was ever seen. His regulation, neatly clipped, black beard did not vary a degree in the angle of its cut or a centimetre in its length from those worn by his myriad counterparts. He exuded the aura of rigid orthodoxy, self-righteous and self-sufficing, possessed by so many priests of all religions and a vague mysticism with, a hint of underlying fanaticism, typical of Islam. In truth, 'he was a verray parfit gentil' *maulvi*. He

9

obviously considered that the odour of sanctity was compounded of garlic and curry powder and he windily propagated this view after lunch.

We drowsed over Urdu primers and readers and wandered along the byways of Islamic theology, history and philosophy. Luckily, he knew practically no English and so our rambling discussions were carried on in Urdu as far as he was concerned. This was another advantage over the professional *munshis* who spent most of their time either teaching their English pupils English grammar or improving their own knowledge of idiomatic English, usually including many phrases not to be found in any textbook.

I have never been able to write a well-formed hand in English and *Maulviji* (*Ji* is a suffix added to names and titles in Urdu to show respect) despaired of the angular irregularities into which I deformed the Urdu script, closely based on that of Persian. Calligraphy is a much-respected art amongst Muslim scholars and from the *maulvi*'s smoothly flowing pen, the graceful curves of the Urdu letters dropped like a necklace of beautiful black pearls. It would have taken a vernier to measure the difference in the curves produced by him and by me but even to the naked eye the effect was grotesquely different. I managed to pass the requisite exams in due course.

I soon settled down to the normal domestic routine. After dinner, Ibn Ali appeared and suggested the menu for the next day. This was approved or amended and, at the due time, appeared on the table faultlessly cooked. He went to the market on his bicycle very early every morning and bought such articles as meat, poultry, pigeons, quails, teals, partridges, fish, fruit and vegetables. Eggs, milk (sold by weight), cream and bread were delivered by their various suppliers. Dry goods and groceries such as sugar, tea, flour, jam, etc. were obtained from shops. Rich or improvident sahibs gave their cooks a rupee a day (then equivalent to about 8p) for all the goods mentioned above which had to be purchased from the market. I was too careful for that and every evening, or as often as I was in, Ibn Ali gave his account of the day's purchases at the same time as settling the menu for the following day. He made no notes but never missed the smallest trifle. No doubt he made a small profit on his accounts but this did not worry me. My daily expenses worked out to about 12 annas and from time to time I replenished the cook's imprest as necessary.

I started off my two admirable servants on 23 rupees a month rising on an incremental scale of a rupee a month for every year's service. They found their own food and being orthodox Muslims never had the slightest desire to touch mine. These rates of pay seem pitifully low but they must have put these two in the upper income brackets for India. About the same time I saw an advertisement in a Lahore paper for an Indian woman doctor to do *zenana* work (that is work confined to women) with no private practice at a starting salary of 30 rupees a month. Maula Baksh and Ibn Ali and their large families lived on less than a third of their pay. They were in a position to save money and become men of substance.

The relationship between servant and master was patriarchal. Service was given from early morning to late night with unfailing courtesy, dignity, cheerfulness and efficiency. Indeed it did not stop even in the middle of the night. When the terrible Indian hot weather developed I took to sleeping out of doors under a tree. (Some Indians thought it was very dangerous to sleep under a tree and fully expected me to contract some inexplicable but dangerous illness.) I had a reading lamp and a fan wired to the tree. I slept with the fan on except for about an hour before dawn when the night watchman turned it off. It rarely rains in the north of India for the six months following Christmas but there are occasional violent thunder or sandstorms. Maula Baksh invariably appeared like Aladdin's genie at the side of my bed at the outset of any storm – sometimes before I was awake myself. Sometimes he might have been woken up by the first clap of thunder, sometimes called by the night watchman. On other occasions it seemed little short of miraculous that he was ready to save my bedding before the first drop of rain could fall on it and to carry it and the bed into the house.

The washing was done by a professional *dhobi*, or laundryman, who called twice a week, unless specially called. I gave him a monthly contract at a fixed rate equivalent to about 63p to wash all my clothes and household linen. An alternative arrangement was an anna (equivalent to one old penny) an article, irrespective of size or shape, with two annas for the 'flying *dhobi*' service or the return of the article the same day.

I always thought that the work of the *dhobi* was one of the most miraculous of all the strange occurrences of the East. They washed the clothes in water, which was often quite muddy, dried them on the muddy banks of rivers and produced them whiter even than the white of any detergent advertisement. Maula Baksh, of course, checked the clothes out and in from the *dhobi*. He also continuously checked, brushed, pressed, aired, mended and sewed buttons on my clothes. Whenever I travelled he packed with professional perfection and an unfailing memory of where he had put everything. There was no need to tell him what to pack or to check that nothing had been left out. All that was necessary was to say where I was going, for how long and what I was doing. He had travelled widely all over India as a gentleman's gentleman and his knowledge of the climate at different latitudes and altitudes in that great subcontinent was invaluable. Quetta, Lahore and Bombay in the Christmas season, for example, were in three distinctly different climatic zones – respectively, the very cold with night temperature far below freezing, the bracingly cold and the rather hot and muggy. On a long journey it was cumbersome to take unnecessary clothing but distinctly uncomfortable not to have clothes that suited the climate.

Maula Baksh ran many errands for me when I was at home. He also made small purchases in the bazaar for me, probably making some minute commission. As the price to me was less than if I had attempted to buy the articles myself I regarded the commission as legitimate bearer's perks. He often accompanied me on long journeys and exacted the correct respect and service befitting what he considered was my exalted station. It was at a far higher level than I would have ever considered appropriate myself. He also insisted on due respect to his own august position.

He was a good horsemaster and could exercise the necessary supervision over the *syce* or groom to see that he was looking after and exercising my horse properly and not eating part of its rations. He could control junior servants with Olympian hauteur.

He was always at the door when I entered the house. He usually insisted on taking off my shoes, chafing my feet and bringing me a pair of slippers. He massaged me if I was stiff from too much riding or violent exercise.

There were very few modern bathrooms in Lahore. Most bathrooms consisted of a brick-floored room with a brick ledge behind which was ensconced a zinc tub. I got the largest I could find in Lahore.

One of many essential functionaries in the Indian system of servants was the *bhisti* or 'Heavenly One'. Gunga Din was a *bhisti* and is his prototype. Perpetually bowed under a heavy goatskin of water he was a ubiquitous figure on the Indian scene. Where there was no piped water supply the women would go to the wells to get their domestic supplies but the *bhisti* was a professional water carrier – sometimes employed by the community or an institution but often selling his water by the skinful or cup.

Although there was no piped water for bathroom or lavatory there was a piped drinking supply on the Aitchison College compound. There were a few *bhistis* on the establishment. Their main duty in the hot weather was to go around sprinkling water on the roads and paths to lay the dust and on the verandas and floors of houses, which were all brick built, to reduce the heat. In the cold weather their main duty was to collect and heat bathwater in drums or four-gallon petrol tins and bring it to the bathrooms. Maula Baksh naturally ensured that the volume and temperature of the water was just right. When satisfied he came in and announced 'Ghusul taiyar hai, Sahib' – 'The bath is ready, Sahib.'

Behind the bathroom was another little room with one article of furniture – a commode or thunderbox as it was more commonly called. This was usually of imposing size and often of polished mahogany. The commode was attended by the sweeper, the lowest of all castes in India but, as customary in India in all such matters, invariably and euphemistically called *jemadar* or *mehtar* – that is chief or leader. Without them the whole country would soon come to a standstill as was proved years later when they went on strike in Delhi. It almost paralysed the Indian war effort. In central and south India the sweepers are often women. In the north they are men – often dark, hairy and small, showing in their appearance their non-Aryan, sometimes aboriginal, origin, and, in their

13

perpetual air of apologising for their untouchable presence, the centuries of servitude which their conquerors had imposed on them by all the religious, social and economic sanctions of the caste system.

After I had been living with these two servants for some time a realistic Hungarian friend I had made suggested that two full-time servants plus the *bhisti*, *jemadar* and others provided by the College were excessive for a bachelor even in India. He suggested that I should ask Ibn Ali if he would do bearer's work or Maula Baksh if he could cook. I certainly did not want to lose Maula Baksh and so I adopted the latter course. This paragon then confessed that he had once been the second cook at the best hotel in Lahore – run by an exacting Italian manager. He had kept very quiet about it as he preferred bearer's work. I said that he would have to do the cooking as well for a few rupees a month extra. In addition to all his other qualities he turned out to be a superb cook. He was naturally also a polished waiter and competent organiser of parties, arranging for extra help and equipment if necessary.

With a large number of young bachelors in Lahore, club life was quite a prominent feature of our mode of existence. There were three European clubs in Lahore. The most senior, sedate, exclusive and expensive was the Punjab Club of which I had no aspiration to become a member. The largest club, to which the majority of Europeans and a few Indians belonged, was the Gymkhana. This was typical of the large gymkhana clubs of a big centre in India. It had an imposing Palladian-mansion-like building with a ballroom and a smaller room for cocktail dances, bars, facilities for billiards, badminton, table tennis, a good library and extensive subscriptions to English periodicals and magazines. Around the club building was a fine cricket ground and about 30 tennis courts – half in use and half under irrigation turn by turn. Incidentally, the Indian clubs had a system of 'markers'. They were Indian professionals in all the games played at the club who would play with any member when desired for practice, and were also capable of coaching. The markers were superb games players and could play any type of shot desired for practice at tennis or squash and bowl any type of ball in the cricket nets. They were brilliant at billiards and snooker.

14

I saw a Pathan boy in his very early teens, playing in baggy *shalwars* and not very good shoes, with a rather badly strung racket, completely trounce the champion of the Army in India in a practice squash game. The excellence of some Pathans at squash was not widely known then but since the war, of course, their pre-eminence has become widely known.

I took to staying at the Club rather late on occasions and hit upon a mutually acceptable arrangement with Maula Baksh. He did not mind how late I came back provided on return I ate the excellent dinner he always had waiting for me. The Club provided a very good dinner at a reasonable price. There was always a great deal of impromptu hospitality and so sometimes I did not want to eat at home. All that Maula Baksh requested was that I should ring him up by ten o'clock to say whether I was coming back to eat or not, and, if I was coming back, if anyone else was coming with me.

Cooks in India always seemed to prepare meals somewhat before they were needed. An indispensable adjunct to any kitchen was therefore a hot case. This was a portable cupboard-like affair lined with zinc with perforated shelves. The cooked food was placed on the shelves with pots of glowing charcoal in the bottom. The food was thus kept warm indefinitely and did not seem to be any the worse when eaten. One must admit that, in the hot weather, meat and fresh vegetables had lost most of their taste.

Another remarkable feature about Indian cooks was that in addition to being able to produce a meal in a reasonable condition hours after the even normal late dinner hour, they could at short notice turn a dinner for one into sufficient for two, three or four. Perhaps, normally, food was wasted.

Maula Baksh was thus prepared from early morning to late night to perform a multitude of functions with unfailing efficiency, honesty, loyalty and cheerfulness.

In return for these manifold services all I had to do was to pay him regularly and to be his 'mother and father'. For example, when his family home was destroyed by a flood he naturally came to me for an advance to build another and naturally I gave it to him – a hundred rupees sufficed.

There was a great freemasonry amongst Indian servants. If one was giving a party and had insufficient glasses, crockery, or any other equipment, it was all arranged by the servants who borrowed from other servants without their masters being aware of the arrangement.

However, I must say that I was very surprised one night when I was asked to dinner at Government House and I found that the table decorations were based on roses which I was pretty sure grew nowhere else but in my own garden.

I have mentioned before that one could find a contractor in India for every human need. Later, when I moved into a bungalow in the College grounds, I had my garden maintained by a contractor. For 13 rupees, one pound, a month he cut the lawns, kept the tennis court marked, the flower beds neat with basic cuttings and seeds supplied by himself and also kept me similarly in basic vegetables grown from his own seeds.

Life and work at Aitchison College were very different from and more interesting than at an English school. The College compound was the biggest in Lahore and had the best grounds and gardens, surpassing those of Government House. The school and residential section of the compound was divided into quarters by two long drives, one of which was flanked on both sides by peepul trees and the other by the banyan or Indian fig. These two stately avenues gave a sense of form to the compound. Beds of beautiful flowers rotated through the seasons. Some of the most colourful were the beds of cannas, scarlet, orange, maroon and yellow splashes of colour which were very heat-resistant. In the cold weather thousands of potted chrysanthemums were laid out round the quarters and school buildings. The head groundsman supervised this and took a great pride in his careful arrangement of colour effects.

The main school building consisted of an Indo-Saracenic style building adorned with minarets and cupolas. In the centre was a large marble-floored assembly hall, flanked on either side by three not very large classrooms. There were two boarding houses for the senior boys each accommodating about 40 boys (I was the housemaster of one of these) and a somewhat larger house for junior boys largely under the control of English matrons. There was also a contingent of day boys. Each boy in the senior houses had a spacious suite of his own and each boy had his own servant accommodated in servants' quarters at the back of the house.

The different races, castes and clans of the Punjab usually had a distinctive style of dress. Most even tied their turbans in special ways. This emphasised the likeness between some of the boys and their servants who had a great deal of influence over their charges – a mixture of loyalty, respect and yet authority which is found only in an old family retainer. Some of the servants had remarkable facial likeness to their young masters and I suspected that they were often their father's unacknowledged illegitimate half-brothers.

There was a mosque for Muslim boys and staff; a temple for Hindus and a *gurdwara* for the Sikhs. Later a more modern classroom block and a laboratory were built. There were fields for hockey, cricket and soccer, a large number of tennis courts, a riding school, stables and huge cavalry parade ground, a swimming pool, staff quarters of all kinds, hospital, farm and a total population in the compound of about a thousand.

All the playing fields except the cricket field, and all the tennis courts were in duplicate. Because of the long rainless hot season it was necessary to irrigate playing fields on alternate weeks. Thus one set was in use one week whilst the other was under water and drying out. Irrigation was so arranged in Lahore that every Thursday was a dry day. It was thus hoped to check the breeding of mosquitoes. (There were still myriads, however.) Some of the best turf I have ever seen was grown under this system of irrigation – without it grass was impossible in the dry season.

The children and young male relatives of all the princes in the north of India, with the exception of the Maharaja of Kashmir, came to the College. Theoretically, entry was confined to certain families whose names were inscribed in a register of the princes and landed gentry of the north of India. However, attempts were being made by the Principal to extend the field of entry and I think that it was in reality open to most who could afford the fees.

The premier prince of the Punjab (and the Chief and leader of all the Sikhs in existence) was the Maharaja of Patiala. He was an Old Boy. Like a number of other princes he maintained a town house called after the state – in Lahore. He had five sons (by

17

different mothers) at the College when I was there. Some had already passed through – others were coming on. Like other princes he had a Guardian's Department, invariably headed by a European, to look after his children. The Patiala princelings lived in Patiala House and were driven to school every day in a venerable Rolls Royce from the Maharaja's stable of cars, of the vintage that looked like a huge cigar-box on wheels. It had a very high ground clearance. I later did some shooting trips in it and we would often drive across country on the flat Punjab plains completely ignoring roads or tracks. Once we got stuck in a ditch and were pulled out by the strange combination of camel and buffalo yoked together.

The Nawab of Bahawalpur, the premier Muslim prince of the Punjab, maintained a house actually in the College compound where his sons lived. They were Haroon-ur-Rashid and Abbas Ali. The ruling family of Bahawalpur can trace descent from the Abbasid Caliphs of Baghdad and it was a source of great satisfaction and interest to me that I was teaching English to the descendant and namesake of the famous Haroon-ur-Rashid. He certainly possessed the same high degree of intelligence and was modest and pleasant. Apart from the princes, most leading public figures in the Punjab had also been to Aitchison College. When the war broke out the grandsons of the Governor of the Punjab and the children of several senior European Government servants were enrolled. The school was controlled by a Board of Governors of which H.E. the Governor of the Punjab was *ex officio* Chairman. The princes retained a very keen interest in their old school and responded generously to any appeal for help – financial or otherwise.

There was considerable inter-communal fanaticism in the Punjab and we hoped that the influence of the school reduced this. All communities mixed and ate together at school. This latter was a considerable achievement and although the food for Muslim, Hindu and Sikh boys was prepared and cooked separately they all sat down together haphazardly at one table and ate together. This was probably the only place in the Punjab then where all communities would eat at the same table. Many of the old boys became Ministers in provincial governments and the inter-communal co-

18

operation that they had learnt at school softened the rivalry of public life and politics.

I gradually became acquainted with the fascinating multiplicity of racial types in the Punjab and the complex and minutely graduated hierarchy of Indian occupations.

Although Sikhs were not the predominant race in the Punjab – these were the Punjabi Muslims – they were in a majority at the Aitchison College. This was chiefly due to the large contingent from Patiala headed by the Maharaja's own family. Most of these Jat Sikhs were fine physical specimens – tall, well-built, fair, handsome and good athletes. Many became Army officers, either in famous north Indian regiments of the Indian Army proper, or in the Patiala State Forces. When I visited the College after the war as a captain, at which rank I had stayed during three and a half years in Japanese prison camps, I found a number of my former fourth form pupils were majors. The Sikhs, of course, never shave or cut their hair and the elder boys had incipient beards and side-whiskers, which looked rather untidy. In general they had large lustrous eyes and lashes which would be the envy of any film star – as long as panthers' whiskers. When young and in their native dress with their long hair flowing over their shoulders it is sometimes impossible to tell Sikh boys from girls.

The Punjabi Muslim boys were a little fewer in numbers than the Sikhs. Apart from the sons of the Nawab of Bahawalpur we did not at that time have the children of any major Muslim prince from the Punjab. They were chiefly from the families of lesser princes and great landowners. Solid, straightforward boys, tough and vigorous – of the stock that formed the backbone of the Indian Army.

There was also a fair sprinkling of Hindus. There were some sons of rulers of important Hindu states in the Punjab but they were chiefly the many minor princes of the Simla Hill states or their sons. They were mostly proud, conservative, withdrawn Rajputs alhough a few who had been more exposed to modern influence were humorous and sophisticated. When the Muslims extended their conquests in the north of India, most of the Rajputs had withdrawn to the protection of the deserts of Rajasthan. Some had carved out small kingdoms in other inaccessible parts of

19

India, and so many Hindu states had Rajput rulers (including Nepal) whereas the common people were of quite different stock. This applied to most of the Simla Hill states.

One of these boys, the heir to a remote petty principality in the Simla Hills, was so orthodox that his servant alone cooked for him and he ate alone in a corner of his room facing into the corner. It was said that if the shadow of anyone else fell on his food he could not eat it. His father spoke no English but always came and chatted with me when he visited the College, invariably carrying a silver-headed walking stick. What is more he shook hands with me with apparent pleasure. This I took to be a sign of true courtesy, as I believe that it entailed the considerable inconvenience of a ritual bath afterwards.

One of the Hindu boys was the young Chamba prince. His family claimed, with I believe a good show of reason, to have persisted as a ruling dynasty in their state longer than any other in the world. The claim went back well before Christ and apparently in those days they paid tribute to China. The boy was a sickly only son. He had a European guardian but never seemed to want to take part in the rough and tumble of sport. In this he was encouraged by his father who was unlikely to have any more children and wished to preserve the line with a fervour in which family pride was reinforced by religious beliefs. Like many other heirs to eastern power his life was thought to be in some danger and there was a constant guard of his somewhat outlandish native soldiers on Chamba House, where he lived as a day boy. I can still picture his skimpy body and thin, pinched, anxious face under his turban tied in the characteristic peaked style of his native parts. He was not over-intelligent and his general burden was increased by the fact that it was considered only fit and proper that in keeping with his high position and orthodoxy he should have special instruction from a Pandit in Sanskrit – a subject that was not normally taught.

Some of the Hindus were fat, flabby sons of an immensely wealthy family of Lahore *Lallas*, a merchant caste. The sons of the *Lalla* had similar Sanskrit lessons – doubtless as part of a social climbing campaign.

We had a sprinkling of Pathans – tough, intelligent, race-proud and as temperamental as violin strings, and a handful of uncouth, hirsute, jungly, incomprehensible and uncomprehending Baluchis, who were, of course, all Muslims. Some were so uncivilised that they had never even played cricket before coming to school! One would become the Khan of the inaccessible state of Las Bela, in the deserts of Baluchistan, when he became of age. He joined the school well beyond the average age of entry. Before joining he had had private tutors, some of whom were French, and his French was rather better than his English. As he was generally backward the other boys in his class were younger than he was. He rather resented this, and school discipline in general, and took refuge in questionable French novels. I had to be rather strict with him and I used to wonder what would happen to me if I ever found myself within his jurisdiction.

Another Baluchi boy, Khwaja Baksh, was a fat, jolly boy who eventually made the cricket team, which distinction was never achieved by the first cricketing Nawab of Pataudi. Although later an outstanding test cricketer, I was told he was better at hockey at school. Khwaja Baksh was the son of a Baluchi *tumandar* or tribal chief whose raids and general unreliability had caused considerable trouble to the British raj. He was finally pacified and one clause in the settlement was that he should send his son to Aitchison College on a scholarship said to be worth 5,000 rupees a year.

After the boy had been at school for a year, the old chief turned up at my house one day accompanied by a band of the most ferocious desperadoes it is possible to imagine. They were all armed either with modern rifles or long *jezails* whose sharply angled butts were mounted with chased silver (I looked anxiously for notches) and all had the tribal sword or *talwar* pushed through cummerbund, or waist-sashes, or festooned in some manner around their middle person. Some had long spears to complete their armament. None of these could speak a word of anything except Baluchi, which is unknown in Lahore, some 700 miles from their native area. The son tactfully said that his English was inadequate to do justice to his father's eloquence, which I quite believed. I eventually found someone who could speak Baluchi and Urdu – I then found that my Urdu was unequal to the father's or the interpreter's eloquence. Finally through another interpreter

21

from Urdu to English, I learnt that the father had arrived to claim the 5,000 rupees said to be the value of the scholarship for a year. It was then the turn for my eloquence and patience to be tested.

When eventually I had made the position clear the old chief accepted it philosophically enough but with obvious inner misgivings as to the Sahibs' system. He may, of course, have been pulling my leg or just trying it on. His fruitless journey had taken the better part of a week, consisting of a day's ride on a horse, a similar ride on a camel, a long, bumpy 100 or so miles in a car over desert tracks, crossing the Indus in a steamer and then about 400 miles by train to Lahore.

There was a vast army of College servants, which would have been the despair of any organisation man. British trade unions have not even begun to appreciate the subtleties of job demarcation compared with the skill and tenacity built up by Indian castes over about 3,500 years. Each was a cog in the wheel and each had his niche in the vast edifice of caste and creed. Two with whom I came into early contact were the *daftari* and the chief *chaprasi*.

Daftar means an office in Urdu. The functions of our *daftari* were to give out paper, exercise books, textbooks, chalk, rulers and similar impedimenta. He was in clothes, manner and beard a simpering affectation of the *maulvi* of whom he was obviously an aspirant acolyte.

A *chapras* is a large brass badge or plate, in the middle of a belt worn round the waist on which is inscribed the name, initials, insignia or coat of arms of the firm, Government department, institution or individual for which the *chaprasi* acted as a messenger. *Chaprasis* were usually illiterate. This was an oriental tradition. They could not therefore read even nameplates or simple directions but their local knowledge was encyclopedic, their memory infallible and, within their convention, their integrity unimpeachable. There were several at Aitchison College. The doyen of the *chaprasi* corps was a short, slight Punjabi Muslim version of Sir Thomas Beecham called Mohamed Sorba. He was permitted a slightly more luxuriant beard than a *maulvi* or *daftari* and an air less bowed down by the affairs of God or state. He combined the dignity of an ambassador with the speed of movement of a mongoose. When not darting about on foot or bicycle on some errand or delivering some chitty, *chaprasis* kept watch outside the office door of those to whom they had been assigned. It was said that they exacted *dasturi* or customary tribute from all who would have audience of their masters. The amount was in direct proportion to the officer's seniority.

The rank and file of *chaprasis* (and similar menials) jumped off their bicycles at their own insistence about forty yards before they met me on a College road and walked a similar distance past me before remounting. Those junior in the scale of things to *chaprasis* increased the distance slightly and Mohamed Sorba, reinforced by the dignity of age and many years of service, decreased it slightly without ever overstepping the immutable boundary fixed in his mind between dignity and impertinence. Distances were, of course, increased in the correct ratio for those senior to me. The chief *chaprasi* was reputed to keep hens and produced objects, which he claimed to be hens' eggs, which he sold to me for a few annas a dozen.

A *chaprasi* from Lloyds Bank in Lahore once walked right into a class where I was teaching and presented me with a letter from the Manager telling me that I was overdrawn.

The chief groundsman was Jalal-ud-Din (Grandeur of the Faith) a long thin Muslim, swathed in an ankle-length cloth as worn by Punjabi Muslims of the type that work in the fields. He had a multitude of coolies under him but always seemed to be on the run between one urgent job and another – supervising the marking out of tennis courts here, the setting up of cricket nets there and of some other equipment elsewhere. It was said that he kept himself going by eating opium.

The riding master was a Rajput Muslim, a retired *dafadar* from a crack cavalry regiment. Magnificently moustachioed and always impeccably accoutred and turbaned he was the epitome of smartness in his bearing and movements and exuded that air of really professional military virtue that seemed to reach its apogee in Viceroy's Commissioned Officers of the Indian Army.

The electrical *mistri*, like every other electrical *mistri* in the north of India, was a Sikh. The Indians had largely turned modern occupations into castes. Baba Singh appeared at call to deal with fused lights and other emergencies. He also appeared to herald the approach of the hot weather by fitting ceiling fans, which, for reasons unknown, were stored away in the cold season. He was bulky and bush-bearded and his taciturnity was broken only on rare occasions but always to disclose some domestic trouble.

The chief clerk was a small, podgy Punjabi Muslim whose bulging eyes always seemed to reveal some inner sorrow. I suspected him of taking drugs. His manner was a compound of extreme obsequiousness tempered by flashes of supercilious scorn when I occasionally queried some deduction in my monthly salary. He was invariably correct.

It was mid-October when I arrived in Lahore, the onset of the cool season, and the cool season in the north of India is one of the most delightful climates in the world. The days are warm and sunny, without being oppressively hot, and the nights are cold and bracing. Three blankets are often required. As the cold weather progresses a very considerable difference develops between the sun and shade temperatures so that one can be playing tennis or cricket in hot sunshine and on walking into a building one is struck by a sharp drop in temperature. There is also a very sharp drop of temperature as soon as the sun sets.

All the masters used to take their share of coaching games in the evening. One of the reasons that I had been appointed to Aitchison College was my supposed ability to play cricket. This proved somewhat embarrassing as I found myself coaching boys from Patiala, including some of the Maharaja's sons, who had just finished a course of coaching under English professional test match cricketers. I considered that their technique, style and natural ability were considerably better than mine. However, they were respectful, tolerant and keen to improve even further. I was very interested later to see that one of the Patiala boys that I had coached played for India and two Muslim brothers played for Pakistan – one opening the batting and the other the bowling for Pakistan. I do not flatter myself that my efforts had much effect on their ability.

Masters usually had three duty evenings a week, either playing with or coaching the boys. I always played some game on the other evenings of the week. There was usually some sport going early every morning somewhere in the school compound – swimming in the swimming pool, rugger touch, P.T. or tent-pegging. Rugger touch was a game that I have never seen elsewhere but was played a lot at Aitchison College. It was based on rugby without any scrums or tackling (which would not have suited the Indian temperament). The player with the ball had to pass immediately he was touched or when he had carried the ball five paces. The game was very fast. I normally played some sport every morning as well as evening and so kept very fit.

2

Elephanta, Ellora and Ajanta

During at least one holiday every year it was the custom for a party of boys to proceed on an educational tour in the charge of two masters. It fell to my lot to go on one of these during the Christmas holidays at the end of my first term, and my companion in charge of the party of about 25 boys was Chaudhri Ata Ullah. We were to go down by train to Karachi, thence by ship to Bombay, do some sight-seeing in Bombay, visit the old cave temples at Ellora and Ajanta and then return by rail to Lahore.

To get to Lahore Station we had a whole fleet of *tongas* – those light Indian vehicles designed to seat four, two facing forwards and two backwards. The driver crouched on the shafts if the four seats were taken; there was room for a suitcase or so under the seats. These vehicles were drawn by equine hacks, which were encouraged to move by queer obscene noises made by their drivers in what phoneticians would call labial plosives. The *tonga* ponies urged themselves forward by a system of jet propulsion, which they had discovered long before it was utilised to propel aeroplanes and which was facilitated by the poor, mouldering fodder given to them.

The advance party arranged the luggage in the right compartments and the rest of us followed later. We had a flashlight press photo taken on the platform and about 9.40 p.m. the great train pulled out on its 800 mile run to Karachi.

First of all the route followed the line of the Ravi across the broad, relatively fertile plains of the Punjab – gradually running into sandier country with a lower rainfall until we reached the

26

valley of the Indus proper. After that came the Sind desert, sand and camel thorn, where cultivation was only possible by means of irrigation. The railway then ran through desert and semi-desert country for the rest of the way to Karachi.

My bedding roll was laid out for me for the night but it was very cold and the blankets kept slipping off and I did not get much sleep. At 5.30 a.m. the next morning it was still very cold as we drew into Multan. We made a quick contract with a pleasant-mannered, bespectacled, English-speaking young fellow for *chota hazri* for the whole party. This consisted of the inevitable fare – smoky toast with rancid butter and bitter tea. By the time it had been prepared we did not have sufficient time to finish it before the train pulled out. This was no unusual occurrence and the waiters simply travelled with us to the next station where they got out with the trays and crockery.

A great deal of life is very public in India and no more so than on a railway station. The greater railway stations in India are huge transit camps with dozens of families camping for days on the platforms waiting until they can find room on a train or for other purposes known only to themselves. I found that every big station had a smell unique to railway stations in India. It was not very pleasant and seemed to be comprised of sooty smoke, steam, hot engine oil, dust, sweat and urine.

There was always bustle and noise at every station. Pedlars selling tea, milk (hot and cold) and all kinds of food – all these in two varieties, one for Hindus and one for Muslims. So fierce was religious fanaticism in the north of India that Muslims and Hindus had to draw water from different wells in each village and the same principle was extended to watering-places on railway stations. There was one for Muslims at one end of the platform, another for Hindus at the other. For religious purposes it was different water but if one traced the pipes back a little way they usually joined the same main not far outside the station. However, honour or prejudice was thus satisfied.

Ice and soft drinks were raucously hawked to the cry of '*Soda baraf wallah*'. *Pan* was stridently advertised and also cigarettes – both European and Indian – to the tune of '*Pan, biri, cigret*'. '*Garm cha pi Hindu*' denoted hot tea to be drunk by Hindus and

27

'*Garm cha pi Mussulman*' the same for Muslims. Hot milk for Muslims was hawked around to the low bass strains of '*Dudh, shudh Mussulmanion*' which was an effective contrast to the strident, high-pitched notes of most of the salesmen. ('*Dudh*' means milk, '*shudh*' has no meaning whatsoever but follows a rather whimsical and pleasant usage in Hindustani that some words are sometimes coupled with a meaningless rhyming word. With proper Hindustani words the accompanying word always has to be the same but I once heard an Indian say '*Cabaret, mabaret*'.) Amidst all the competing cries in Hindustani, at one station one hawker went slowly along the platform muttering 'Very good, decent food'.

We stopped for lunch at Khanpur where we had local Muslim food, which the non-Muslim boys seemed happy to eat – chicken curry, rice, *chapattis* and curried mincemeat balls, with a sweet largely made from rice. This was ladled out on the platform with half the local population looking on and commenting. The quality was not very good but I lived up to the appetite expected of an Englishman in India by eating a lot, as I was quite hungry by then.

After Khanpur we were right in the Sind Desert and except for irrigated areas nothing grew but scattered groups of stunted camel thorn. Here and there deep wells had been dug in the desert to reach underground water. This was brought to the surface by what is known in India as a Persian wheel. This consists of an endless vertical chain of buckets, usually made of goatskins, sometimes of cowhide or large earthenware pots, fastened to a great wooden wheel with a diameter big enough for the bottom of the wheel to reach water-level. This was geared to a wheel on a horizontal plane, which was turned by the endless plodding in a circle of a camel or bullock. The water came to the surface a few gallons at a time. A good proportion was lost by leaking or overflowing from the buckets before it spilled into a runnel whence it flowed away on its life-giving mission. The screech of the un-oiled Persian wheel was heard in irrigated areas all over the Middle East.

The apparently dead sand of the desert was very fertile and wherever the water reached luxuriant growth sprang up. We passed numbers of these little oases of mango and citrus trees, sugar cane, grain and pulse crops together with rice. There are huge irrigated areas in Sind supporting towns on what was formerly barren desert. We had earlier passed a junction on which there was the strange noticeboard reading 'Change here for Baghdad, Kut-ul-Amara and Sulaimaniya', all the names of towns in Iraq. These were irrigation colonies that had been developed after the First World War and settled by ex-soldiers from the Indian Army who had been in Iraq and gave these names to the little towns they founded. These development projects had been remarkably successful chiefly due to the fact that they were run on sensible lines backed up by discipline based on military tradition, often with former Viceroy's Commissioned Officers in positions of leadership.

By dinner time we had reached Rohri, the nearest station to the great Sukkur Barrage across the Indus. This is not very high as the waters of the mighty Indus are not impounded by it but only partly diverted, but the Sukkur Barrage feeds, I believe, what is still the greatest area in the world irrigated by one dam. It is certainly a far greater area than that irrigated by some of the famous and spectacular high dams in the USA.

Dinner was waiting for us in the refreshment room at Rohri but we decided to see the Sukkur Barrage first. We walked across the railway bridge over the Indus just as the sun was setting. The soft pink tints of the setting sun threw into picturesque silhouette the strange outlines of native fishing boats on the broad bosom of the Indus and gave a fairy-like glow to the islands in the river and the great barrage stretching across the horizon.

We had had to walk further than we anticipated and there was some danger that we might lose our train. Luckily a local train passed us very slowly. I think that the driver must have sensed our predicament and that a combination of Indian helpfulness and the informality of trains in India led him to slow down. We all clambered on to the running boards of this train. However, it was stopped by the signals before we got into Rohri. By the time we had run to the station our train was due or overdue to leave and we still had not had our food. The stationmaster readily agreed to hold the train until it was put on board. Such practices are commonplace in India. Indeed, it was the custom for the stationmaster on smaller stations to ask a European he considered of any standing,

29

'Can I please now start train, Sahib?' Only a few trains a day ran on the long distance routes. The journeys were measured more by days than hours and minutes. Thus, important trains were known by names such as *The Frontier Mail, The Deccan Queen*. Others were given numbers such as the '7 Up' or the '13 Down'. I once heard an irate Indian, whose long wait had exhausted even Indian patience, sarcastically ask the stationmaster, 'Is this today's "7 Up" twelve hours late or tomorrow's twelve hours early?'

After we had all showered and changed on the train, as we were hot and sticky from our exertions, dinner was served by travelling waiters. It was much the same as lunch but of a considerably better quality. One of the waiters knocked over a large iced-water container and flooded the carriage. As he left he asked me for a chitty commending his diligence and efficiency. They certainly displayed nerve and agility as they often balanced on the running board passing trays through the windows as the train was travelling, even opening the doors and passing in and out of the carriages and the servants' compartment at the end, which was serving as a pantry.

I had a friend at the RAF station at Drigh Road, a station before we reached Karachi, and I had arranged for him to meet us there and show us round the aerodrome. We arrived at about 6.15 a.m. and were met by my friend. Our *chota hazri* this time was provided through Service channels but was exactly the same as the previous day. It appeared to be a well-established tradition in India that Europeans and the more well-to-do Indians on long train journeys could only start their day on smoky toast, rancid butter and bitter tea. In the course of my journeys I got so used to smoky toast that eventually I found toast that was not smoked rather insipid.

Luxurious Chevrolet taxis drove us to the aerodrome, the chief feature of which was the 200 foot mooring mast built for the ill-fated airship R101 which was destroyed in flames at Beauvais on its journey out to Drigh Road. It was built and based at Cardington in Bedfordshire and when I was at school I often saw it passing overhead on practice flights. I never thought then that I would see the tower built to receive it at the other end of the earth.

There was also a huge hangar – 980 by 200 feet – built for the airship. The Hannibal airliners, which were then the largest in use and used for the flights from England were completely lost in this hangar. We also saw the Atlanta-type monoplanes, which made the journey from Singapore to Karachi.

We reached Karachi by train about 10 a.m. and were besieged by the usual mob of coolies fighting to handle our luggage. It was all stacked up outside the waiting room and as we had some time before we had to board the ship we left the luggage in charge of one coolie, unpaid so that he would not be tempted to leave, after the usual fierce battle with the others over their tips.

Although a good proportion of the personnel in the Royal Indian Navy came from the north of India, it is a long way from the sea and thirteen of the boys had never seen the sea. We therefore dashed down to Clifton Beach and it was very interesting to see the reaction and hear the comments of those who had never before seen the 'black water' as Indians call the open sea.

Back to the station, where we could not get all the luggage in the available taxis and so we had to have two Victorias – those old-fashioned horse-drawn vehicles named after the Empress of India, which were still common in Karachi and Bombay although they had long disappeared in the land of their birth.

We erected two soaring unstable pyramids of luggage on these two rickety vehicles and each was surmounted by a triumphant servant. Needless to say we had taken some servants with us. It was really necessary to have servants on any long journey in India as, although, or perhaps because, millions of people seemed to be constantly on the move, India was not a country geared to modern travel facilities or comforts. It was really a great boon to have some help in getting food, cool drinks, ice to cool the compartments, defending them against intruders, making one's bed, controlling coolies and generally acting as a buffer between one's self and the heat, dirt, noise and general unreliability of any arrangements.

As we reached the docks we had once more to force our way through clamouring coolies before we could get on board. I left a guard on the luggage and went ahead to check on the berths. This done I returned to find a fight in progress between two rival gangs of coolies both anxious for our patronage. We managed to settle this and get the baggage safely on board the British India ship *Vita*, of 4,961 tonnes, built on the Clyde an indeterminate number of years earlier.

It may be wondered why we were taking a ship from one major city in India to another but the answer is that it was the only reasonable way to go. India is a vast country and although the British built a magnificent railway system some of the natural obstacles were so great that there were big gaps in it. Karachi and Bombay are separated by the vast swamps and waterways of Kutch, impassable to road or railway. The boundary between the provinces of Sind and Gujarat ran through this region in those days. It was not very clearly defined in places. Thus this area of swamps, worthless except for some poor seasonal grazing in the dry weather, became, ironically, a cause for one of the wars between India and Pakistan. Above these swamps stretch the deserts of Sind and Rajasthan and the rocky mountains and boulder-strewn jungles which lie between the deserts and the plains of Central India. It was possible to go by narrow gauge railway through Hyderabad (in Sind and not the dominion of the Nizam in the Deccan) up almost to Jodhpur and down again to Bombay but that was very slow. The quickest rail route would have been to retrace our steps 800 miles back to Lahore and thence 1,200 down the trunk route through Delhi, Kotah and Baroda to Bombay.

I woke up next morning to find the ship lying off Mandvi. There was an indescribably motley collection of people fighting their way on and off the ship with their women, their babies, their bedding, their luggage, some of their household furniture, their food, their water-pots and last but not least their noise and their smell.

Plying between ship and shore was a collection of very graceful native craft. High at both ends, they had one stiff stumpy mast. From the mast, suspended at the point of balance and lying, as it were, diagonally to the mast was a long boom. This was fastened to the mast by some primitive but effective type of universal joint, which made possible a full manipulation of the large, single, triangular sail, which was fastened to the boom. Sailors swarmed up and down the boom and mast to reef and unreef the sail with the speed and agility of cats. They climbed hand over hand up a rope, which they held between their big and second toes.

32

We lay off Okha about 9 a.m. where there was a repetition of the earlier performance but on a smaller scale, and passed Dwarka about noon. We lay off Porbander about 4 p.m. I found all these ports, somewhat off the beaten track, very interesting.

About noon the next day we reached the outer harbour at Bombay and passed a graceful fishing fleet of vessels similar to those met previously on the voyage. When we came to disembark at Bombay the confusion and struggling amongst the coolies was worse than ever before – far worse than when I had arrived on the ship from England. We finally got the baggage off and proceeded to the Cathedral School where arrangements had been made for us to stay. It was there that the boys and I had our first taste of another type of Indian food. This was *mouli*, a delicious, sweetish, mild fish curry cooked in the cream squeezed out of the flesh of grated ripe coconut. I met this type of cooking later in Fiji.

The next morning we set out to sail across the harbour to Elephanta Island to see the famous caves. It was a lovely trip but very hot. It took us nearly two hours to reach the island, which was very tropical in its vegetation and the contours of its hills, and in great contrast to the brown, arid austerity of the Punjab.

The caves were at one time a Buddhist hermitage. Like many places with religious associations in India they had changed hands between Buddhists and Hindus. In the seventh and eighth centuries A.D. a considerable number of Hindu images and religious carvings were made in the caves. The two most important were the Trimurti or combined representation of Lakshmi, Shiva and Vishnu and the Shiva Nataraga or Shiva dancing. The latter gives a great sense of power and rhythm and yet the expression on the face is one of normal serene calm.

The caves were great places of pilgrimage and like all such places in all countries collected crowds of people who battened on to the pilgrims. We were met by a crowd of these as we stepped ashore. They varied from a group selling walking sticks at prices from the equivalent of a halfpenny upwards to a whole battery of snake charmers each with his flat-covered basket and an evil-looking cobra. Most of the snakes were rather dormant and I gathered that although it was warm enough for us just down from the Punjab, it was too cool for the snakes to be very active. One fellow, eager for our money, played his pipe madly and slapped the basket several times without arousing the snake.

These were the first old Hindu shrines that I had seen and I must confess that although the caves and carvings were most impressive I got a most uneasy feeling of being completely steeped and overwhelmed in primitive beliefs.

The mud and sand of the flats near the water's edge were covered with small crabs insolently aware of the orthodox Hindu's aversion to taking life. There were stairs to the top of the hill and palanquins could be hired by the lazy or feeble. We climbed to the top and had a delightful view across the harbour to Butcher Island and Bombay.

During the next few days in Bombay we went round the Mint, *The Times of India* press, a big cotton mill and one of the many film studios around Bombay. At this time industrial slums in Europe were deplorable but the few I had seen were not nearly as bad as some of the evil-looking and evil-smelling quarters that we saw around Bombay. In one place cows and goats were sharing a room with human beings who looked dirtier than the animals. At the cotton mill we were shown with pride 'an ideal canteen' for the workers, which I thought was indescribably depressing and shabby.

Walking back to one suburban station after a visit to a works we came across vast swarms of the gigantic fruit bats, or flying foxes, that in India take over certain large trees that appeal to them. They kept up an incessant high-pitched twittering and squealing, the sum total of which was so great as to make conversation difficult. They hovered around in the twilight, fantastically silhouetted against the sombre sky in the flames coming from fires made of cow-dung pats, and seemed to me to be incarnate spirits of evil.

Officials of the very efficient Bombay Port Trust, which had its own fire brigade and generated its own electricity, showed us all around the harbour and its installations. Bombay had berths for the largest liners east of Suez and until the building of the King George V dry dock had the largest dry dock in the world.

We went to lovely Juhu Beach and drove along the Marine Drive up to the high-class residential area on Malabar Hill where most of the houses are owned by Parsi merchant princes. The word Parsi means Persian in Hindustani and the Parsis originated from Persia whence they were driven when Islam rose to power in that country. They fled to India and maintained the old Persian religion of Zoroastrianism which is based on the worship of the sun, fire and light. They are a relatively small community for India numbering only a few hundred thousand but they are largely wealthy merchants. They were mostly confined to Bombay and its environs and in India were seldom found outside Bombay Presidency. Some established big businesses in Aden and elsewhere. Although they did not appear to be very interested in politics their wealth gave them considerable influence. In a country where millions were on the verge of starvation the two poorest Parsis that I came across were the engine-driver of an important train (a job of considerable standing in India) and a taxi-driver who owned his own taxi. They have a great reputation for honesty as well as astuteness and in an environment which is not noted for honesty in commerce they seem to have proved the maxim that honesty pays. They are very fair in complexion and their women are often of outstanding beauty and sophistication. The Parsis are a proud and closely-knit community. One has to be born a Parsi, as they do not accept converts and intermarriage with other communities is frowned upon.

The Parsis have unusual customs with regard to the disposal of their dead. I was informed that when a Parsi dies they break the bones of the corpse in a peculiar way and smear the body with *ghi*. The first dog that is found is then introduced into the room and if it licks the body it is regarded as an omen that the soul will find peace in Heaven. After this, the body is placed on metal grills in tall round towers fitted above pits of quicklime. It is not long before the bones are picked fairly clean by vultures and kites, which abound everywhere in India but particularly in the neighbourhood of the Towers of Silence on Malabar Hill. The bones fall through the grill and are absorbed by the quicklime.

It is said that afternoon tea-parties on the lawns of the Malabar Hill are sometimes disturbed by a frightened vulture or hawk dropping a partly eaten limb at the foot of the tea-table!

We left Bombay about 11 p.m. one night on the Lucknow Express. This was a fast electric train and was the then acme of comfort in rail travel in India. We had a fine corridor coach with a full-size bath in the bathroom. Most of the boys had not seen electric trains before they came to Bombay and were fascinated by them.

Our journey on this swift, smooth and comfortable train did not last very long as about 3.30 a.m. we reached Manmad and had to change over to a steam train on His Exalted Highness the Nizam of Hyderabad's metre gauge railway which was to take us on the next stage of our journey to Aurangabad in Hyderabad State. Aurangabad was named after Aurangzeb who was the sixth Moghul emperor and lived from 1682–1717. Akbar, the greatest of the Moghul emperors, had been amongst other things a great administrator and a ruler of tolerance. He built so well that in spite of inadequate successors his administrative structure lasted a century after him. Although becoming progressively weaker it survived in significant details into the British raj. Aurangzeb was a superstitious religious fanatic. He used Aurangabad as a base in his operations against the Deccan at the end of the seventeenth century. His operations here were successful on the whole but combined with his campaign against the Rajputs and his enmity to the Sikhs, started the dissolution of the Moghul Empire.

Near Aurangabad is the fortress-city of Daulatabad, which means the Fortunate City. This was founded in 1338 by Mohammed Shah Tughlak, King of Delhi. He thought that Daulatabad, which had then another name, was an auspicious place as the climate suited him. There was also the threat of a famine at Delhi. He therefore decided to move his capital from Delhi, 600 miles to the north.

Tradition says that with typical oriental despotism he ordered every living soul to leave Delhi and that all except two – a blind man and a cripple – obeyed. The blind man was taken to the top of a tower and pushed off. The cripple was tied to the tail of a cart and dragged off on the start of the long journey at the end of which only a leg arrived. The project was a failure and the capital reverted to Delhi.

The focus of the great complex at Daulatabad was one of those many high, steep, flat-topped hills that rise abruptly 500 feet from the plains of Central India. Great cubical cliffs formed a series of

36

plateaux superimposed one on the other like a column of children's bricks in descending size. Each face of the massif was like a giant staircase cut out of the natural rock.

A great outer perimeter wall ran for miles around the base of the hill. It had enclosed palaces, a residential area, a mosque with a soaring minaret, baths, bazaars, barracks and a huge Hathi Hauz or pit where the war elephants were kept. Little remained of all this.

Each successive tier had its perimeter wall and fortifications and they were crowned by the final citadel on the top-most peak. The only way to get from one level to the next was either to scale the cliffs and the walls or to go through a tunnel cut through the rock and protected with massive wooden doors scaled with murderous spikes to discourage the use of war elephants as battering rams. Every approach was guarded by ancient cannon with a bore of 10–12 inches. At the time of any assault on the tunnel, if it appeared necessary, charcoal fires were lit at the head of the tunnel and deadly carbon monoxide fumes were wafted down on to the attackers with huge fans.

This was a grim reminder that war is savage in all ages. As a contrast not far away we visited the tomb of an old Muslim saint. Like a somewhat smaller Taj Mahal in its symmetrical setting of stately rows of formal cypress trees, with its beauty duplicated by reflection in its flanking marble-lined pool, it was a welcome oasis of peace and coolness amid the surrounding heat and dust.

The next items on the programme and the highlights of the tour were visits to the world-famous cave temples at Ajanta and Ellora. The Ajanta caves were dug out and carved and painted from the fourth to the sixth centuries A.D. The mighty caves of Ellora were carved out of the solid rock in the seventh and eighth centuries.

Both places were somewhat off the beaten track and we arranged to visit them by car. The caves and images of Ajanta are carved out of the hardest type of rock on a tall, almost vertical cliff, which forms one side of the valley of a small river. Towering horseshoe cliffs shut off the end of the valley, which must have been a place of real seclusion at the time when the unbelievably difficult work was carried out. At each of these places the senses were overwhelmed at the boldness of the conception and the

37

magnitude of the effort which must have been needed to complete the work. Both at Ajanta and Ellora, caves and temples of Buddhist, Brahmin and Jain origin are found. At Ellora there are 34 in all. Some served as monasteries, some as temples and some as hermitages.

Strangely enough, the first Hindu Vedas apparently wrote against image worship and the construction of images. Originally Buddhism also was opposed to the representation of the Buddha in sculpture or painting. Later this outlook was changed and art and religion became intimately connected as in medieval Europe. Religion inspired art; and painting and sculpture taught religion to an illiterate peasantry. This educational aspect of art seems to have been successful as the illiterate Hindu peasantry have a deep understanding of Hindu culture and religion.

The Buddhist caves were adorned mostly with representations of Buddha only, in the various conventional poses – usually sitting cross-legged and typifying contemplation. The Jain caves were relatively simple and austere. The Brahmin caves had a wealth of statues and some were somewhat oppressive with carving and detail. All alike, however, were true works of art of an arresting verisimilitude and many showed an irresistible verve and *joie de vivre*.

The famous 'Cathedral' cave at Ajanta was amazingly like a cathedral. Even the rock of the roof had been carved. A cave I found noteworthy at Ellora was a Buddhist monastery with a dining room in which refectory table and benches had been fashioned from the rock.

In addition to the sculpture, the Ajanta caves have frescoes painted by Buddhist monks. Buddha himself taught his followers to avoid women, not even to look at them for in that danger lies and one may be diverted from the true path. These monks must have forgotten what their master said as there are many paintings of women of all kinds at Ajanta – princesses, beauties, courtesans, dancing girls, singers, musicians – standing, seated, lying, walking in processions, attending court, making themselves up – women of all types in all attitudes and poses, some of which are not considered religious in the West.

There are also paintings of the conquest of Ceylon (Sri Lanka), showing ships transporting war elephants. In fact these old monks, although supposed to be living a life of seclusion and contemplation, seemed to be intimately aware of all facets of human nature, current affairs and past history. All the hustle and bustle of contemporary Indian life is portrayed as well as the calm, serene detachment of the Bodhisattva.

The Ajanta frescoes had a powerful and lasting influence on Indian painting and still arouse the keen interest of the art critic as well as the historian and archaeologist.

After the visits to Ellora and Ajanta there was little left to do but to make our way back to the main railway line and return to Lahore via Bhusaval, Khandwa, Jhansi, Agra and Delhi.

The tour was meant to be an educational tour for the boys. It had certainly been educational for me also. I had had my first glimpses of the fascinating variety of scenery, climate, race, religion and way of life of the teeming sub-continent that was India. I determined to extend this knowledge at every available opportunity.

3

Settling in

I soon learnt that I was the first European on the staff of Aitchison College who had not been to Oxbridge and a major public school. No one was in any way unpleasant to me over this but I was a little inhibited at first. A good proportion of the box-wallahs were also public school but not university types. On the whole they had more self-confidence and social poise than I had but I did not find any evidence that they were better educated from the academic point of view. Europeans in India had a very different way of life from anything to which I had previously been accustomed and I was, by nature, rather shy.

I had invitations to a considerable number of dinner parties and got to know a good number of people. Some of the invitations were to rather formal dinners. I was amused to see that, if there was any doubt, the ladies were rather anxious to see who was considered the 'senior lady' and seated by the host on his right. It was her duty to lead the ladies out to the drawing room when dinner was finished whilst the men had a few more drinks and a smoke. She also decided when it was time for the party to break up. It was not 'done' for anyone to go home before her.

There seemed to be an obsession with precedence or seniority in India. I saw tables of precedence hanging from the wall in some *dakh* bungalows or government rest houses. I never found out the significance of their provision. They integrated civilian and military officers into one long hierarchical list. Perhaps if there were a clash for accommodation the junior officer would have to pack up and go elsewhere.

Young women were greatly outnumbered by young men in India. When I became a little more known, a hostess would sometimes ring me up and say frankly that, for once, the men were outnumbered at a dinner she was arranging and ask me to come along, sometimes at short notice, to preserve the symmetry of her table. I had some quite good evenings in this way. Mrs Barry had a degree in domestic science and was an outstanding cook, caterer and hostess. She herself did not, of course, cook in India but she knew how to superintend and train her Indian cook properly and got very good and varied meals from him. She devised good menus and kept a note of guests at all of her parties to ensure that guests did not get a similar meal twice running.

Apart from the heat and difficulty of cooking in Indian kitchens, Indian servants would have resented any undue intrusions into the *bawarchi-khana* or kitchen by the memsahib. Indeed, it was really a case of 'what the eye does not see the heart does not grieve over'. Indian kitchens for European houses were primitive and not very hygienic and always in separate outhouses at a little distance from the house. The stove was a block of dried mud with round holes in the top. The cooking was done by charcoal placed in these holes over which the *dekchis* or aluminium saucepans with a flat lid were placed. The *dekchis* and lids had no handles but protruding rims running round. Roasting was also done in these vessels when the charcoal was heaped up around them. They had the advantage of stacking one in another in descending order of size. I was always astonished to see how Indian cooks could pick up very hot utensils without seeming to feel the heat. It was either oriental stoicism or sorcery.

Barry himself hardly ever took any classes being very busy with many administrative matters. The burden of teaching was not onerous on any of the staff. Classes were small. I had about four or five classes a day.

The recommendations and testimonial of my tutor at the Institute of Education had played an important part in my appointment. He was anxious that I should not let him or the Institute down and, therefore, tried to get me briefed as well as possible before I left for India. As a result of discussions that I had with him and specialists in teaching English as a foreign language it was agreed that the best books to use were an Oxford series on a word frequency basis. That is, the early lessons were based on the most frequent words in the English language. English vocabulary was gradually extended, used and learnt in the order of the frequency of its use in the language. After I had discussed the matter with Barry these books were bought and put into use. The series had special editions for a number of countries, including India, for which they were intended so that the subject matter would be suitable and not cause cultural or historical clashes. The stories were reasonably interesting.

The boys were very keen to acquire a good English accent. Many of the sons of the princes came into contact with quite a number of well-educated Europeans who were on their father's personal staff or civil servants of their state. With a fairly good English accent and a reasonable command of the language they were rather snobbish towards those Indians who spoke with a *babu* accent. (One of the Indian staff spoke to me critically about a European we had on the staff for a short time who had a regional accent.) Some of the boys who had not come into contact with Europeans at their homes before coming to school, or some who lived in more outlandish parts where there were very few Europeans, were not so good at English and spoke with an 'Indian' accent.

I could never quite understand why some professional and academic Indians who had a complete and fluent mastery of English, both formal and idiomatic, and often considerable powers of oratory, never lost their *babu* accent. I suppose that it was because they had been originally taught by Indians, or even self-taught, and had not mixed enough with native English speakers at the formative stage of their English accent.

The general method that I adopted was to read a passage and then get a boy to read it. I would then correct any pronunciation mistakes and we would practise the correct pronunciation. New words would be explained and discussed and I, and then the boys, would use them in oral sentences. Sometimes I would make them do oral and written exercises to illustrate English idioms, constructions and the use of words. Formal grammar was kept to a minimum but I ensured that they knew enough to understand the essentials of the construction of an English sentence and the principles of punctuation.

I taught them the basis of sentence construction on a simple analogy, which occurred to me. The sentence was a train, the verb the engine, the nouns the coaches, the conjunctions were the couplings, the adjectives were the different classes of coaches, the adverbs showed the way in which the engine was run and the interjections were the bangs of the buffers. I gave them dictation and also essays to do in class and as prep. Prep was done in the evening and occasionally I looked in to see how things were going. I gave them written English examinations at the end of every term.

As I gradually acquired a knowledge of Urdu, learning a significant amount in discussions with the boys, I came to appreciate the differences between the constructions and idioms of that language and English which caused pitfalls for Northern Indians trying to learn English. I adapted and, I hope, improved my teaching accordingly. Eventually I drafted a book based on my experience to help Northern Indians to teach themselves English or to help Northern Indian teachers with their subject. Unfortunately the draft was lost or stolen when I was on war service. This was a pity, as undoubtedly it would have sold well amongst the millions of school children in that region eager to learn English.

There was an avid and never-satisfied thirst for learning amongst Indian students. Qualifications of some kind were the only way that many Indians had of rising economically above the hardships into which so many of them were unfortunately born. Many Indians also had very keen minds and great intellectual curiosity. They sought learning and wisdom for their own sake and for the prestige they carried. Indian publishers exploited this to the full by printing never-ceasing streams of text-books. These were mostly written by Indians but sometimes by Europeans. On occasions Indian publishers managed to get Europeans in the teaching world to give their names to textbooks that they had not actually written or, less reprehensibly, got fairly prominent Europeans to write forewords recommending such books.

A snigger ran around educational circles in the Punjab when a book of the former category, actually written by an Indian, but purporting to be written by a senior European in the Education Department, contained in the preface an acknowledgement by the real author thanking another European in the Education Department for correcting the English of a book ostensibly written by his senior colleague.

I had been warned about these dangers and was soon exposed to them. A plump, smooth-spoken Sikh publisher called to see me one evening and said, 'Sahib, if you are writing geography textbook for me, I am giving you rupees three thousand.'

'Geography is not my subject.'

'No matter, book is already written. All I am wanting is your name.'

It then came to light that the book was written in Urdu.

I said, 'My knowledge of Urdu is such that I could not possibly fully understand the book or claim to have written it.'

'No matter, Sahib, I will get book translated into English. Then if you approve it, we can say that you wrote it in English and I got it translated into Urdu for publication.'

Any European with a degree could have accepted such offers but in my case the fact that I was on the staff of 'The Chiefs' College' would have sold a large number of copies. He was most persistent and it was a pity that I could not take advantage of such an easy way of making money.

Apart from teaching English, I was supposed to teach that mysterious subject known as 'General Knowledge and Current Affairs'. The school had a good library, including a wide selection of papers and periodicals, and we used to retire to the library for this subject. The boys would study the papers and magazines, ask questions and informal discussions would develop on topics of interest. I used to try to use these as pegs on which to hang little lecturettes, which I hoped tended to stimulate their intellectual curiosity and to broaden their knowledge and outlook. The discussions broadened mine.

I gave all forms an examination in general knowledge at the end of each term. To come top carried considerable prestige as the boys thought it was a sign of their sophistication and westernisation.

I suppose that this was the foundation of my own interest in, and acquisition of, general knowledge which enabled me to get into the semi-finals of *Mastermind* many years later.

There was another aspect of routine which differed from an English school. The hunting of jackal with a pack of foxhounds was a well-established sport in the north of India. This took place in the cold weather and in Lahore the meets were about 5 a.m. on Sundays and Thursdays. I found that if I could arrange to have the first period free on Thursdays I could hunt on Thursday as well as Sunday. It gave me time to finish the hunt, shower and breakfast and take the second period of the day in good time. The College authorities were very sympathetic and arranged my timetable accordingly. The school timetable started at 7 a.m. in the hot weather but not until 9 a.m. in the cold weather.

Jackal hunting was good exciting sport. We had some fast gallops over the flat Punjab countryside and some very good jumps over minor irrigation canals. However, there were no fences as in the English countryside, only a very occasional dried mud wall.

Sometimes on Sundays after the hunt we would all assemble at someone's house for a sociable breakfast.

Another pleasant Sunday diversion was to ride out a dozen miles or so to one of the very comfortable bungalows that were sited at intervals along the main irrigation canals. We used to start early in the morning. By the time we arrived the sun was fairly hot and we gave ourselves and our horses a most refreshing swim in the great Bari Doab irrigation canal. Its waters moved without a ripple but the current was so swift that only the strongest swimmers could hold their own against it. Then sausages, bacon, tomatoes and eggs, fried over a campfire, with some cold beer. After this a rest – and we could motor back in the cars, which had been brought out by drivers who had also brought out the *syces* who rode the horses back home.

Towards the end of the hunting season but before the onset of the hot weather proper, we used to have a few mounted paper chases on Sunday. These were good fun.

The Auxiliary Forces (India), which were the equivalent of the Territorial Army, contained a number of Light Horse regiments of which the Punjab Light Horse was one. A good proportion of the Europeans in Lahore belonged to this unit. The chief role was, I assumed, internal security. I do not think that its military value otherwise was very great. However, there was a noticeable *esprit de corps* and social unity amongst its members and it enabled one to play cheap, second grade polo and so I soon became Trooper Hill. I remained Trooper Hill for several years and found my eventual promotion to Lance Corporal and Section Leader far harder to achieve in peacetime than it was to rise from Second Lieutenant to Captain and Company Commander in war.

I have stated above that the Punjab Light Horse did not appear to me to be of great military value. There was an Urdu jingle about us which went —

> *Ek hath men zin*
> *Ek hath men ras*
> *Kis hath men kirch*
> *Punjab Light Harse?*

which can be translated —

> One hand on the saddle,
> The reins in the other,
> Which hand is the sword in
> Punjab Light Horse?

This was said to be an Indian appreciation of our military efficiency but I believe that, with fairly typical British self-mockery, it was written by a member of the unit. I think it would be fair to say that in a real battle, like Wellington's troops, we would have frightened our commander more than the enemy.

We wore brown riding boots with spurs, khaki riding breeches, khaki tunic with a bandolier for cartridges, chain mail over the shoulders and a heavy protective *topi* or Wolsley helmet. This was a fairly practical kit for riding and looked quite smart, but riding boots are quite unsuitable for dismounted action as anyone who has tried to march any distance in riding boots or cross ground rapidly on foot whilst trying to take cover when necessary will

46

soon find out. It was obvious that in this respect efficiency had been sacrificed to smartness. However, we did little dismounted action.

Personal weapons for troopers were swords and rifles (carried in a leather bucket on the right side). One of the first things that had to be learnt was never to dismount without the rifle in the right hand. We also practised with lances and revolvers. Various NCOs and all officers had the latter. We had one or two Hotchkiss guns carried on pack horses. There was also a motor section, which we in the cavalry ignored and despised.

I found the standard skill at arms test interesting and exciting. One began at the starting line with sword drawn, took a brush jump, engaged a dummy on the right side, took another jump, and then engaged a dummy on the left side, leaving one's sword in the second dummy, then drew a revolver, loaded with blanks, from one's holster and shot balloons in various positions on the ground and on jumps. By this time one should have arrived at a lance with its butt stuck in the ground. This was pulled out of the ground and grasped at the point of balance and also gripped under the arm as one's horse was galloping towards a ring suspended at a height between waist and shoulder to a mounted man. This ring, about 3–4 inches in diameter, was supposed to be picked off by the lance, after which one continued on a straight gallop, picked a peg out of the ground with the lance and continued on to the finishing line. There were points for accurate performance of these tests and penalty points for exceeding the time limit.

We all went through the set cavalry riding school, as the ability to stay on a horse, and do most things on a horse, is not considered an ability to ride in the Army unless it is done in the Army style. I eventually passed the course but the Staff Sergeant Instructor (SSI) made it clear that he regarded me as far from being a star pupil and his theme song was ' 'ill, your 'ands and your 'eels'. I learnt after the war that a school friend of mine, with whom I used to do my first riding in Huntingdonshire, later became Equitation Officer in the Life Guards, but even that would not have impressed my tyrannical tutor.

The first horse that I acquired had already been in a cavalry regiment and knew the drill far better than I did. Like most

47

experienced cavalry horses he could also pick out the words of command and provided I maintained my seat in a completely passive manner he went through the required movements like a blasé ballerina.

We had many hilarious incidents whilst on parade. On one occasion we were practising mounting. We had the command 'Prepare to mount' *ad nauseam* but each time someone did something slightly wrong. It became ineffably tedious. In order to prevent a mental breakdown I decided to vary the monotony by placing the ball of my right foot in the stirrup. I did this several times without being spotted as the SSI was concentrating on an even duller boy than myself. I thought it would be some time before we got the final command. However, to my horror there came a staccato and stentorian roar of 'Mount'. I do not quite know what flashed through my mind in the split second between command and execution. If I had not obeyed it would have been a very awkward fumble to change feet and I should never have arrived in time. I suppose that reflex action really decided the issue. I flung my left leg over the horse's head and neck and found myself in the saddle after a fashion but, of course, back to front. The Staff Sergeant Instructor never varied the assessment of my IQ that he made on that occasion.

I had become friendly with a charming Irish couple. He was a retired major from an Indian cavalry regiment and a real horse master. They gave me a celebrated horse called Blotto. Some years before, he had got into the final or semi-final of the Qadir Cup – the celebrated annual All-India pig-sticking championship in which the horse not the rider is entered. To do as well as this in this very gruelling event meant that the horse and rider had to have the very highest cross-country ability. Blotto was also good in the cavalry riding school, at showjumping and on parade. I did not look him in the mouth but I should have been warned. He was absolutely and unalterably vicious but far too clever to be consistently vicious, choosing his moments, one of which I shall describe.

I rode Blotto to one early morning parade at the Punjab Light Horse riding school. The parade consisted chiefly of going down the set jumping lane, with its different types of jumps, and unbuttoning and buttoning up our tunics as we did so. Blotto performed perfectly which was better than I did. During one rest period I vaguely heard the fellow next to me say that I had my horse on too tight a curb chain. I was beginning to learn about Blotto then. I always kept him on a very tight chain and took no chances. I paid no attention to the remark.

After the parade I walked Blotto out of the riding school, through a few back streets and on to the Mall – the *Thandi Sarak* or Cool Road as the Indians call it – the long, wide, tree-lined road that runs through Lahore. Like most of these roads in Indian cities, it had a tan riding track down one side. I thought I would take a slight risk and let Blotto out into a controlled, a very controlled, canter. I slackened the reins slightly and in three paces he was doing a split-ass gallop down the side of the main street of a city of half a million inhabitants. He was quite uncontrollable and I then realised that my neighbour in the riding school had completely slackened the curb chain. I was, of course, using the standard cavalry double bridle. If the curb chain is kept reasonably tight the lower rein can exert such leverage that a horse has to stop or run the risk of having its jaw broken. The upper rein has the effect of a straight snaffle and if the curb chain is too slack the lower rein loses all its leverage also.

We galloped flat out down the Mall. The sentry outside Government House gate took several rapid and rather unmilitary paces backwards. I then realised that we were approaching quite a busy crossroads and apart from traffic hazards I would have to pass a fairly wide expanse of smooth tarmac before I regained the riding track. I tried everything that I knew to stop Blotto – such as sawing the bit and pulling one side with both hands but it never even caused a falter in his stride. Luckily it was still fairly early and there were few pedestrians or vehicles. A traffic policeman was on duty. Very sensibly he gave me right of way. We skated across the tarmac at high speed. I had no more control over Blotto's direction than over his speed. Shortly after the crossroads, he took a side turning and I guessed that he was returning to the home of his former owners. This was a narrower road with no riding track. We were galloping down the earth side of the road. I saw to my horror that we were approaching a telephone pole with a wire stay

49

running diagonally down the track at almost the height of my chest. Blotto was heading straight for the opening between metal pole and wire. I lay down as low as I could along his back and neck and felt very thankful that I was wearing a heavy protective helmet or *topi*. We passed through without a scratch.

The next obstacle was a series of deep gravel pits, some with several feet of water in them. I decided to try to steer Blotto towards them, thinking they must, if not stop him, at least slow him down. He liked the look of them and went for them himself. He then showed the qualities that he must have shown in the Qadir Cup. The only effect that they had was a slight shortening and irregularity of his stride as he sailed from one bank to another across several hundred yards of these formidable obstacles.

We were now approaching his former home but I was far more tired than he was. As we reached the gate of the house he was still doing a pretty good gallop after over two miles of assorted terrain. He jinked violently through the gate. I was too exhausted to retain my seat and fell heavily on the drive just as my friends were coming out for their morning ride.

They told me afterwards that they had been out for several preceding mornings with a guest who was learning to ride. There had been an incident each morning in which their guest had got into a bit of trouble. Just before I landed with a crash on their drive the wife had said that they would be able to have a quiet ride by themselves that morning at least.

I had recurrent trouble with my back for years afterwards which must have been caused by this fall. Twenty years later my back was x-rayed and the bones found to be bent.

When the staff of regular cavalry instructors heard of my fall they said that there was nothing wrong with Blotto but it was only that I could not ride him properly. A sergeant with long service in a British cavalry regiment offered to take over Blotto for a bit and show how he should be ridden. It was not long before Blotto put him off and broke his leg. This gave me considerable satisfaction in view of the persistent sarcasm I had endured from the sergeant on parade. The only person who could ride Blotto properly was the wife of the couple who formerly owned him. He was like a lamb for her. Possibly Freud could explain this.

Annual camps were tremendous fun. We had various mounted competitions including jumping and there was always a grand finale enacting Red Indians attacking the United States cavalry or Arabs the Foreign Legion or something which gave a lot of us an excuse to gallop madly about screaming at the top of our voices.

There was also a concert at the end of every camp. At one of these a war scene was being enacted. A scientific but absent-minded friend of mine was in charge of noises off representing cannon fire. He was firing off blanks in small saluting cannon. He absent-mindedly touched one of these off just as someone was passing fairly closely in front. The victim had most of his trousers either blown or burnt off. A vital part of his anatomy was also burnt and he was in hospital for several weeks.

At one of the Church parades I noticed the Anglo-Indian next to me, who was not noted for his religious fervour, putting his heart and soul into a hymn. I was somewhat surprised. When we came out, he mounted his horse but went straight over the top and off the other side and I realised that he was dead drunk. However, he remounted, managed to retain his seat this time and completed the parade without being detected. Another advantage of being in the cavalry.

We carried out various manoeuvres which mostly simulated dispersing rioting mobs or guarding vital points. On one of the latter, Trooper Hill, alone with his charger, and twenty rounds of ammunition, was dispatched to guard an important bridge on the outskirts of Lahore. I remember thinking at the time that it was a token force rather than a task force. There was a friendly Punjabi village nearby. The villagers looked after my horse. I remembered to retain my rifle and sword but spent most of the day chatting with the villagers and sitting with them on *charpoys* in the welcome shade of great trees. They gave me some *lassi* to drink – the buttermilk beloved by the Punjabi peasantry. As evening drew on, I realised that the day's manoeuvre was drawing to an end and that someone had blundered by not recalling Trooper Hill. Unfortunately, I showed the initiative that has always got me into trouble in such circumstances. I withdrew myself and returned to headquarters. This was accepted at the time as reasonable but I

51

realised later that if I had waited for orders I might have spent a more comfortable and peaceful war than I actually did – forgotten and vegetating in that quiet village; at least until the partition of the Punjab.

It was very wet at one of the camps. We had a real old-timer with us. One general during an inspection said 'Were you in the war?' He answered, 'Which war, sir, Boer, Great or Third Afghan? I was in all of them.' He was devoted to his horse and put it in an empty tent to shelter it from the violent rain. The Commanding Officer, accompanied by the RSM, was extremely surprised to walk into the tent on inspection and find himself *vis à croup* with the horse.

I had one of the Supreme Court judges in my section. On one occasion a rather pompous general was inspecting us. He stopped in front of the judge and said 'What are you in civil life?' He was completely flabbergasted to receive the reply 'Acting Chief Justice of the Province, Sir' – a position senior to the general's. On another inspection the Commanding Officer saw human ordure on the parade ground. This was the huge cavalry parade ground belonging to Aitchison College and open to all and sundry. The C.O. said 'Some poor devil got dysentery, I suppose,' but the RSM, more cynical and experienced in such matters, retorted 'Looks to me as if it was done with a heffort, sir.'

Lahore was a social centre for a radius of 500 miles or so and there was a very gay Christmas season. There were races (which the Governor of the Punjab opened by driving down the Course in a state carriage drawn by camels), polo tournaments, cricket matches and a round of parties. Civil servants and service officers swarmed into the city from outposts of the Empire. All hotels, clubs and private houses were full of guests but accommodation was required for hundreds more. This was solved by contractors who erected tents in gardens, private or public, and any other suitable open ground. The word tent hardly does justice to the magnificent movable palaces that were erected. They consisted of entrance hall and lounge, dining room, bedrooms and dressing rooms as required, bathroom and toilets, all interconnected. They often had wooden floors and carpets. In the background were cooking huts if necessary and servants' quarters. Sometimes there was a shortage of Government quarters and some officers lived for some time in such accommodation.

If necessary one could have *chaprails* erected. They were houses made of a tough, thick grass woven together in a very ingenious way by a caste specialising in such work. They were very comfortable – cool in the hot weather and warm in the cold. The climax of the season was the New Year's Eve Ball at the Gymkhana Club which was often marked by such incidents as riding a horse or driving a small car onto the dance floor.

The Sovereign's Birthday Parade was always held early in the morning on New Year's Day in India – probably for climatic reasons. The Punjab Light Horse were always on parade. Most of us used to stay on at the New Year's Ball until as long as possible, then go home, shave if necessary, change into uniform, have a little nap if time permitted and then go on parade. Of course, although most of us were nominally troopers, we all had *syces* to look after our horses and take them on parade. We could motor to the parade ground and mount our chargers there. *Syces* would then flick imaginary specks of dust off our riding boots and we would form up on parade.

There was a most amusing incident on one King's Birthday Parade. There was normally at least a division of troops stationed in Lahore and the parade was usually taken by a senior general. One year, for some reason, all the generals were absent and the senior officer in Lahore was a colonel in the Indian Medical Service. There were always several cavalry units on the large parade ground and the parade commander was always mounted. The colonel had not ridden for many years.

The parade went normally until the artillery started firing the salute. The parade commander's horse leapt into the air at the first round. He managed to control it for a bit but after a few more rounds the horse leapt about more and more wildly and finally set off at full gallop round the outer perimeter of the huge cavalry parade ground which must have been a circuit approaching a couple of miles. Having completed one lap the steed went straight to an Indian Lancer Regiment from which it then became clear that it had been borrowed, took up a perfect dressing on the flank of its own squadron and then refused to budge.

The British squadron commander in front of his troops could not see what had happened. He half-turned his head and muttered to his Indian *Dafadar* Major '*Kya hogiya, dafadar sahib?*' 'What has happened, *dafadar sahib?*' There was not the slightest sign of recognition on the latter's face that it was a somewhat unorthodox call from the parade commander as he answered '*Ek sahib a-gae, huzur*' – 'One *sahib* has arrived, Sir'.

Every year the Lahore Hunt had a point-to-point meeting and I used to enter for the Punjab Light Horse event. It appeared that one year the jumps would be so stiff that a number of people would have nasty falls and that the next year they would be lowered. It would then be said that they were too easy and they would be raised again.

The Punjab Light Horse race was for catch weights. I had a very game Indian-bred horse on which I used to attend the Punjab Light Horse parades, play polo and hunt. I was very gratified one year to come in third over a stiff course in the Punjab Light Horse race to two English thoroughbreds ridden by considerably lighter and more experienced riders than myself.

Most major Indian cities in the north of India, which had more strategic importance than the south, had a tripartite structure. There was the old native city, then what was called the Civil Lines, and finally the cantonment. Aitchison College was in the Civil Lines, which lay between the old city and the cantonment. The cantonments were usually some miles away on their own and with their own railway station.

Most of the bazaars were indescribably crowded, noisy and dirty. The old streets of Lahore were narrow, dusty, stinking and fly-ridden. Kipling adopted the title 'City of Dreadful Night' for Lahore. Throngs of pedestrians strolled down the middle of the streets oblivious of the tongas, bullock carts and cars that tried to push their way through. When I got a car I soon learnt that it was counter-productive to blow the horn – that indicated that you had probably seen the obstruction and were paying it some attention. The secret was to go steadily on at a moderate pace; pedestrians then took fright and opened up.

The bazaars had many mutilated and deformed beggars who were very, very persistent and obtrusive. There was one – the remains of a man, who pulled himself along so fast on a low wooden trolley that he would catch up a car several times when it stopped to make purchases. Some of the most horrific sights were emaciated figures sitting in mute appeal with eye sockets sometimes empty but always surrounded by a mass of tiny flies known as 'eye flies'. I went to the bazaar once or twice to see what it was like and made a few purchases. I always felt infested and infected when I came back. I invariably gargled and sometimes had a bath. The main bazaar in Lahore was known as Anarkali, which means the bud of the pomegranate. I never learnt why such an unsavoury place got such a lovely name.

All the trades and commodities were grouped together. There were bazaars for silversmiths, goldsmiths, shoemakers, sellers of saris and everything else. Most of the shops were very colourful and the traders infinitely patient, unrolling bolt after bolt of cloth to tempt the purchasers.

Some of the shops with narrow unpretentious fronts were Aladdin's caves inside with a huge stock of fine quality goods at very competitive prices. Similarly, some of the merchants had magnificent houses behind the grimy facade abutting on the bazaar. Fairly lengthy haggling always took place and a reasonable command of Urdu was worth at least 20% off any price that would otherwise be obtained. One shop amused me. The sign above it read: ALLAH BAKSH, MASTER SADDLER, QUALIFIED H.M. PRISON LUCKNOW.

Other signs that one saw offered services of various kinds that needed a knowledge of English, and, to strengthen their qualifications, the advertisers sometimes put 'BA failed' after their name. This certainly seemed bizarre by the standards of Europeans, many of whom scoffed at it. However, if one looked at it from the Indian point of view it showed that amongst the tens of millions of illiterates the advertiser was not only literate in an Indian language but had reached a reasonable degree of proficiency in English.

I arrived in Lahore at the time of the *Shahidganj* trouble. These were religious riots and inter-communal strife between the Muslims and Sikhs in Lahore. There was an average of about ten murders a week for a long time. There was no attempt at concealment. One day a Sikh would go to a Muslim *abadi* or quarter with

55

a sword or similar weapon and run down the street killing as many Muslims as he could before he himself was struck down. A few days later a Muslim would retaliate in the same way against Sikhs.

The source of all the trouble was a place called *Shahidganj*, which means the Martyrs' Burial Place. The Muslims claimed that it had originally been a Muslim holy place and the Sikhs that it was sacred to their religion, as the Muslims had massacred some Sikhs in that place.

The dispute had been quiescent for many years when secretly, overnight, several hundred Sikhs built a small *gurdwara* or Sikh temple on the spot. In the *gurdwara* they deposited a copy of their holy scriptures – the Guru Granth Sahib – which made it doubly sacred. It took little to start inter-communal trouble in the Punjab at any time and this provocative challenge was immediately taken up by the Muslims.

The matter was also taken up in the law courts. The Muslims won in the High Court of the Punjab but the Sikhs appealed to the Privy Council. The Muslim case, which was argued by Jinnah (who became the first president of Pakistan) was that once a place had been dedicated to Allah, which they claimed this had, it remained so dedicated for ever. They called expert witnesses to reveal the will and laws of Allah. However, this time the Sikhs won and the judgement was largely influenced by the finding of bones in a well on the spot, said to be those of the Sikh martyrs.

However, the whole affair, and particularly the High Court judgement, badly upset the Sikh community. A company in a Sikh battalion in Malaya, of which a friend of mine was the company commander, carried out what was probably the most brilliant and dashing single action against the Japanese. In a magnificent bayonet charge they completely overran the Japanese position and killed a large number of Japanese. These very men were the first of the Indian Army to join the Indian National Army and side with the Japanese after the fall of Singapore. I believe that the *Shahidganj* affair had a lot to do with this.

There were several militant religio-political parties in the Punjab. The Sikhs had their *Akali Dal* or Deathless Army. They appeared in deep blue robes with yellow sashes. They had the *chakkar* round their turbans and usually carried a long spear and a *kirpan*, the Sikh sword. The *chakkar* is a ring of flat steel about 18 inches in diameter and $1\frac{1}{2}$ inches wide; it is about $\frac{3}{8}$ of an inch thick on its inner blunt edge but its outer edge is sharpened to razor sharpness. It was one of the traditional weapons of the Sikhs, which they hurled at the enemy at fairly close quarters often with devastating effect.

Every true Sikh is supposed at all times to have on his person the five *kakas* or things beginning with the K sound in the Punjabi language. The first is the *kes* or hair. No Sikh is ever supposed to cut his hair or shave his beard. The traditional origin of this was so that they could be ready to fight at any time. In the Indian army all Sikhs had to roll and neatly comb their beards under a string tied over the head and under the chin. This habit had been adopted by most Sikhs of any standing. The combing out and rolling of the beard usually took much longer than shaving would have done.

The second was the *kach* or drawers. This was also supposed to be a sign of martial readiness and to distinguish Sikhs from such unmartial races as those who wore the *dhoti* or Indian loincloth draped round and between the legs. An orthodox Sikh was never supposed to be without his *kach*. He was even supposed to take his bath in it. Certainly some wore them beneath swimming trunks. It was said that the orthodox would keep one leg in their old *kach* whilst putting the other into a clean pair.

The third *kaka* was the *kara* or thin iron bracelet, which every true Sikh always wore round his wrist to signify the unity of the *khalsa* or Sikh community, asceticism and dedication to its defence.

The *kanghi* or comb, usually worn in the topknot under the turban was the fourth *kaka*.

Last but not least was the *kirpan*, or sword, whose significance was obvious. So much trouble had been caused by the Sikh *kirpan* that the British raj said that it was not to be carried. The Sikhs retorted that it was a specific tenet of their religion, as it was; that they must carry the *kirpan* at all times and invoked Queen Victoria's promise that the religious beliefs of her Indian subjects would be scrupulously respected.

The counter to this was brilliant in its simplicity. It was pointed out to the Sikh community that nowhere in their religious beliefs was the length of the *kirpan* laid down. The Government would therefore permit the carrying of *kirpans* but restricted their length to 4 inches. This was accepted by most Sikhs and they carried a small token *kirpan* usually in their turban with the *kanghi*.

But not the members of the Akali Dal. They openly paraded with long *kirpans* hanging from their sashes. They were sometimes relatively peaceful religious fanatics courting arrest and publicity or even martyrdom. They quite often did this singly and were sometimes ignored by authority. Only occasionally did they congregate in bodies and make some well publicised march on some town. When this occurred there was usually a clash with the police or a rival Muslim band.

The *Khaksars*, or Humble Ones, were a fanatical, arrogant Muslim movement basing their beliefs on inspiration derived from the wellsprings of Islam. They had obviously learnt a great deal from the Nazis in Germany also. *Khak* means earth or dust in Urdu and the word *khaki* is derived from it. They paraded in smart *khaki* military uniforms and were organised exactly like an infantry battalion. One of their ostensible objects was to carry out public works like the Nazi labour groups and they were all equipped with spades. I never heard of their doing this but the curved spades were filed around every edge until they were like razors. They marched through the streets in military formation and drilled to Persian words of command. They were most impressive and appeared on most big public occasions ostensibly to help in crowd control. However, they were obviously militant and the constantly heavily-charged inter-communal feeling became electric whenever they appeared at the Muslim religious festivals of various *Ids*.

It appeared that they must have had special drills in street fighting. There was one terrible day in Lahore when they went into action with military precision with their spades and killed a number of policemen, including a European officer. The police had to open fire and over 50 people in all were killed before order was restored.

Many of the great religious festivals were times of inter-communal tension. The festivals which called out the greatest number of people were the great Id festivals of the Muslims. It was said that one *lakh*, that is 100,000, Muslims attended the Id prayers in the great courtyard of the Jami Mosque in Lahore, one of the biggest in the world. However, as the Ids were festivals of rejoicing and the *Id-ul-Fitr* ended the long fast of Ramzan there was reduced tension at these times.

Most of the adult male Muslims of Lahore and its surroundings converged on the *Jami Masjid* at Id. All Muslim servants had time off to go to the mosque to pray. I was taken to the great Mosque by a Muslim friend to see the spectacle. Of course, I could not enter the mosque proper or its courtyard but we were given places of vantage in the great arched gateway, which led to the courtyard.

As we approached the mosque the crowds converging on it from all over the great city of approximately half a million inhabitants became thicker and thicker. As we got to the steps leading to the gateway we saw the shoes that the crowd had discarded before entering the mosque. It was a strange sight to see tens of thousands of pairs of shoes just lying around with no attempt at any order or anyone to look after them. Eventually, when the prayers were over and everyone had emerged all the shoes gradually disappeared and no one was left around looking for missing shoes. This seemed to me to be a typical example of many such incidents that I was to see later in the East in which there is often a loose underlying order in what seems complete chaos to a European.

It was estimated that 100,000 attended the prayers the day I saw them. The estimate by the Muslim authorities was invariably 100,000, which made one inclined to doubt its accuracy. However, the vast courtyard was completely packed with the congregation of the faithful and I had no reason to doubt that they were less than the figure given. Everyone was wearing his best clothes, new if they could afford them. Many, including nearly all our boys, wore *achkans*, the long Indian frock-coats, made of gold brocade. Many others had fancy coloured waistcoats. There was a dramatically changing kaleidoscope of colour during the various movements of the Muslim prayer. At one moment the eye met 100,000 gold coats or fancy waistcoats, at the next all that could be seen was the snowy expanse of 100,000 white backsides as the faithful prostrated themselves in prayer – they all, of course, wore the traditional orthodox white, baggy Muslim trousers.

One of the times of greatest tension was when the Shia sect of the Muslims held the Mohurram procession to commemorate the martyrdom of Hassan and Hussein by the Sunni sect in Iraq in the early days of Islam. Devout Shias walked in procession all through Lahore from dawn to dusk. Most pounded their bare chests until they were a blood-clotted, soggy mass. They walked forward in unison shouting 'Hassan, Hussein' and after calling out the two words dealt their chests five sickening rhythmic thuds with the inside of the clenched fist. They struck the right breast once with the left hand, then the left breast once with the right hand, then a double punch on the right and a final blow on the left. It was quite a sickening sound to hear the dull but quite loud sound of thousands of fists hitting thousands of breasts simultaneously.

The more fanatical flagellated themselves on the back with chains, bunches of keys, penknives and any excoriating piece of metal they could find, tied on to chains or cords. A few women took part also.

The Muslim religious calendar is a lunar one and so their festivals moved round our solar year. When Mohurram came in the hot weather it tried tautened nerves to the uttermost. The stench of mingled sweat and blood in the narrow airless streets was nauseating.

The climax of the procession was a white horse and the *tazia*. The horse represented the steed that Hassan was riding when he was killed and which is reputed to have brought his body back to his followers. It was always liberally daubed with blood. The *tazia* was a wood, paper and tinsel erection representing the tomb at Kerbala where the martyrs are buried.

The sight of these two portents was liable to send a religious maniac completely off his balance and make him attack any non-Shia – a Sunni Muslim, Hindu, Sikh or Christian.

The month-long fast of Ramzan was a period of trial and tension for Muslims especially if it came in the hot weather when the day lasted from about 4.30 a.m. until 7.30 p.m. From the time when it was light enough to distinguish between a black thread and a white thread until such time as it was not possible to do so, no orthodox Muslim was supposed to eat or drink. The really strict considered it incorrect even to swallow their saliva, which led to ritual spitting, increasing the eternal oriental expectoration. Some would not even take medicine.

Naturally, like nearly all Europeans who had not long been in India, I was anxious to see some of the world-famous performances of the Indian *sadhus* and mystics. One such came to perform at the College. He was a small, slightly built but well-articulated Hindu with fairly good muscular development.

He gave his performance in the main hall of the College, which was quite a sizable room. His first item was a display of archery. From one end of the hall, he shot and cut with an arrow a silk thread on which a small weight was hanging at the far end. He then hung two such bobs on silk threads. One was stationary and one swinging to and fro like a pendulum. He cut through both threads with an arrow as one was passing the other. He then repeated the performance with his back to the target, bending down and shooting between his legs.

Next he lay down on the traditional bed of nails. A large flagstone was placed on his chest. On the flagstone was a length of railway line. Two brawny fellows with heavy sledgehammers, one of whom was the master Shahbaz Khan of ox-like strength, then cut through a steel rod held on the railway line.

After this the *sadhu* bent the steel rod in his hands, round his arms and round his neck.

His next performance was to hypnotise members of the audience, including a number of Europeans.

Finally he said he would stop his heart. After a few deep breaths he apparently did so. Two doctors in the audience examined him with their stethoscopes and agreed that his heart had stopped. After a short interval he jumped up as if nothing had happened.

I was very impressed with the performance. This and a number of other incidents that I came across led me to believe that some of these people – yogis, sadhus, faqirs and the like – have remarkable powers.

There was a widespread belief amongst Indians, including the educated and sophisticated, that some such people had the powers of withstanding being buried alive for considerable periods. There were constant reports of such performances but I saw none myself.

61

On one occasion the school team went to Chail to play cricket. Chail was an enclave of Patiala state set on a peak opposite Simla. The Maharaja always said that Simla rightly belonged to Patiala.

We went on the broad gauge railway to Kalka where the narrow gauge railway to Simla started. The sidings at Kalka usually had an imposing collection of private railway coaches reserved for the Viceroy, Commander-in-chief, Provincial Governors, Heads of Department of the Imperial Government and maharajas. As so many exalted personages passed through Kalka the refreshment room was a brilliant affair and the cuisine was as good as a first-class international hotel. We had a very good meal there.

The narrow gauge railway writhed round and through the hills on a spectacular journey towards Simla. I think the journey is about 80 miles and that there are over 50 tunnels – some quite long. The little train looked just like a coiling snake on occasions when one could see its tail quite easily by glancing out of a window in a compartment near the engine.

We were met by a fleet of state cars at the station for Chail and motored through magnificent hills covered with pines and deodars until we got to the township and one of the summer palaces of the Maharaja. Here we were welcomed with typical Patiala hospitality.

The cricket ground, over 8,000 feet high, was claimed to be the highest in the world. It was really the top of a truncated peak, which had been cut down and levelled off to make a cricket ground. It was mostly surrounded by a loose stone wall. In places if the ball cleared the wall it had a good chance of dropping about a couple of thousand feet and so 'lost ball' there had a very definite meaning. The Maharaja himself was a mighty hitter, who had played for India on occasions, and delighted in putting balls over the wall at the most effective spots.

We played the match – Aitchison College v. Old Boys – and it was rather strenuous chasing balls at this altitude, as we had had no time to become conditioned to the height. Although it was very much cooler than the plains, the effect of the sun was, of course, much more severe and we found we soon had burnt noses and ears.

I cannot remember the result of the match but I well remember the dinner we had that evening in the pavilion. About 40 of us sat down to eat on either side of a long table. In front of each of us was a *thal* or round solid silver tray about 18 inches in diameter. On the trays were a collection of little silver dishes filled with a variety of the most delicious meat and vegetable curries imaginable. It was a wonderful sight to look down the table at the rows of gleaming silver surrounded by dark beards and brilliant multi-coloured turbans. The quality and variety of the drinks available matched the food and played their part in a memorable evening.

Maula Baksh accompanied me on this tour. At that time there was a touring English cricket team whose manager, Major Britton, had received some publicity. The boys nicknamed Maula Baksh 'Major Britton' and he never lost his soubriquet. I can still picture his hawk-like face, straggly beard and blazing eyes, as he sat atop the pile of baggage of which he was self-appointed guardian as the baggage lorry swung and swayed round the sharp corners of the mountain road. At one place we had passed a notice that warned that one Bhagat Singh had gone over the edge to his destruction – apparently through falling asleep at the wheel – and advising others not to run the same risk.

Another unusual sporting experience that I had was when the Afghan Soccer team came to Lahore. The Government of Afghanistan had decided that one sign of a modern state was to have a national soccer team. They raised a team and sent it on a tour of India. Soccer is played very little in the north of India although it is a popular game in other parts. In winter in the north the Europeans play rugby or hockey and the Indians, of course, hockey.

The Afghan team played a match or so in Peshawar and then came to Lahore on their way to their fixtures proper in Bombay, Calcutta and Madras and the surrounding regions where soccer was popular. They said that they wanted a training match in Lahore and asked if a team could be raised to play them. A scratch team was got together and entitled 'The North of India'. It consisted of three or four Europeans, including myself, who had played soccer, completed by masters and boys of Aitchison College. Afghanistan beat us only 3–2 in a dreary match of a very low standard. By stretching the imagination a bit I can therefore claim to have played in an international soccer match.

I spent two holidays in Patiala through the kind hospitality of the Maharaja. I had become very friendly with an Australian and a Sikh major in the Patiala army both of whom were serving in the Maharaja's Guardian's Department and looking after his sons at the College. I stayed with them in one of the palaces at Patiala and it was a memorable experience. The hospitality was overwhelming. The best way in which I can describe it is that it was like a luxury hotel of the highest possible standard – with the slight difference that it cost us nothing. The Maharaja had a Goanese chef and a Czech head-waiter. We had, at every meal, a range of choice European and Indian dishes backed by a superb cellar. There was a magnificent dining room in the palace with lounges and ante-rooms served by an ever-open bar. Cricket, tennis, small and big game shooting, riding and expeditions to places of interest were organised to entertain us.

The nobles and officers of the State, both civil and military, were a most impressive cross-section of north Indian aristocracy and there was usually some celebrated personality, Indian or European, as a fellow guest.

Patiala had formerly been one of the great polo-playing states of India but the Maharaja's interest had later turned more to cricket. There were still one or two old polo players around who had been amongst the best in the world in their day. One old major in the state army, with a ten handicap, had gone on tour with a polo team raised by King Alfonso of Spain and at the same time after dinner every evening he would describe in identical words a famous galloping movement executed by the King and himself which ended with his scoring a brilliant goal. It was always worth hearing as he told it with such verve and dramatic effect and with such evident but honest and justified self-satisfaction.

We went on a few partridge and duck shoots. There was a lake in the State famous for its thousands and thousands of ducks. Most of them used to stay out of range in the middle of the lake. Boatmen were sent in to drive them out and we were supposed to shoot them if they came within range. The Maharaja vied with King George V, with whom he shot in England, as one of the best small game shots in the world. The first duck that came off the lake came over me at a great height, which I thought was obviously out of range, and flying at a tremendous speed. I pointed my gun vaguely in the air and pulled the trigger. To my surprise the duck plummeted to the ground. Everyone else took it as a normal commonplace shot but I never repeated the performance.

After one cricket match at Patiala, I was talking to the Maharaja. I noticed that the band had started to play but I did not give it much attention and in any case I am very unmusical and probably might not have recognised an unfamiliar tune if I had been paying attention. I then noticed that all the other guests had discreetly retreated to the background. The tune was apparently the Patiala Anthem and the Patiala Army consisting of two battalions of infantry, a cavalry regiment, field battery, field ambulance, etc. was about to march past in review order. I felt like someone in an H.M. Bateman cartoon and slunk away as best I could.

I was at Patiala on another occasion when it was the Maharaja's birthday. There was a floodlit parade in the evening. The lights were turned off during the *feu de joie*, which made it a much more spectacular affair than one held in daylight.

The Patiala infantry were the descendants of the dour Sikh soldiery who at the battles of Sobraon and Chilianwala, during the Sikh wars which led to the conquest of the Punjab, had given the British some of the toughest infantry fighting they had ever encountered. Well-built men in scarlet tunics and turbans adorned with gold braid and encircled with gleaming steel *chakkars* they were an impressive sight and seemed still capable of giving a good account of themselves.

I took part in one sport in Patiala, which I never met elsewhere. The Maharaja had had a fine roller skating rink built and the sport of playing hockey on roller skates developed. We used ordinary sticks and ball and it was a fast, exciting and somewhat dangerous sport. I once went clean over the fairly high metal barrier that surrounded the rink. The Indians displayed the same legerdemain in their stick work in this game as in ordinary hockey.

It was said that some of the Patiala princesses were very good skaters but, of course, they were in purdah and had special sessions reserved for themselves.

65

A Frenchman who had some business in Patiala came to join us once. He could speak no English and no Indian language and I had the strange linguistic experience of trying to interpret between French and Punjabi. When he had found a pair of skates that suited him he gave an exquisite display of what might be termed figure skating on roller skates but he disdained joining the hurly-burly of a hockey match.

The Aitchison College sports were one of the highlights of the Lahore season. The beautiful array of saris and coloured turbans set against the lovely grounds of the College formed a most spectacular scene. The fathers' race in which most of the princes of the north of India took part was very popular amongst the spectators.

The climax of the afternoon was the tent-pegging competition and final display in which boys pulled out a series of pegs with attachments which, on the end of their lances, became guidons in the College colours.

All in all, life in Aitchison College and Lahore was full and interesting for a young bachelor. There was a satisfying job and always something to learn about the history, customs and traditions of the complex mixture of races and religions in India. There were the ample school holidays, and in particular the long vacation, which enabled one to travel to various parts of India and its surrounding countries.

4

Kashmir

The hot weather in Lahore was very trying. By mid-April the temperatures began to soar and very soon, until about mid-October, heat became a real enemy. The maximum shade temperature in the hot weather in Lahore was seldom below 114°F (45°C). Sometimes it was rather more, sometimes a little less. The nights were hot also and sometimes did not fall below 90°F (32°C). Occasionally there was an overcast day. Often it was a prelude to a sandstorm, which was very unpleasant, filling most orifices of the body, houses and furniture with fine sand or dust. Sometimes it was just clouds shutting out the sun. There was a tradition at the College that if, at the beginning of a working day in the hot weather term, the temperature was below 100°F (38°C), we had the day off and masters and boys went on a quickly-organised picnic usually to the Moghul Gardens at Shahdara on the outskirts of the city or to some other similar site on the banks of the Ravi. This lucky event never happened more than once a year in my experience and not at all in some years.

We were very lucky in our vacations at Aitchison College. We had shortish breaks at Christmas and in the spring but eleven weeks from about mid-July until the first half of October. Thus, although we had to endure about three months of the hot weather, this was nearly all before the monsoons broke. It seemed to me that it was even worse in Lahore after a rainstorm in the hot weather. The rain cooled things down for a bit but after a few hours the heat built up again and the increased humidity made conditions even worse. I got prickly heat on occasions, which was

67

rather unpleasant. The College doctor was a mild, bespectacled little Hindu. He was dedicated to helping suffering humanity and after a time he left the relatively well-paid job in the College to help the poor peasants in the countryside and subsist on the small amounts they could pay. Most Indian doctors preferred urban practices. He prescribed baths to which silver nitrate solution had been added but insisted that the water be kept so that he could recover the expensive silver nitrate.

Because of the shortened time we had to endure the hot weather we did not have any breaks during that term except for religious holidays. These were literally sacrosanct in Lahore where we were particularly lucky as Muslims, Sikhs and Hindus were all well represented in the Punjab. The British had to show equal respect to their great religious festivals and so we had a lot of statutory holidays. I remember one year that I felt we had been a little unlucky as Good Friday coincided with a Muslim and a Hindu festival and thus we lost two days' holiday.

Most European women who were not wives of those in academic jobs left for the hills for the hot weather. The breadwinners joined them for short local leaves as they could.

Kashmir was the most popular hill station for Lahore. There were several reasons for this. Firstly its size, that of France, and its accessibility by the standard of distances in India. Other attractions were its marvellous scenery which offered facilities for fascinating but strenuous mountain treks; polo, golf, tennis and other sports; lotus-eating beside the lovely lakes and Moghul Gardens near Srinagar and what was known in Anglo-Indian slang as 'poodle-faking'. This was a term that baffled me the first time that I heard it. The dictionary defines it as 'seeking women's society'. As hill stations were the only places in India where European women outnumbered the men, their company was not hard to find.

Even by early July I was feeling the strain of the Lahore hot weather and I managed to make arrangements to leave in the second week in July and for various sets of examination papers to be sent on for me to mark.

I was quite excited as I left Lahore on the night train for the railhead at Jammu. The full title of Kashmir state is Jammu and

Kashmir. Jammu was a separate state before it was incorporated in Kashmir and the town of Jammu was the capital of the state of that name. It is just over the border from the Punjab, at the beginning of the foothills and as far as the railway can penetrate.

I slept fitfully until we reached the railway junction at Wazirabad. I woke up very thirsty and walked down the platform. I was disconcerted on my return to find that the section of the train in which I was travelling had disappeared. I found the station-master who reassured me that it was only some complicated shunting that was going on. Under his persuasion I had a bottle of tepid beer in the waiting room. This was served by the Muslim *khitmatgar* or butler after the stationmaster had woken him up from his sleep on the platform.

The train arrived at Jammu at 5.40 a.m. and I contacted the North Western Railway's out-agent who arranged onward trans-port by car to Srinagar. I was to have three Indian fellow passengers. I had some tea in the minute waiting room and sat there impatiently waiting for them to be ready whilst they were waiting, no doubt patiently, for me to finish my tea. Even after this was clarified we had, of course, to wait a little time for the driver to be ready. We set off, but not for long. We had to make a customs declaration at Jammu City and whilst the formalities were being completed I wandered round the bazaar with my three fellow Indian passengers.

After this we got started on the journey proper and as on all journeys in India we introduced ourselves. My companions were a Hindu film director from Lahore, a Pathan and a Hindu from Indore. They immediately set about to find out all they could about me without revealing so much about themselves. However, the Pathan could not, for long, restrain his racial patriotism nor con-ceal the fact that he was not a friend of the English as a ruling power, although friendly to individual Englishmen.

We had not gone very far when we had to shelter in a tunnel from a terrific storm, which rose very suddenly. Just before the storm closed down visibility we had seen a small flock of most beautiful wild peacocks.

We rose steadily with the noise of rushing streams almost con-stantly in our ears. I was soon to learn that it was unusual to sleep

69

in Kashmir without the sound of running water to lull one to slumber. As we rose the air became cooler and the scenery grander and wilder.

On and on and up and up went the road until at a height of nearly 9,000 feet we were running through beautiful pine forests with their aromatic, invigorating scent.

We then dropped down a steep descent to cross the Chenab by a fine suspension bridge. The roaring, frothing, creamy-grey, glacier-fed waters far below us were full of logs floating down to Wazirabad where the river becomes less tempestuous and they are made up into huge rafts on which shelters are built for the lumberjacks and their families as they continue their long, leisurely journey across the vast plains of the Punjab.

After the crossing of the Chenab and passing Ramban the ascent became very steep again. In places the road followed a narrow shelf blasted out of the cliff face. The country became wilder and wilder. We passed through several huge, dangerous-looking screes with glimpses of the gleaming Chenab in the valley now far below us again. In one place the road zigzagged up a huge mountainside and we could see three parallel stretches of the road at different altitudes thousands of feet above our heads.

It was a tough, inhospitable country. Vegetation, man and animal showed signs of the unrelenting struggle for existence. The style of dress had changed from the Punjab. Instead of turbans the men wore embroidered skull caps. Their beautifully worked caps seemed to be the only example of energy that was not expended on the mere effort to survive. The men were prematurely aged and bowed with labour – dressed in rags, they often held out their skull caps as begging bowls. The women were ugly and toil-worn but wore loop after loop of silver wire in their ears. I suppose that this represented the family insurance policy. Bad goitres were commonplace.

We then dropped down to a more favoured area where laboriously-built stone retaining walls supported narrow strips of terraced plots growing maize and rice on slopes which seemed too steep to support cultivation. Even steeper slopes were grazed by goats and small cows not much bigger than Great Danes. It seemed almost impossible that the animals could find a foothold on the terrifying slopes and it was obvious that both animals and herdsmen must have been immune to vertigo.

In this area the people – men, women and children, seemed to augment their living by working on the road. They prised off great blocks of stone from the rock face and then broke them up by crowbar and sledgehammer to metal the roads. In other places where the rock on the cliff face was completely unyielding they carried up stones from the river beds on branches laid across their shoulders. Some of the slopes would have been a severe test for most able-bodied people unencumbered with any burden. These stones were also manually broken to provide road metal. At one place in this section the road dips and turns and on approaching this spot it looks as if one is about to set off on a journey into space. We passed many large lizards sunning themselves on the side of the road and also a number of snakes, probably preying on the lizards.

Shortly after Batote we had to pass through the customs again on the entry into Kashmir state proper, as distinct from Jammu. We paid three rupees in road toll. We were asked various questions by the state customs officials who were Kashmiri Brahmins. Seventy-three per cent of the population of Kashmir were Muslim but there was a Hindu raj and the vast majority of the state officials and nearly all the Army were Hindu.

Various laws were on the statute book based on Hindu religious beliefs, some of which protected with legislation the Hindu devotion to the cow. If a European killed a cow in a motor accident in Kashmir he was immediately required to leave the state. The penalty for locally-born Muslims who killed a cow, by accident or otherwise, was seven years' imprisonment. This was not uncommonly enforced but not for motoring accidents as hardly any Kashmiri Muslims would be able to afford a car.

We passed a river where we heard the jingling of the pebbles being perpetually rolled down by the strong current and shortly afterwards an unstable scree with the ominous crunching and crackling of boulders endlessly on the move.

Shortly after this the road gave up the heavy task of attempting to climb the Pir Panjal Range, one of the buttresses of the Himalayas, and plunged into a long tunnel below the Banihal

71

Pass. The view on emerging was one of the most dramatic I have ever seen. The Golden Vale of Kashmir was spread before us like a beautiful oriental prayer mat below the dome of our mountain-mosque. Long rows of poplars lining the straight roads formed the main outline of the pattern, which was inset here and there with the flashing jewels of the paddy fields; masses of fruit trees in blossom added a variety of delicate pastel shades whilst the eye was led by the silver thread of the Jhelum to the opalescent hues of the Dal Lake which in the far distance formed a background to the whole view.

We still had some distance to go before we reached Srinagar and we stopped for a substantial tea at the foot of the mountains. The drive along the valley was in marked contrast to the austerity of the mountains. The fields were bursting with fertility. The beautiful, shady, poplar-lined road ran through fields of maize, rice, peppers, melons, pumpkins and vegetables of all descriptions and groves of mulberries, walnuts, peaches, apricots, plums and apples in bloom.

I left my fellow passengers in Srinagar and continued along the winding picturesque road to join my friends camping on the lovely slopes of the Nasim Bagh, wooded with *chenar*, the Indian plane, which ran gently down to the beautiful Dal Lake.

Theo was the Principal of one of the Colleges of the University of the Punjab and Carl was an American missionary teaching in University College in Lahore and we had decided to spend our summer vacation in Kashmir together and to include a trek in our programme.

First of all there was plenty to see around Srinagar which was the summer capital of Kashmir, the largest state in India but not the most populous or first in precedence – that honour going to Hyderabad.

Kashmir controls several routes between India and Central Asia and has been considered of strategic importance from earliest recorded history. It has had many rulers – Moghuls, Afghans, Rajputs, Sikhs and Dogras amongst others, but rarely have the major indigenous race ever ruled the territory, which probably accounts for their somewhat oppressed, downtrodden attitude. It is now, of course, an issue of contention between India and

Pakistan and the position is probably made more difficult by the fact that the Nehru family is of Kashmiri Brahmin origin.

Modern Kashmir was founded by Maharaja Gulab Singh who lived from 1792 to 1858. On the break-up of the Moghul Empire in the first half of the eighteenth century, the petty Rajput princes who held sway in what is now the province of Jammu gained some measure of independence. But this independence was short-lived because as the Moghul authority in the Punjab broke down the Sikhs took over. Soon the great Sikh ruler, Ranjit Singh, the Tiger of the Punjab, established a far-flung domain from the Pamirs to Sind and from Peshawar to the Sutlej — which included most of Kashmir. Before Ranjit Singh established his empire, the exploits of Gulab Singh, one of these Rajput princes, on the battlefield whilst only a boy of 16, had aroused the interest and admiration of his Sikh enemies. To clarify the position for readers not familiar with Indian names — all Sikhs and some Rajputs take the suffix 'Singh' (meaning lion) to their name. Ranjit Singh sent for Gulab Singh and the latter became a great captain at the Sikh court.

Gulab Singh subdued Jammu, which had always been considered an unruly and difficult province and was given it to farm in 1820. He reduced further outlying provinces to Sikh rule and was rewarded with the hereditary grant of Jammu and the title of Raja. By 1835, Gulab Singh was the most important feudatory of Ranjit Singh. In 1839, Maharaja Ranjit Singh died and his empire relapsed into anarchy. Gulab Singh retired from the intrigues and struggles for succession and returned to his own dominions. It is said that he carried off with him the accumulated treasures of Ranjit Singh stored in the Lahore Fort to the extent of 16 bullock carts full of silver rupees and 500 bags of gold *mohurs* each given to a trusted horseman.

In 1841 disaster befell the British at Jalalabad in their war against Afghanistan. There was a very real danger that the Sikhs would turn against them also. Gulab Singh was in a very strong position, which he exploited to the full. He managed to persuade the Sikhs not to attack the British whilst at the same time retaining the friendship of the Sikhs.

Gulab Singh went through many vicissitudes of fortune before the British finally beat the Sikhs in 1846 at the Battle of Sobraon – the most fiercely contested that the British ever fought in India. He managed to hold his own by a mixture of cool nerves, cunning, bravery and evasive, dilatory tactics without which no Indian prince seemed to retain his power for long. As a result of the Battle of Sobraon the British became undisputed masters of the Punjab and the whole of the Sikh Empire. In the Treaty of Amritsar in 1846, for a consideration of 7.5 million rupees, they confirmed Gulab Singh in his possessions, which by this time had been extended by conquest to include Baltistan, Ladakh and parts of Western Tibet.

The plateau of Ladakh is part of the main Tibetan tableland and for a long time before its conquest by Gulab Singh it had been ruled by a dynasty which was Tibetan in origin. The population is mainly of Mongolian origin and the religion is Lamaistic Buddhism. It is one of the most elevated areas in the world – the average height is about 12,000 feet and there are peaks up to 28,000 feet.

Baltistan is part of the same geographical area as Ladakh and the people are the same racially but Muslim in religion. These regions were as accessible from Tibet and Sinkiang as from India and the emperors of China long exerted political influence there. For example, I have mentioned that the rajas of Chamba are said to have paid tribute to the Emperors of China at one stage. These are some of the outlying regions of India where sovereignty is contested by China.

It can thus be seen that Srinagar was a fascinating meeting place for Central Asian types of the most diverse kinds. The Jhelum River wound its serpentine course through the city and was crossed by seven elaborate wooden bridges. The best way of giving a location in Srinagar was 'near the Third Bridge' or 'under the Seventh Bridge' as the case might be.

In the caravanserais one saw tall, wiry, fair, loose-turbaned horse-dealers from Afghan and even Russian Badakshan with their strings of tough horses from the upland pastures which crossed with a little blood make outstanding polo ponies; dark, squat jade and turquoise dealers from Tibet wearing their distinctive felt hats with flapping wings over the ears, shaped like a

74

triangular pyramid in the middle – they still wore their thick long-sleeved robes but, belted round the middle, they usually had one shoulder and arm free as they always felt hot and oppressed at any altitude less than 10,000 feet; felt dealers from Ladakh with their round, flat-nosed, cunning Mongolian faces and their own brand of skull cap; carpet-dealers from Persia and Baluchistan – the former smooth, suave salesmen, the latter of the take it or leave it type; European-looking people from the mountain fastnesses of Gilgit and Hunza where Alexander's army is said to have left its mark, wearing their unique flat, round woollen caps; Tungans or Chinese Muslims from Sinkiang, whose thin drooping mous-taches, tightly slit eyes and thin lips gave them an air of blood-curdling ferocity relieved by the bright red flowers embroidered on their black skull caps; short, round, fair-skinned smiling Uzbegs, not from Russian Uzbegistan but from Yarkand and Kashgar in Sinkiang, with yet another type of embroidery on their skull caps; tall, fair, high-turbaned, grey-bearded, Persian-speak-ing Tajiks from Tajikistan in Russian Central Asia with an air of melancholy and infinite disillusion which was natural in a race cut off under alien rule from its parent stock and brothers in race, language and religion – some were horse-dealers, others had no visible means of support and were said to be Russian spies; a few outlandish Kirgiz from the high Pamirs wearing another type of winged hat, some selling horses; swaggering, bullying Pathan moneylenders; cunning Kashmiri pundits and last but most numerous the ordinary downtrodden, sweated Kashmiri Muslim.

A great variety of handicraft and material was on sale – all at very reasonable prices because, regrettably, it was produced by men, women and children working crowded together in ill-lit, ill-ventilated rooms and suffering from malnutrition, chest troubles, trachoma and numerous other diseases brought on by sub-standard living conditions.

Not only do the great groves of walnuts in Kashmir produce the most wonderful walnuts I have ever tasted, with paper-thin shells, but the wood is the basis for a great furniture-making and wood-carving industry. One could furnish a whole house with Kashmiri walnut furniture for a few hundred rupees – the drawbacks were that sometimes the wood had not been properly seasoned and usually hinges and other fastenings were of inferior workmanship. In addition to major pieces of furniture, trays of all sizes and descriptions, boxes, chests, candlesticks, carved trees, plants, fruit and other objects (but not figures, in deference to Muslim belief) were produced en masse and anything could be accurately copied. Most of the tools were primitive.

Oriental carpets and rugs of all types were displayed in the stores. There were the usual range of woven rugs – Persian, Baluchi, Turkoman, Chinese and others and also felt rugs from Ladakh, Tibet and China decorated with somewhat primitive embroidery or appliqué – very cheap and attractive.

Papier mâché work was very common – a popular item being a smoking set – a container for a tin of 50 cigarettes, matchbox and ashtray. The designs were exquisite and beautifully executed. Some portrayed kingfishers or other birds in most natural colours – others incorporated gold and silver lacquer and the prices were only 3–10 rupees.

There were sapphire, ruby and gold mines in Kashmir. Jewels were on sale at a price far less than they would fetch in Europe. There was also a wide range of jewellery including a lot of the delicate, beautiful filigree silverwork in which Indian craftsmen excel. Brass, copper and bronze ware abounded in the bazaar. There was a state silk factory and many beautiful silk articles were on sale. It was also possible to buy sandalwood chests, marvellous for keeping one's clothes beautifully scented and insect free (an important consideration in India) and fragrant sandalwood soap. In short, many entrancing hours could be spent wandering around the bazaars of Srinagar at little expense if one had a modicum of cash and reasonable sales resistance, as I had.

Srinagar had many attractions apart from the bazaars. It was a city of delightful waterways mostly connecting with the Jhelum River or the Dal Lake. There were fleets of *shikaras*, the Kashmiri equivalent of gondolas, waiting for hire at all strategic spots. These were sharp, high prowed boats propelled by two, four or six paddlers. They were wide enough to seat two people side by side, were furnished with comfortable fitted cushions and back rests for either two or four with a canopy and curtains. Many of them had rather suggestive names luridly painted across the front such as

Pneumatic Bliss, Aquatic Ecstasy and so on. As we floated along the waterways in *shikaras* we frequently caught the flashing, irridescent flight of a kingfisher between sunbeams and reflecting water and drifted through floating beds of pink, ivory, maroon and magenta water lilies. They yield an edible nut, which the Kashmiris eat but which belies the old legend of the effects of lotus-eating as few people can work harder than the Kashmiris.

One of the most interesting features of the waterways was the floating gardens. These are made from earth and vegetable matter brought by *shikaras* and piled on top of the closely matted water plants floating raft-like on the water. All kinds of vegetables, melons and vines are grown on these floating gardens.

One thing that never failed to surprise me was the filthy, stagnant water, which the Kashmiris drank without apparently coming to harm. The edges of many of the small lakes and streams were dirty and evil-smelling and covered with loathsome green duckweed. The Kashmiris just pushed the scum to one side and filled their vessels without a qualm.

There are three Moghul Gardens in Srinagar – each exquisite and each different in character although conforming to a general pattern.

The most famous and largest is the Shalamar Bagh or Garden of Love. We got up early one morning to visit this and had breakfast on the artificial island on the way. This is an ornamental island about 40 yards square built in three terraces by the Moghuls to adorn the approach to the Shalamar.

After breakfast on the island our *shikara* took us up the canal to the Shalamar Garden. This is a large walled garden in four terraces planted with *chenar* and fruit trees interspersed with lovely beds of flowers. Just as we entered the gardens the waterworks were started. The old Muslim builders – from those who built these gardens in Kashmir to those who built the Moorish palaces and gardens in Spain – had a great feeling for the beautiful effects of falling water and splashing fountains and for the refreshing coolness induced by water in a hot climate.

In the Shalamar Garden the fountains played in the sunlight and the water creamed down from terrace to terrace over different types of stonework each designed to give the water a different pattern of movement. Each waterfall leading from one terrace to another is flanked by a summer house with walls of delicate white marble tracery. It was noticeably cooler in the gardens than outside.

On the topmost terrace is a white stone hall surrounded by a square stone pool filled with fountains throwing the water up in different shapes. There is a veranda running all round the hall pillared in black marble from Pampoor. These pillars make a delightful contrast with the white of the main pavilion and the creaming water of the fountains.

The upper part of the garden was originally set apart for the emperor's *zenana*. The place is worthy of Jehangir's fair queen, Mumtaz Mahal, to whose eye for scenery and good taste whilst alive the Moghul Gardens in Kashmir are beautiful and enduring monuments, but surpassed by that erected on her death by her grief-stricken husband – the Taj Mahal.

The Maharaja of Kashmir used to give banquets in the Shalamar Garden on the King-Emperor's Birthday and on other occasions. The glitter of a myriad multicoloured electric lights set in the trees and fountains and illuminating the bright colours of saris and evening gowns must have made a memorable scene for the lucky guests. Europeans who signed the Maharaja's book were normally invited.

After leaving the Shalamar Garden we came back into the lake and went under a stone bridge to the Nishat Bagh – the Garden of Gladness. The general design is somewhat similar to the Shalamar but the hill from which the terraces are cut is steeper and backed by a magnificent mountain. Like the Shalamar Garden, a great deal of the effect is achieved by the magnificent position between mountain and lake and, like the Shalamar and all Moghul Gardens, a great effect is achieved by absolute symmetry. A *chenar* tree in one corner is reproduced in the opposite corner and the flowerbeds and differently coloured shrubs all take their place in the pattern. The Nishat Bagh was even cooler than the Shalamar and the water fed from a mountain stream felt icy cold. The Moghuls had a palace on the terraces facing the lake but this had disappeared.

The third garden is different. This is the Chashma Shahi or Royal Spring. It is a perfect miniature set in a hollow surrounded by high mountains. It owes its existence to the copious spring of cool, pure water. Its focus is a delightful, large summer house of white stone overgrown with beautiful creepers. Through a Moghul arch one looks out onto the fountains and the spring, again set amidst symmetrical flower beds and trees.

Swimming in the Dal Lake was a strange experience as it was fairly warm near the surface but in places, if one went down a few feet, the water fed by streams from melting glaciers was icy cold. There had been quite a few drownings in the lake possibly due to heart failure or cramp on suddenly meeting this cold layer of water.

We spent a week or two in these ideal surroundings following the idle, carefree pursuits of youth. The surface of our content was only slightly rippled by news of the Spanish Civil War and the rising menace of Hitler. We decided it was time to start our trek into the mountains and we made arrangements to hire tents, camp furniture, riding and packhorses, horsemen, cook and servants.

On the appointed day we were up at 5 a.m. and eager to go. The first stage of our journey was by lorry to the Woygil Bridge. This was the road head for wheeled traffic where we had arranged a rendezvous with the *ghora walle* or horsemen.

Our luggage was loaded on to the back of the lorry and the four Kashmiri servants we had hired, Sohbra, the cook, and the three bearers, Buttu, Aziza and Jamal, were seated with ourselves on rough wooden benches in the front. Some of the horsemen and a local coolie surmounted the luggage at the back and nearly suffered the fate of Absalom from low-hanging branches.

We set off through the fields of white and red rice on the first stage to the village of Ganderbal where we made a slight diversion to the Post Office to see if the exam papers that I was awaiting had arrived from Lahore. The babu at the Post Office, a fat, suave Kashmiri pandit, informed me, 'Nothing arriving for Sahib' and so after an inspection of the neighbouring shop, whose sole stock appeared to be Urdu primers, slates and rubber balls, we set off again.

When we arrived at Woygil our tents, equipment and luggage were unloaded, divided into pack loads and loaded on to eleven packhorses. There was nothing austere about our camping. We had two sleeping tents, a collapsible string bed each, three most ingenious camp chairs designed in India and known as *Roorkee* chairs (which break down into a roll of canvas wrapping up the rounded wooden members), a folding table, commodes, a bath tent with tub and a lavatory tent – not to mention tents for the servants and kitchen.

The road as far as Woygil was classified on the map as 'good' but it was only really a lorryable track. Our trek was to start up the valley of the Sind. This was the original name of the great river Indus and is still retained in Kashmir and Tibet. At Woygil the Sind was crossed by a substantial suspension bridge but it was designed only for animals and was too narrow for motor traffic. We found, in any case, that on the other side of the river the *rasta*, road, track, definitely deteriorated into an animal track which led by gentle slopes up the side of the river.

Soon we had to cross the dry beds of various small tributaries of the Sind which were strewn with large rounded boulders some as high as our small riding ponies and it was obvious that in spate even these small rivers carried an immense force or water. Every little pocket of cultivable land was utilised. Where it could be irrigated, rice was grown and where water would not reach the crop was maize.

Shortly after midday we left the valley of the Sind to enter the valley of its tributary – the Wongat. We had not gone far up the Wongat Valley when we decided that it was so beautiful that we would spend the night there. Soon the packhorses caught us up, the tents were pitched, a fire lit and our *tiffin* being prepared. I made an arrangement for a coolie to leave at four o'clock in the morning to go back to Ganderbal to wait for the examination papers.

After this we all sat back and drank in the marvellous scenery. Just in front of us was a mountain stream full of trout. Steep, pine-clad hills formed an amphitheatre behind us and far away in the hazy distance towards Tibet we saw snow gleaming on the peaks of some Himalayan giant. In the middle distance the silhouette of the Pir Panjal Range, which acts as a rampart jealously guarding the Golden Vale of Kashmir from unwarranted intruders, fretted a delicate tracery against the deep blue sky. This was the first of many camping places of rare beauty. I felt a very definite spiritual exultation as I looked at it and could well understand why the Hindus consider that the Himalayas are the abode of the Gods.

The only slight snag in our contentment was the fact that the saddles were rather uncomfortable and I found that the ponies were so short that I had difficulty in keeping my long legs out of the way of the pony's front or hind legs and once nearly tripped up my mount.

The next morning we were off to an early start, after having our breakfast and watching the camp struck and loaded on the ponies.

The track climbed steadily all the time, usually steeply, sometimes gently. In the steeper parts it was indistinguishable from a small mountain stream and runnels of water gushed down it. Sometimes it crossed swampy but steep hillsides which held the water like a constantly dripping sponge; sometimes it threaded through trees which we had the greatest difficulty in avoiding, sometimes it was a narrow ledge at the edge of a precipice. At times we slithered precariously across greasy, shaly screes or squeezed between boulders; at others we passed sedately through mountain hamlets where the children, at best dressed in rags, sometimes stark naked, looked at us with eyes popping half in wonder, half in fear as they screeched out *'Salaam sahib, bakhshish dedo.'* 'Welcome Sahib, give bakhshish.' Although small, the ponies were very sturdy and sure-footed and I think that there was nowhere I could have climbed, without using my hands, that the ponies could not have covered.

In spite of the exiguous nature of the track in many places, we were constantly reminded that it was one of the main traffic routes of that part of the world and, indeed, before the erection of the Iron and Bamboo Curtains, had carried a great deal of trade between India and Central Asia. We met or passed several long caravans mostly consisting of packhorses or donkeys, occasionally mules or coolies and once we saw a long line of sheep all carrying a little bag of sugar on each side. That was the only time in my life that I saw such a sight. We also saw a coolie carrying a sick, consumptive-looking girl to the nearest medical attention. They had already been over a week on the road.

We camped for the night on the upper of two mountain terraces

81

with a view of the Wongat several thousand feet below. The place was called Nar Nag and was near the ruins of a Hindu monastery. It must have been an important foundation as the ruins were quite extensive and included a large rectangular pool lined with dressed stone. A mountain stream had originally been led into it but the channel was blocked up.

When the time came to light the lamps we discovered that some parts were missing and a great deal of paraffin had vanished. This was the first depredation of our henchmen. They were most indignant when branded as *chor* or thief. We had a terrific scene, which must have made it clear that we would not tolerate any further losses and we had no further trouble of this kind.

I was woken up next morning by Carl saying that the exam papers had come. I spent the morning marking them and then sent them back to the Post Office by the same coolie, giving him 1 rupee, 10 annas for his long double journey. That was 8 annas for each day's trek and 10 annas bakhshish after his insistence that the custom was '*hamesha bakhshish*' – always a douceur.

Later in the morning an old man called to say that his grand-child was ill. Kashmiri is a language in its own right and quite distinct from Urdu. I could not understand it at all. Occasionally some of the villagers who had come into contact with Indians from elsewhere or who had worked in other provinces spoke Urdu. This old man had some Urdu and said '*Meri poti bimar hai.*' 'My grand-daughter is ill.' He had not brought her.

We carried a few simple drugs and pills as there was always such a demand for them. It was quite pathetic the way all Europeans were besieged for medical help and the implicit faith placed in one's ability to diagnose and cure. We could not completely understand the old man's story even if we had had the medical knowledge to diagnose the trouble and the correct drugs with which to treat it. We gave him quinine, aspirins and laxative with explanations as to the use of each. The last was always a great favourite, which led one to think that there must be something in their way of life that kept the Kashmiris constantly constipated. A good purge seemed to have as great a spiritual as physical effect.

The old man appeared again in the afternoon carrying the child on his back. It was fairly obvious that she was suffering from malnutrition and had a high fever. We thought that she was probably tubercular and advised, '*Usko Mangaum ko lejao, taki doctor Sahiba usko dekh sakke.*' 'Take her to Mangaum so that the lady doctor can see her.' A lady missionary doctor called there at intervals. This was a day's journey over a difficult track but very close for medical service by the standards of Kashmir.

The old man must have known about the doctor. The illness was obviously of long standing and he had not troubled to do anything before. We thought that probably he would do nothing in the future. After all she was only a girl. It might have been worth while making some effort to come to us but not much more.

We were off next morning to an early and smooth start. By this time the men had become used to striking the camp quickly and the pack for each animal had been established and each animal resigned to its load. The ponies had to be particularly carefully loaded for this stage and the most awkward articles such as bath tubs and the long poles of beds had to be distributed amongst coolies specially hired for this stage.

The track led immediately up a very steep hill and we climbed steadily for several hours, zigzagging up as steeply as it was possible to go. By this time we had gained the brow and immediately the path led between thick pine and fir woods at a height of about 10,000 feet. At about 11,000 feet the only arboreal vegetation was the slanted mountain juniper. Lovely alpine flowers filled the spaces between the trees and threw brilliant splashes of colour against the sombre masses of rocks that outcropped here and there.

We then dropped down about 1,000 feet and found the most entrancing alpine meadow opening up in front of our wondering eyes. Scattered over the upland immensity of grass and flowers were Gujar families with vast herds of sleek cattle and spirited ponies. This was a surprising sight at a height of 10,000 feet, accessible only by a most difficult mountain track. Our own ponies had been stretched to their limit to make the climb – struggling and heaving for a precarious hold from one boulder to the next. At one point, when the steep track, heavy load and rarefied atmosphere had brought them almost to the point of breathless collapse, the pony men brought out skewers from their sleeves and plunged them into the ponies' muzzles. This seemed very brutal treatment but I believe that it has some scientific basis. The ponies staggered on with a little more energy.

The Gujars are a hardy, upland pastoral folk of a distinctly Semitic appearance. They are Muslims but of a different race from the Kashmiris proper. Legend has it that they, like so many others, are the lost tribe of Israel. Throughout the centuries they have gradually established their rights to a type of transhumance which gives them a rough but self-sufficient and self-satisfying existence on the mountains of Kashmir. In the short summer season they monopolise the upper mountain pastures. As the snows approach, the Gujars drive their flocks to the lower level. Naturally there is sometimes a conflict over the rights to the lower pastures and there is little love lost between the Gujars and the Kashmiris proper.

As we rode over these meadows, the lush grass and tall flowers came knee high to us on our small ponies. The scent of the flowers and the humming of the bees gathering nectar filled the air and wheeling high against the blue sky were hawks and eagles intently watching for birds and small animals on which to pounce. Now and then far below us we could see the silver thread of the Wongat lined on each side by poplars and ahead of us were the towering snow-capped peaks of some of the mightiest mountains in the world.

When we reached the end of the meadow we stopped to have our lunch surrounded by wild roses, asters, blue mountain poppies, forget-me-nots, harebells, spiraea, geraniums, foxgloves and other flowers. It reminded me that many flowers leading a sedate life in a domesticated flower bed had been brought by early botanists from the wild heights of the Himalayas.

On the distant heights we saw what appeared to be vast ploughed fields covered with large brown clods. In due course as we reached the place we saw that it was a gigantic moraine of brown boulders.

This spot had a lovely view and although it was rather exposed we decided to camp there. We had had a fairly strenuous day, could see no more promising sites in view and had a very wide range of vision. The expanses are so great and the air so clear that anyone with sufficiently good eyes concentrating on the right spot can pick out a caravan threading its way down a distant mountain-side and looking no bigger than a train of small brown ants with scarcely discernible movement.

Every locality has a name in Kashmir and the name of our camping spot was Trankhul. Just behind us rose the austere, disdainful peak of Haramukh, 13,400 feet, and before us the slopes showing typical glacial contours over which we had climbed earlier in the day. To one side of the slopes leading up to Haramukh were several hanging valleys down which rushed torrential streams, finally plunging in waterfalls down the cliffs into the main valley which had been scooped out and deepened by a glacier. Gujar huts were dotted about the mountainside and their stock filled the valley floor.

When the pack ponies arrived we found evidence of the difficulty of the track. The waterproof canvas covers of my bedding roll had been badly gashed against the boulders on the track and similarly the sides of my tin trunk had been bashed in. It was necessary to take the small ubiquitous Indian tin trunk if one wanted to keep something safely dry from the occasional but sudden and violent mountain storms. Several of the ponies had fallen and grazed themselves quite deeply. We had to pay off the special coolies engaged for this stage but the whole Gujar community had great difficulty in producing change for a five rupee note.

The chilly night made our fine camp fire very welcome. We set out our gramophone and medicine chest on the camp table. Shy silent figures gradually stole down in the dark from the mountainsides to listen to the music. None of them had previously heard a gramophone, radio or telephone. The women were dressed in black robes from head to foot, with turbans or cloths round their heads and the children were similarly dressed. The men wore black turbans, wound around a *kula* (or stiff dome-shaped inner cap worn by Muslims in the Indian subcontinent inside a turban and projecting above the open middle of the turban), rough home-spun waistcoats, jackets and s*halwars*. Each had a rough loosely-woven blanket, which was used as overcoat, mackintosh, bed-coverlet and poncho. When it is cold they crouch down and draw the blanket around them. In the really cold weather, like all Kashmiris, they carry around a little earthenware pot in which

85

they burn charcoal to keep themselves warm. They place this up against their stomach as they squat down and wrap the all-embracing blanket around pot and body. The constant contact of hot pot and body leads to a very high incidence of cancer of the stomach.

For a long time they sat mute and wondering at the strangeness of the Sahibs' magic. At length there was some subdued muttering amongst themselves which finally crystallised into requests for laxatives passed to us by the old men who had a smattering of Urdu. Ultimately the really sick cases were produced. A little girl who was obviously very ill and looked like another TB case; an expectant mother who said that her first three children had died and who appeared to be yet another TB case. We repeated our advice that they should go for proper medical attention but this was not well received and they clamoured for pills. We therefore gave them some of our stock remedies, aspirin, quinine and laxatives. They were touchingly grateful and it was obvious that they were far too fatalistic to walk over the mountain for medical attention.

We had decided to make Trankhul our centre for several day trips, the first of which was to visit the two celebrated lakes at Gangabal, which have thick slabs of perpetual ice floating on the surface of the water on the side of the lakes protected by high cliffs from the sun. We made an early start as usual as it was always advisable to have a few hours in hand to avoid any risk of having to spend the night in the open at such a high altitude.

We climbed diagonally up a long mountain slope fording a few small streams as we came to them. Then came a steep rocky descent to a roaring mountain river crossed on the two halves of a long pine tree split roughly in two with the flat sides laid on top. On the edge of the river were the skeletons of several ponies that had obviously slipped off the narrow bridge. Topping a small rise we saw the first and smaller of the two glacial lakes in front of us. This was semi-elliptical in shape and about half a mile long. It was a lovely shade of peacock green with the white peak of Haramukh reflected in the water.

A track led on up to the mountainside over several arêtes to the larger Lake Gangabal. Here we had to wade through part of the stream as the bridge had broken down and the stepping stones were covered with water. As the stream was issuing from the glacier only a few hundred yards away the water was numbingly cold. Gangabal is a place of pilgrimage and, as its name implies, is reputed by many Hindus, but apparently incorrectly, to be one source of the Ganges. We were told that it is considered desirable for a visit to Gangabal by the close relatives of the deceased to form part of the funeral rites of every pious Kashmiri Hindu.

Haramukh was usually obscured by mist and only revealed itself occasionally, but always its fleeting appearance gave an impression of austerity and remoteness as befitted one of the reputed homes of the Gods. The main lake, like the smaller lake, was a typical glacier formation with a terminal moraine of boulders and a clearly defined lateral moraine. The spot was thickly carpeted with snowflowers, ground-ivy, buttercups, oxlips, house-leek and many others unknown to me. We walked through several large meadows of yellow crocuses, from which saffron is obtained, and also wide flats of springy, peat-like moss which is used to fill up the chinks in the rough log bridges and give them some kind of decking.

On the way up to the second lake we had come to a bridge without any of this decking. The one pony we had brought along with us had slipped off and had been swept away some little distance. It had just managed to scramble to its feet and half flounder, half float to safety and so avoid adding to the skeletons. We, ourselves, had crossed by linking hands together with a coolie and edging carefully over.

In the evening more Gujars came to listen to the gramophone and to ask for medicine – it was difficult to know which was the chief attraction. We bought a sheep from one. His asking price was 6 rupees, 8 annas but he agreed to sell it to us for 5 rupees if it was killed on the spot and he could keep the fleece. The village headman killed it and we had some of it for dinner. Later on on our trek we bought another sheep for 5 rupees and it accompanied us for several days until, somewhat reluctantly, we had to put it in the pot. It was killed, skinned and neatly jointed with an axe. These Kashmiri sheep fed on the aromatic herbage of the mountains formed the most delicious mutton I have ever had.

The mountain bowl in which Trunkhul was placed seemed to

collect a great deal of rain and the next day it rained steadily and depressingly all day. We could do little but spend a miserable day in our tents. Carl told me about the parts of America that he had travelled in and I described what I knew of England. The next day it cleared up and the Gujars took advantage of the fine weather to ask for a matinee performance on the gramophone.

In the evening we visited a Gujar's hut, a rough log cabin plastered with clay and peat. The mountainside is used as the back wall, logs form the sides, front and flat roof. The inside was fairly clean but about a dozen people and three calves occupied a fairly confined space. There was a separate higher ledge, which was used for eating and sleeping. This was spread with small fir branches to form a mattress. This is a type of couch that I have tried myself in India when sleeping out on army manoeuvres and is fairly comfortable. We were surprised to find a clean up-to-date sewing machine in one corner. The dense smoke soon drove me out. The Gujars are not particularly addicted to using water for any purpose except drinking and as they are so constantly kippered by the smoke of their huts they have a rare old patina and rich redolence.

Next day the track began a long steep ascent to a snow patch about 20 yards wide but about 1,000 yards long. We had to plough through its length to reach the pass as the track being in the lowest and most sheltered part of the col was the very part where the snow had not melted. At the pass we fell in with a caravan of red-bearded Muslim merchants with their coolies carrying their merchandise on their backs. The pass was 13,000 feet high and we were glad that we were not encumbered with heavy loads like the coolies.

On the way up we looked back to some fine views of Trankhul and the Gangabal Lakes. The pass was a desolate, windswept, completely uninviting spot. The rocks were mostly bare but covered in places with a scraping of soil and a few inches of hardy lichenous turf. Like many passes it had no real view as it was too long to give a view of either valley and was completely shut in by high peaks.

We zigzagged down a shallow, boggy basin and then a very steep descent to Mangan Dob. In addition to the steepness the

surface was a slippery shale and the pack ponies had a very difficult time. However, the Gujar coolies that we had again employed
for this stage to lessen the loads on the ponies did not find much
difficulty and left the track in places to take short cuts down the
even steeper face of the mountain. When we reached Mangan Dob
we paid off the Gujars who immediately set off on the difficult
stage back to Trankhul with no more ado than a city man going
round the corner to the tobacconist.

Even below the pass with some degree of shelter our camping
ground was a desolate spot. Not far from us was a Kashmiri skin
tent sheltering between two boulders and anchored down by
rocks. To our astonishment we saw two completely naked children
outside the tent in the bitter wind. We spent a very cold night
constantly woken up by the banshee howling of the wind.

Off by eight o'clock on a beautiful morning with a stiff breeze
blowing, we passed a flock of sheep and the shepherd, on enquiry,
told us there were two thousand.

Shortly we came to another of those beautiful mountain
meadows carpeted with all manner of flowers which caressed us
with scented embraces as our horses brushed through them. In the
distance the beautiful shape of Nanga Parbat, the Naked Mountain, dramatically thrust its 26,600 feet into the sky. This
mountain, the fourth highest in the world, was the focus of all
landscapes for the next few days. It seemed to be no nearer at the
end of a day's march than at the beginning. The main massif of the
mountain is a great upthrust mass of rock so steep that it holds no
snow, which gives it its Hindustani name. This characteristic and
its abrupt rise from relatively level upland meadows gives it
unique, dramatic beauty.

We had our lunch near a lonely Gujar tent and went on after
lunch until we found an inviting hollow near a lake in which to
pitch our tents. The next day we decided to do two stages in one
and press on to within a short stage of Sonamarg. I started off on
foot and after walking about a mile went down to investigate a
lake, which was said to be covered with ice for the greater part of
the year. I found cakes of packed snow floating on the water but no
ice. I had a fairly stiff climb back to the others who waited for me
and I then got on my pony and we continued together. We rode for

some distance over rolling country and then came to another stiff climb. We all had to dismount and climb on foot. I felt rather tired near the top and had a peg of brandy. Finally we had to climb a fairly stiff snow pass. All around the pass were masses of yellow hyacinth-like flowers. From the pass was a fine view of a lake and gradually descending upland *margs* or meadows.

The descent was very steep and shaly. After lunch it was first of all easy pony-going. We had to ford two wide, powerful streams and then to start climbing on foot. About this time I felt very queer but walked on for about half a mile; I then had to lie down in the shade of a rock and have a little more brandy. I continued for a short distance on my pony but soon had to get off and climb again. By then the altitude and the long stage had given me a very definite attack of mountain sickness and I had to take things fairly easily over the soft snow. I felt quite light-headed and could not speak rationally or correctly.

When we had got over the pass I mounted again. One of the horsemen led the pony and half held me on its back. I was extremely grateful to him and admired his fortitude as we passed down a steep, boulder-strewn track. He had only loosely-woven grass sandals to protect his feet from the jagged stones.

When we got to the camping place I lay down covered with a blanket. As soon as the tent and bed were up I retired, very shivery, for the night. I had completely recovered by the morning except for a slight headache, which soon wore off.

Next day came a very steep climb up through a birch wood with occasional delightful glimpses of the opposite side of the valley. Emerging from the wood we had a lovely view of our destination – Sonamarg. Sonamarg means 'Golden Meadow' – presumably because of the flowers at certain seasons – but now it was a deep, vivid emerald carpet backed by gleaming glaciers and snow peaks.

We continued down the track, which became steadily easier and obviously more used. Finally, just before we reached the plateau of which Sonamarg is the centre we came to a wide river crossed by a substantial bridge of squared timber, the first that we had seen since we left Woygil. Beautiful groves of mountain poplars lined the banks of the river and decorated its flood plain with their graceful plumes.

Sonamarg was quite a mountain metropolis and an important centre for caravan routes. Scattered over the extensive pastures were vast herds of cows and yaks and small self-conscious groups of *dzos*, the result of free love between the two former species of animal on the mountain slopes.

We found a delightful little side valley and pitched our camp under some trees and within striking distance of a small glacier. It was an entrancing site and we decided to spend some time there. Therefore, we paid off the coolies and the horsemen and then walked to the Post Office to fetch our mail before settling down to a lovely moonlit night.

The next day we luxuriated by having breakfast in bed and then walked to Sonamarg passing some lovely, gambolling colts on the way.

We saw some Ladakhis who had made a primitive open-air forge and were mending their horses' shoes. We also listened to a Ladakhi band dressed in strange uniform with wild, outlandish instruments producing sounds which were harsh and discordant even compared with our previous experience of other oriental music. Later on we met a wedding party with a bigger and louder band and a group of men mumming and dancing led by one very tipsy old fellow. The bride was in a palanquin, the bridegroom on a fine white horse. We joined the dancing group and the spectators rolled on the ground in agonies of merriment at our efforts. A little later we came to the camp where they were cooking the wedding feast. We were invited to join but thought that our digestions would not be strong enough.

On the way back I bought a tiny, roughly-carved jade Buddha for a few annas. We came to another encampment of Ladakhis wearing thick sheepskin coats, which seemed to be their uniform dress either for the sub-zero nights at 17,000 feet or the hot, sunny days at 10,000 feet. Some seemed very Mongolian but others had finer features. Men and women were all burnt a most peculiar blackish shade by the strong ultra-violet rays of the mountain sunlight. They had some of those fierce but delightful Tibetan sheepdogs like giant snow-white chows. Their job is not to shepherd the sheep but to head off wolves and, if necessary, bears, at night. They are strong and fearless.

91

The next week we spent making day treks up the lovely valleys, which radiated from Sonamarg. Sometimes we took Buttu to carry our tiffin basket. First light saw us on our way after breakfast in the dawn twilight as we did not want to risk a night in the open at these altitudes. Sometimes we were back in time for a bath before a late lunch and a shorter walk in the evening. Our last day at Sonamarg was washed out by rain, which only served to point our good fortune in the previous ten days' perfect weather.

The road back was the busy main route following the valley of the Sind. The first day the track followed fairly level ground close to the river through many leafy groves of lovely Kashmiri walnut trees. We met large caravans of pack ponies carrying grain up from the plains and several other trekking parties – the first that we had seen. The road gradually rose, winding round the shoulders of hills until it reached a fair height above the river. We then passed through a rock cutting and emerged onto a shelf cut from the face of the cliff and widened by a plank structure built up on ledges from beneath the level of the road.

Our first night's stop was at Gund where we pitched our tents in the neat willow-bordered compound of the rest house. We were joined by two other European parties. One was very tired after doing two stages in one day. We gave them water and tea. We were intrigued to see a double camp bed being erected for one party – something I never saw before or afterwards.

The going was relatively easy and we decided to double up two shortish stages on foot. By evening we were tired and sore-footed although we had become so fit that we could walk 20–25 miles a day indefinitely over difficult country. We camped by the side of the Wongat river only a few hundred yards below where we had camped on the first night of our trek. Buttu emptied our last tin, Heinz beans, on to a foundation of mountain mutton, onions, marrow, potatoes and tomatoes and we had a delicious stew. A long search had produced some milk and we finished our meal with a cup of steaming chocolate.

We had arranged for a lorry to be at Woygil at nine the next morning and so we started out at seven o'clock. We arrived in time but, needless to say, the lorry was not there. But it soon arrived, before our pack ponies.

92

When they arrived an incident came that could only happen in India. It may seem strange to those not used to social and religious customs in India – amongst Europeans as well as the Indians – but we had been accompanied on all our journeying by a commode. No servant would have accompanied a European who was so unseemly, even in the remote mountain fastnesses of Kashmir, as to defecate straight on to Mother India. Likewise no ordinary servant would touch a commode and so we took along with us a patient, cheerful fellow of the sweeper caste whose mission in life was to handle commodes and their contents and heat bath water.

When it came to loading the lorry it was discovered that this fellow, who had completed his last sortie and had been paid off after breakfast, had been allowed to slip away without finally loading the commode onto the lorry. Everything else had been loaded but the lonely commode, a sorry and solitary eyesore, stood neglected on the village green. At first all the other men refused to load it. I then said that if they would not put it on the lorry I would do so myself although such is the power of prejudice that I would have been reluctant to do so. They were obviously horrified at the suggestion and after a hurried consultation decided that it would be even worse to let me do it than to do it themselves. One fellow, more independent-minded than the others, then strode forward and, tensely watched by all the others and handling the offending object as if it were a time bomb, gingerly placed it on the lorry. The strange thing was that they were all Muslims and theoretically quite untouched by the caste system. However, so strongly pervasive is caste in India that it tends to affect Muslims, Europeans and Indian Christians. Indeed, in some Indian Christian churches, particularly in the south of India, the Christian congregation still segregates itself into groups according to caste origin.

Thus ended our trek in the most beautiful country that I have ever seen. I cannot imagine there can be scenery, grander or more beautiful than Kashmir anywhere in the world. I still carry in my mind's eye scenes encountered on that trek.

We set up our camp for a few days on our old site and it was very enjoyable and cooling to have an itinerant barber cut our hair and shave off the beards we had grown on our trek.

After a few days we decided to hire a houseboat from one of the agencies. For about five rupees a day we got a craft with three bedrooms, a lounge, bathroom and lavatory. There was a sun deck with awning on the roof. Ours was a relatively modest affair. Some of them approached floating palaces. The terms included a kitchen boat anchored in the neighbourhood and a cook.

The houseboat was sited on the Dal Lake but nearer to the centre of Srinagar than the camping site. We luxuriated in the life of lotus-eaters figuratively whilst we constantly saw the Kashmiris literally eating the nuts of the lotus or local water lily.

Swarms of pedlars in boats plagued us daily; persistently and obstinately offering their wares. Almost anything that Kashmir could produce and would fetch money was on sale. Amongst the items offered were vegetables and fruit; meat, poultry and milk; store goods of all descriptions; a variety of the lovely Kashmiri wood-carvings and small articles of furniture; a wide range of papier mâché articles, silk goods from Kashmir, Central Asia and China; woven rugs and carpets from Persia, Turkistan, Baluchistan, Kashmir and China; rugs and other articles made from *numdah*, the special type of felt made in Ladakh and Tibet; articles from *pashmina*, that very lightweight fleecy but warm woollen material made from down specially plucked from the under parts of sheep; embroidery work; ivory and bone carvings and a wide variety of other interesting and beautiful items.

One day a Turkoman rug dealer came along with his last rug for which he asked a fairly reasonable price but I had little money left. He then asked me what I would offer and I said thirteen rupees which was the first figure that came into my head. It was quite a ridiculous offer and I hoped it would send him permanently away. However, he came back every morning but I never varied my offer and finally got a lovely rug as a great bargain.

I also bought a pair of old Persian brass stirrups with wide foot plates, a very beautiful fretted bronze mosque lamp, a lamaistic brass inkwell shaped like a pagoda and a votive candlestick like those used in Tibetan temples.

We did a little more wandering around the bazaars and interesting buildings of Srinagar. We visited the Hari Parbat Fort on its hill dominating the city and the Jami Masjid with an outer arch and wall of brick but with the main inner building a soaring timber construction and the tallest and most complex wooden buildings that I had seen until I went to Japan.

We climbed the thousands of weary steps to the Takht-i-Suleiman, Soloman's Throne, on its peak dominating a corner of the Dal Lake. It is said that this was a place of worship 2,000 years before England became Christian. It had become a mosque from the time that Kashmir became Muslim.

The surface of the lake was so clear and calm that the surrounding peaks were perfectly reflected in every detail and it is difficult to tell which is the right way up of some of the photos that I took. We watched the Kashmiris fishing in the lake from dawn to dusk. One of the favourite ways of fishing was by throwing out a big round cast net, with small weights on its circumference. This was given a spinning motion as it was thrown so that it opened out and the weights, when they sank, pulled the net in, catching any fish inside. The throwing of the net was a very graceful movement and the rays of the sun falling on the drops of water caught on the net made them sparkle like jewels. As dusk fell the long line of fishing *shikaras* would file back across the lake, the outline of the fishers silhouetted against the setting sun and their strange plangent chorus keeping time with the rhythmical rise and fall of the paddles.

It was fairly hot at Srinaga, although at a height of about 8,000 feet, and so after a week or so we decided to go up a few thousand feet higher to Gulmarg, the summer capital of Kashmir.

We got seats in a local bus, which was not very comfortable but it was a fairly short and pleasant journey. First of all we went along a straight road lined with poplars and raised on a *bund* above the rather low-lying countryside. Not until the last four or five miles did the road begin to climb.

There was a motor road all the way to Gulmarg but only the Viceroy, the Commander in Chief and the Maharaja of Kashmir were allowed to use cars in Gulmarg. Thus a lovely beauty spot was preserved from noise and petrol fumes. Everyone else had to leave their vehicles at Tangmarg and either walk, ride on ponies or use horse-drawn buggies or man-drawn rickshaws above this place.

We decided to walk the three or four miles from Tangmarg, the Narrow Meadow, to Gulmarg, the Meadow of Roses. There was a horde of coolies clamouring and struggling for work and we left it to a policeman to pick out four for our luggage. Just after we started a violent storm burst on us. Carl had no mackintosh or other protection at hand and a coolie absolutely insisted on giving him his blanket.

We found the scenery different from the other parts of Kashmir that we had seen. There were many more coniferous trees and the whole effect was very much like Switzerland when we reached the township of Gulmarg with its wooden chalets, shops and hotels.

Gulmarg lived on tourists. It had several hotels run by hoteliers famous in Lahore and elsewhere in India, a number of boarding-houses, two golf courses, and facilities for tennis, cricket and polo. The golf courses were most scenic, especially the lower one running up Leopard's Valley. Sometimes the All-Indian Championship was played at Gulmarg.

Like all Indian hill stations, it had lovely walks radiating to different beauty spots and a famous outer circular road which was a lovely walk four or five miles long through fir and pine woods through which one could get magnificent, distant views of Nanga Parbat and Haramukh and occasionally of Mount Godwin Austen, as it was then called, second only in height to Everest.

We spent a quiet life at Gulmarg, eating wonderful food at a lovely chalet boarding house run by a European lady and going for walks. We walked one day up to Khillanmarg to the site of the hut belonging to the Ski Club of India, which was shattered by an avalanche in the 1935 winter. Several Europeans and Kashmiris sheltering in the hut at the time were killed.

The time slipped by all too quickly until we had to return to Lahore and work. We all agreed that it was the most wonderful holiday we had ever had. Not only were we very fit physically but the lovely scenes from the Abode of the Gods were printed on our memories and for me at least formed a spiritual reservoir from which I would draw refreshment in the years to come.

5

Gaining Experience

Muslim, Sikh and Hindu boys normally attended the mosque, gurdwara and mandir, respectively, first thing every morning and at the appropriate time in the evening, which varied with the seasons. There was nothing in the College rules to enforce this but such was religious conviction and convention in India, and probably the influence of the respective priests, that absentees were unknown except for illness. The College employed priests, in the loose sense of the word, who presided over the various services and attended to the spiritual needs of their community. Some families, particularly those with pious aspirations, arranged and apparently paid for special religious teachers to instruct their children and protect them from any threat to their orthodoxy. These priestly pedagogues existed in the strange limbo of so many in India whose status is not clearly defined and whose means of existence is exiguous. When not engaged in their instruction they stalked around the College, their eyes blazing with fanaticism, searching for religious peccadilloes amongst their charges and glaring at infidels.

Most days, after lunch, the *maulvi* came to give me Urdu and Persian lessons. I was sometimes quite sleepy as I would have been up since five and often not in bed until one o'clock the night before. The hot weather routine made everything later in the evening. After the *maulvi* left I would lie on the bed in a sarong, read a little, and then fall asleep until Maula Baksh brought some tea. Then I would bath, change and go out to take my turn on games duty or to play tennis.

I cannot say that I educated myself as Winston Churchill did by instructive reading whilst lying on a bed during these long hot Indian afternoons.

The boys normally wore khaki shorts and white open necked shirts in the hot weather. Formal wear for them was the *achkhan*, the long Indian coat which buttoned round the neck and went down to the knees. In the hot weather it was made of light, white silk and in the cold weather of black cloth. They could have gold buttons if they wished. It looked very smart either way and was a useful and economical dress for Indians as it was accepted for different occasions when Europeans would have to wear either ordinary or formal suits, dinner jackets, tails or morning dress. Sikh boys, of course, always wore turbans except for strenuous sports for which they took off the outer turban and retained the *pagri* or inner turban with their top knot tied up in a handkerchief. For everyday wear the turban was optional for other boys. If worn, it was slate coloured for all boys. For formal occasions all boys had to wear the *firozi* turban so called from the Urdu name for its beautiful turquoise colour. It was specially dyed for the Chiefs' College and I never saw the exact shade anywhere else. This turban was a great length of gauze and almost colourless when stretched out. As the turban was bound round the head the colour gradually built up. I have already described the Sikh turban. The Hindu boys tied their turbans in different styles according to their tradition. Some Rajputs rolled up the end of the turban into a rope-like form and had several rows of this more or less horizontally at the side of their head. I thought this looked very untidy. The Muslim boys always wore a *kulah* or type of skull cap round which the turban was tied and sometimes stitched. Low dome-shaped for most Punjabis it was high and pointed for Pathans; for both it was embroidered with gold thread. It was a very striking sight when the boys were all assembled in their formal dress.

At Basant Panchmi, the Indian festival of spring, all the Hindu and Sikh boys and masters wore yellow turbans associated with the mustard crops that came into flower at that time.

The staff could wear shorts or slacks and open-necked shirts in the classroom in the hot weather. Medium weight suits and ties were worn in the cold weather. Some of the older Indian staff wore suits for teaching throughout the year. For formal occasions the Indian staff wore Indian or European dress according to their taste.

As in all good boarding schools, an important part of the educational process both for boys and staff was in what might be called the extra-curricular activities.

One of these at the college was called the Council of State after the body representing the princes in the consultative, legislative and administrative machinery of the Indian constitution. About once a month in the College hall we had an enactment of a session of the Council of State. Boys were given various roles to play and different policies and resolutions to propose or oppose. They had time to do some research into the subjects and prepare their speeches, which they were not supposed to read. On the whole they did quite well but there was a tendency among some to make cheap debating points.

Indians as a whole are not usually at a loss for words. At one social occasion at the College, Bakshi Narain Singh, he of the crab-like gait on the tennis court, spoke for about 25 minutes, with hardly a pause for breath, merely thanking the retiring secretary of the staff tennis club. When he had finished he said, 'With these few words I resume my seat.'

There was tennis available every evening for members of the staff who were not in charge of some game and who wished to play. The Raja of Sheikhapura, an old boy of the College, was an honorary member of our club and hardly an evening went by without his attendance. He was a finely built man of about six foot two with broad shoulders, beetling eyebrows and huge handlebar moustaches. Of the more conservative school of princes, he wore a diamond clipped into the bottom of one nostril, the only Indian man that I recall doing so. The rest of us wore shorts but he always wore long white trousers, and a massive gold ring with a huge emerald. He was a very keen and competent player with a powerful accurate service and firm well-placed shots. His weakness was that as the game proceeded, and particularly at crucial points, his foot faults became more and more blatant until he took a definite step with his left foot into the court as he started to serve. None of the Indian masters ever said anything to him either out of politeness or respect or fear of his rank and influence. These factors did not affect me. He always arranged the doubles himself, usually choosing the strongest player present as his partner. This was not often me. I would ignore his encroachments for a game or two then at a critical moment as he was serving I would shout, 'Foot fault, raja sahib.' He never contested this but sometimes gave me a rather old-fashioned look. I was never asked to his state and might have been slightly uneasy to accept his hospitality. After a protest by me, he would respect the base line for a few games and then gradually begin encroaching more and more.

Zulfiqar Ali and I entered the doubles every year in the Lahore tournament and did quite well.

It was on the Gymkhana Club courts at Lahore that I saw an amazing demonstration of a tennis player's confidence in his own accuracy. Tilden, Cochet, Ramillion and Burke, who were all professionals then, arrived to play demonstration matches. Big Bill Tilden was playing singles against Cochet and served several double faults. He said, 'I don't serve doubles. Can we have the court measured?' This was done and the service court was found to be about six inches too short. They moved to an adjoining court and Tilden, the originator of the 'cannonball service', placed all his serves just inside instead of just outside the line.

There was table tennis in the house and I used to play quite often with the boys and occasionally with Gwynn. There was also another game on which the boys were very keen. This was *carom*. It consisted of flicking draughtsmen so that they cannoned off others into pockets in a specially made table with a hard, smooth surface. It was popular in India but I have never seen it elsewhere.

It was understood that I would eat the evening meal with the boys whenever I felt like it. I found this quite enjoyable. They were good, lively company and I soon came to like Indian food. They all came into the dining room when mealtime came and took their places without regard to religious communities. Naturally the more senior and junior boys tended to segregate themselves.

Although the boys' food was prepared in three separate kitchens by cooks of the Muslim, Sikh and Hindu faiths there seemed to be little difference in what was served at the table except that the Muslims had larger *chapattis* (the Indian unleav-

100

ened bread, something like pancakes) than the others. Each type of food was served by a servant of the related religion and each boy, of course, took his food from the correct dish. One or two Hindus confined themselves to vegetable dishes. No Hindu would eat beef and no Muslim pork. Out of deference to each community neither of these was served at the College and seldom elsewhere in India. Thus, meat dishes were mutton, chicken, duck, wild fowl and goat. Amongst the less well-to-do Indians goat was commoner than mutton as it was cheaper.

The meat that the Muslim boys ate was, as strictly enjoined in Islam, killed by the *halal* method of cutting the windpipe. (Muslim *shikaris* would usually *halal* any game shot on the theory that it was not dead before they did so.) Sikh and Hindu boys ate meat killed by the *jhatka* method of cutting off the head. (These differences were enough to cause riots in Lahore.)

My conversation with the boys was naturally in English but I picked up some Urdu from them in these talks. There was a tradition in the College that English was the universal means of communication amongst the boys and between boys and teaching staff. (The servants could not speak English and were addressed in their own tongue.) There was no formal rule about this and no punishment if the convention was breached. This only occurred occasionally amongst newly joined boys in the junior forms. The boys themselves welcomed this practice as they were very keen to improve their English. I encouraged them, in and out of class, to use words that they had newly learnt, stressing that one could not acquire mastery of a vocabulary merely by learning meanings but that it was necessary to use words and read as much as possible to gain a command of the subtle distinctions of usage in a language with such a rich vocabulary as English.

The general attitude to school work was very different from that of British boys. They were nearly all keen to learn and hard-working. There were never any disciplinary problems. One or two boys were rather slow-witted, found it hard to learn and were inclined to slack.

Education and knowledge had great prestige amongst all classes in India. Even the sons of great princes who would never have any economic need to be well qualified to earn a living worked well simply for the prestige of being well educated. Similarly, teachers received considerable prestige. The boys showed a marked respect to the Indian masters and to myself. I found it incongruous and surprising at first to be referred to by Indians outside the College as 'professor at the Chiefs' College', especially as 'master' had been borrowed by Urdu to mean a teacher. Some boys, not including the sons of princes, were inspired to work by a desire to pass the entrance examination for the Indian Civil Service. Here, again, it was as much for the prestige and power of that service as for the pay, although this was a consideration.

As the boys were studying in a language which was not their mother tongue it could hardly be expected that they would reach the standard of a good sixth form in any English school. In general, our sixth form reached the standard of the old Cambridge School Certificate which some of the boys took and passed.

One of the Sikh boys expressed the desire to go to Cranwell and join the RAF. I gave him special coaching and had the satisfaction of seeing him get into Cranwell – the first Indian to do so. He did very well in the Indian Air Force during the Second World War but unfortunately had to fight against some of his former school-mates in the wars against Pakistan.

I gave special tuition also, out of normal school hours, to a few boys who were backward in English. As these were the duller boys it could be rather trying. Their fathers were always keen for them to improve and offered me money for these services. I preferred not to accept it.

I did not think it appropriate to spend more than about two evenings a week with the boys although they tried to get me into meals more often. Some of the other evenings I spent alone in my rooms. I drank very little, if at all, when I was by myself. The other evenings were passed in going out to drinks or dinner, visits to the club where I joined friends and sometimes stayed to dinner or dances, visits to hotels where there was dancing and cabarets and visits to the cinema. There was never any question of dressing for dinner at home according to the stereotype of the pukka sahib in the east. However, if I went out a dinner jacket was de rigueur. In the Punjab the custom was for a dinner jacket to be of lightweight black material; it was worn with white trousers. In other parts of India the colours were reversed. A dinner jacket was considered necessary even if one went alone to the cinema. I thought this rather absurd myself, especially before I could afford a car and went on a bicycle, but the convention was so strong that I never had the strength of mind to break it. The furthest I went was to wear a light, white short-sleeved cellular sports shirt, take off my dinner jacket during the film and loosen my black tie. This was regarded by some as distinctly risqué and few followed my example.

Strict dress convention was part of the all pervasive, subconscious bond amongst the British in India to maintain their prestige upon which their influence, and eventually their sovereignty, was ultimately based. Their numbers were so few among the teeming millions of Indians that British rule in the final analysis depended upon its acceptance by the Indians. This again depended upon several factors – the reputation for justice, integrity and efficiency, which the British had built up and also upon their *izzat*. This last factor was uniquely Indian in its importance. Difficult to translate, it is inextricably bound up with Indian culture. It is a combination of honour, dignity, precedence, prestige, respect, power and good name. The Indians themselves were bound by convention and self-respect and paid great regard to such matters in themselves and Europeans.

One of the senior Sikh boys in my house asked me several times if I was fond of dancing and where I went in the evenings. I had no suspicions of his motive until one night I found him out dancing when he should have been in bed.

In the mornings during term time when I did not play some sport with the boys, which was completely at my discretion, I usually went riding or hunting. In the holidays nearly every morning saw me doing one of the latter.

One Christmas holiday there were several hectic parties and I got to bed very late. For two mornings running when Maula Baksh woke me up at five o'clock with *chota hazri* and said, '*Ghora taiyar hai, Sahib*', 'The horse is ready, Sahib', I just turned over and went to sleep again. The third morning the same call came but this time the *syce* and the horse were in the bedroom. As Maula

Baksh made his usual announcement the *syce* pushed the horse's face into my own. I had to see the humour of the situation. They were a bit uncertain as to how I would take it but we all burst out laughing and I had to go riding.

Many of the *syces* in Lahore were what the Northern Indians rather contemptuously called Purbiyas, that is men from the Purab or east, in other words from the province of Bihar. This was another example of the strength with which certain castes and communities exercised a near monopoly on certain callings. Each horse had its own *syce*. In general they were devoted to their charges. My *syce* slept in the stable when the horse was ill. In a similar manner Maula Baksh insisted on sleeping across the door of my bedroom when I had fever, not only to be ready if I wanted anything but also to inhibit any malign influence from crossing the threshold.

I introduced boxing into the College. This has never been popular in India whereas there is a strong, historic tradition of wrestling. In general, Indians are not keen on body contact sports. Many of them are naturally rather quick-tempered and thought it rather undignified to let someone else attempt to hit them. This was one of the reasons why I thought it was a good thing to get them boxing. It would teach them self-control. I got an open air ring built on baked earth with a canvas covering and found someone in a British regiment to spar with me. This aroused interest amongst the boys. Boxing was completely voluntary but Punjabis pride themselves on their military and manly qualities. Quite a few joined my boxing classes. Some were quite promising and it was not long before we built up a reasonable team and entered various tournaments. The judges and referees were nearly always officers from British regiments and, I regret to say, that in my opinion on occasions they showed racial prejudice against the boys from the College.

I boxed in various tournaments in Lahore in which Indians and a few Europeans took part and became known in boxing circles. Then there occurred a typically Indian incident. I have mentioned that boxing was not a major sport in India. It was based chiefly in the Punjab. All the controlling officials were Punjabis and the winners of all the weights except one in the tournaments in Lahore had been Punjabis. I had won at middleweight. I was approached by the officials of what they called the All India Boxing Association who said that they wanted to send a team to the 1936 Olympic Games and wanted me to box at middleweight. I was surprised on three counts. I did not think that our boxing was up to Olympic standard nor that there was enough money to send a team. Finally, there was a Bengali middleweight with a good record and reputation whom I had never boxed but was probably better than I was. When I mentioned the last point they said, 'We are not wanting Bengali in team. All other members are Punjabis, we are preferring European to Bengali.'

In the end, as I had thought, the proposal to send a team fizzled out chiefly through lack of finance. I think that the proposal to include me had been largely based on provincial and political prejudice.

I once, cynically and somewhat wildly, said that the Indians were so given to factionalism that it was likely that an Indian test cricket team sent to England would split into two factions. That is exactly what occurred shortly afterwards and some were sent back to India by the captain, a maharaja.

The Indians won the hockey in the 1936 Olympic Games. An old boy of the College, Mohamed Jafar, was a member of this team. He was unfortunately drowned whilst duck shooting shortly after his return. He told me that the Indian team had let a German team beat them in one practice game but had trounced the Germans in the finals and won the gold medal, much to Hitler's disgust. The winning team toured India on their return and played all the provinces. They only just beat the Punjab 2–1 in a hard fought game. I think that the team of any major province could have won the Olympic games.

After the incident regarding the boxing team, I was narrowly beaten in the final of one tournament by an Indian student. There were a number of Europeans amongst the spectators. It was quite an exciting fight and enthusiasm was not unnaturally rather divided on racial lines. Some Europeans thought that I had been discriminated against as this time the judges and referee were Indian. I was disappointed to lose but had no real quarrel with the decision. Some Europeans hinted that they thought that I had let the side down a bit by losing to an Indian and suggested that I should not have entered if I had not been certain of winning. I must say I had thought I would win and felt slightly abashed. My only consolation was that the Indian student went to London University, immediately got into the University team and did very well.

There was a very good water polo team at the College who had the opportunity of practising nearly every day. We entered various tournaments. Most of the teams were Indian but several British regiments entered teams. The venue was the pool of one of the University colleges and it was always packed with students who were, in general, the leaders of the movement for Indian independence. They could be very pleasant to individual Britishers but en masse were anti-British. Water polo matches against British regiments allowed them to express this feeling by screaming their heads off and the atmosphere was always very strained. Water polo is a game in which a lot of nasty work can go on and the racial ill-feeling was even more intensified by the crude fouls and unsporting behaviour, which disgusted me, of one British regiment against the team of the very college in whose pool they were playing. The Indians won, otherwise I think there might well have been a nasty incident.

I was involved in another tense sporting event. This time I was refereeing the boxing tournament at the Islamia College (for Muslim students in Lahore). There was still a high degree of tension between Muslims and Sikhs, which only needed a spark to explode it. I saw to my astonishment that in one bout a Sikh (he must have been very brave) was boxing a Muslim student. The Sikh had brought along a British soldier as his second. Apart from the three of us the hall was packed with a vast crowd of fervent Muslim students. Quite a few thoughts went through my mind as to what would happen if the Muslim lost. Luckily he proved a clear winner.

Gwynn and I used to enter the table tennis tournament in Lahore every year – the only Europeans to do so. This evoked a little racial partisanship. I was playing an Indian in the deciding game of one of the semi-finals. At a fairly crucial point my opponent hit a shot which had clearly missed and gone well beyond the table. I caught the ball before it had bounced and the Indian referee immediately gave the point against me. He was formally entitled to do this but I had never seen it done before in the tournament. I thought this was rather unsporting.

The last incident was rather trivial but I have included it amongst the others concerning sporting episodes as I think they were all pointers. In general, the Indians realised that they were a subject race and many of them had an inferiority complex vis à vis the British. Therefore it gave them a greater sense of satisfaction than would otherwise have been the case if they could gain advantages in the sporting field even on nice points of law.

Lahore was the centre for the University of the Punjab. At the time of examinations the Lawrence Gardens, a fine park in the centre of Lahore, were full of students in the shadow of every tree learning their textbooks by heart. Academic qualification was a much sought-after channel out of poverty by most Indians of any ability. Many were financed with great hardship by their parents and family who sometimes crippled themselves with debt to a moneylender. The pressure was such that some sought to succeed by dishonest means. It became strongly suspected that some students were obtaining prior knowledge of examination papers. Security was tightened up but still leaks seemed to occur. Finally the examination papers were printed by one senior European in the Government Printers' Department aided only by a messenger.

Still there were leaks. At last the messenger was caught very much *in flagrante delicto*. When he thought he could not be seen he whipped up his *dhoti*, the Hindu loincloth, and sat with his bare behind on the press. All he had to do then was to sit on a piece of paper and reproduce what the students would eagerly purchase.

6

Iraq and Persia

After spending my first long vacation in Kashmir the goal for my next was Persia. My interest in this country had been aroused from the time when I began to learn a little Urdu and a little of the influence of Persia on a very large part of India, in particular the north and the Muslim population of the north.

Most of the Muslims of the north of India belong to races which entered India long after the main body of the Hindu races and from such places of origin as Central Asia, Persia and Arabia. Of the influx of Muslims, those who most influenced India and indeed whose influence spread well beyond the boundaries of India, were the Persians. The Persian language formed the main basis of Urdu and gave its script to the Urdu language. The Arabic vocabulary in Urdu entered the language through Persian which borrowed it first. It still remains the classical language of the Muslims of the north of India. Persian writing was a source of constant allusion in Urdu literature and Urdu is thickly sprinkled with words and phrases lifted bodily from Persian.

Persian architecture had a great influence on building in India and I suppose it would be true to say, although some claim it was designed by Italians, that the Taj Mahal is the finest flower of Persian architecture.

Khan Anwar Sikander Khan and Chaudhri Ata Ullah had both spent their previous long vacation in Persia together and although they had the advantage in respect of travel there of being Muslims and masters of classical Persian the tales they told me of their interesting and enjoyable trips whetted my desire to follow them.

108

Therefore the end of the summer term in 1937 saw me once again at Lahore station prepared to set off on my travels. I was seen off on the journey to Karachi by Khan Sahib, Chaudhri Sahib, Maulvi Sahib and Maula Baksh.

It was extremely hot but I found myself sharing a compartment with an Indian Army colonel who bought a huge block of ice at every station and reduced the carriage to a temperature that I found somewhat too chilly.

My Air Force friend met me at Karachi and I spent a day with him there before catching a small British India ship for the Persian Gulf. The tail end of a monsoon storm set up a heavy swell and the 2–3,000 ton vessel rolled in a manner which reduced my appetite at dinner the first night.

We had a few hours' daylight the first day which was spent hugging the barren shores of Baluchistan which made even the coast of Arabia and Somaliland appear hospitable.

The only point of interest was the beautiful vivid tones of the dying sun on the bare, stark, high, eroded cliffs. These cliffs which looked so dull, sombre and uninteresting in the full light of day became a fairy kaleidoscope of lemon, pink, green, magenta and deep purple in the rapidly changing light of the tropical sunset.

The ship was the slow steamer that gave one an opportunity of seeing something of the many interesting little ports on the route. Bingham, an old Etonian and the heir to an English peerage, and myself were the only Europeans travelling second class. The rest were deck passengers. The cabins were small but comfortable and I had one to myself. My other fellow second-class passengers were all Arabs or Persians most of whom did not eat in the saloon but prepared queer messes of their own or shared the meals of the Muslim lascar crew. The only first class passengers were a young newly married Englishman taking out his bride to a consular post in the Persian Gulf.

The next morning, as the sun was rising, we reached Ormara one of the two little ports in Las Bela State whose ruler designate was one of my pupils.

Pasni in the Baluchi portion of Makran, the wild desert land shared between Baluchistan and Persia, was reached that evening. The ship did not go close in but was met fairly well out to sea by a small fleet of large, heavily-built species of bandar boat. We unloaded rice and took on dried fish which seemed to be destined to become 'Bombay Duck', those pungent slices of dried fish so often served with curry in India.

The boats and cargo were handled with great skill and energy by boatmen of magnificent physique whose dark skin and negroid features suggested that they were descendants of the African slaves once common on this coast.

The evening of the next day saw us at Chahba, the first port of call in Persia. Nothing very interesting took place there except an interchange of store goods from the ship with strange exotic marine products and one wondered what else such an inhospitable land could produce. The port consisted of a few squalid, heat-drenched, flat-topped buildings set in a shimmering sandy street.

We reached Muscat after lunch the next day about two hours after the expected time and I gathered that this was due to bad navigation and a difficult landfall.

The port appeared to be a sunken volcanic crater. At least it was a lovely curve surrounded by high forbidding volcanic hills and to enter it one had to sail through a fairly narrow passage with old Portuguese forts dominating the heights, as they do so many other strategic spots on the Persian Gulf and the coasts of East Africa, Western India and the other old sailing routes of the past. These Portuguese forts were the scenes of many bloody battles in the past – mostly between Portuguese and Arabs and not with the English and Dutch as elsewhere.

As we entered the harbour a small saluting cannon was fired and the Sultan's flag hoisted. This was not a mere courtesy but is laid down in a treaty with the Sultan.

I went ashore with a local Arab who spoke good Hindustani but no English and he showed me around. I had heard many fearsome tales about the overpowering heat of Muscat but it was not as bad as Lahore in the height of the hot weather. However, it was easy to imagine that it could become hotter as it was so closely sur-rounded by rocks, cliffs and hills and the surface of the land was mostly rock, stones and sand.

The two chief buildings in the town were the Sultan's Palace and the British Residency, the outward symbols and abodes of the only two powers in the land. Both were long buildings flanking the waterfront, both were a painful white in the dazzling sun and both had tall imposing flagstaffs. The Residency was neater and better kept, the palace slightly larger and more picturesque. Everything thus seemed as it should be.

On guard over the Sultan's palace was a motley crew of assorted cut-throats. It is possible that they were more effective than the guard on Buckingham Palace but they were certainly more ragged in every sense of the word. My guide introduced them as *Sultan ke sepahi*, or the Sultan's soldiers. Almost every man had a different type of rifle. I suppose that each man must have supplied his own ammunition as well as rifle as otherwise the Quartermaster's job must have been a nightmare. Each had the wicked looking curved Arab dagger in his *cummerbund*.

My guide left me here and I took a taxi, a twenty-year-old Buick driven by a Persian, out to Matrah which appeared mostly a Baluchi settlement a few miles from Muscat. They lived in a ghastly shanty town set down on a gravel desert and their settlement was one of the least favoured human habitations I have seen. Again, in spite of the apparent grinding poverty, one shack had the ubiquitous sewing machine.

I spoke to one old Baluchi in Hindustani. They were apparently largely water-carriers for Muscat town and the settlement grew up because of the small enclave of Oman State at Gwadar in Baluchi Makran on the other side of the Gulf of Oman which led to an interchange of population.

In addition to the Baluchi settlement, there was a large negroid element in the population. Even many Arab chiefs are quite negroid owing to the constant inter-breeding, until recent generations, with slave women.

On the way back to the ship we passed swarms of dolphins gambolling in the sunlight.

In the evening, the rigid hierarchy of the ship unbent a little and I was invited to join the Captain, Chief and First Officer for drinks in the first-class saloon. There were no public rooms except the dining saloons on these small ships.

Bandar Abbas, 'The Port of Abbas', was reached the next evening. This was a pleasant looking little port in a pleasingly

111

rounded cove. Like nearly all the small Persian Gulf ports there is no proper harbour and we lay off in the open roads. The bandar boats that worked the cargo were of the same design but bigger and heavier in build. They were still worked by men of a distinctly negroid type.

To my surprise, we shipped crate after crate of mangoes until the whole deck space was occupied by them. I bought some and found them delicious. It seemed strange that a ship coming from the home of mangoes should ship some half way on its journey but I suppose that the additional four days on the journey from India would have made them overripe.

Two Persian gendarmes came on board in their faded blue uniform and with their three days' growth of beard, flapping puttees and uncleaned rifles; they were the first and typical of many of their fellows that I was to meet in the future. I found later that one could judge their length of service by the shade of their uniform. Some contractor must have saved money on the dye and fading and washing eventually reduced the blue almost to white.

By this time I had struck up an acquaintance with the Chinese ship's carpenter who told very proudly that he was 'first man in ship after white man'. I wondered what the Goanese ship's doctor would have said to that claim. He reinforced it by pointing out to me on the ship's emergency orders that he was the commander of one of the life-boats.

Like so many Chinese, he seemed to think that it was his mission in life to catch sharks if possible and whilst we were lying off Bandar Abbas he baited a huge hook with a lump of pork and shortly afterwards pulled up a shark that must have been at least ten feet long.

In the morning we were at Lingeh which appeared to be a very impressive looking place with a light-house and a large number of domed buildings clustering amongst groves of palm trees. We were unable to go ashore and the Chief, who had turned into a walking geographical gazetteer, told me that the town had originally had a population of 20,000 but that now it was very much less and that most of the buildings were ruined. He told me of a legend of sea-horses at Lingeh.

The oil island of Bahrain was our next port of call, reached on the following day. This was an Arab sheikdom under British protection but the Persians claimed sovereignty based on an old and somewhat tenuous authority they had once exercised over the island.

I was surprised to find that the passport control officer was a dignified old Bengali Muslim, Jelal-ud-Din Hamid, dressed in Arab costume. I went ashore with him and Bingham, who had arranged to fly on to Baghdad and meet me there. I then went to the office of the American Oil Company to ask them to show me around.

They rang up the camp, some miles out in the desert, and arranged a car to take me out. I was met and shown around by an Englishman.

The story that I was told about the discovery of oil at Bahrain was that one company had employed what were then the very latest scientific methods of exploring for oil and had found none. Another company, American, had employed an old Texan to fossick around. After doing so he had said, 'There's oil in them there dunes.' They had bored and struck it rich.

The camp was very up to date with a club, swimming pool and cinema, all air-conditioned. Many of the quarters were air-conditioned and it was said that there was an air-conditioned brothel.

In places could be seen the old quarters, bare Quonset huts half-buried in the sand to give them some degree of protection from the heat.

The desert road to and from the camp was extremely hot and consisted merely of an oiled strip of sand. However, it was smooth and flat and could be taken at speed. We passed groves of date palms in various small oases but they were not quite ripe.

Before the discovery of oil, Bahrain was noted for two things – its large white riding donkeys and its pearls. The former were highly prized throughout the Middle East for their smooth gait and beautiful dignified appearance. Before so many Arab sheiks rode in Cadillacs it was considered quite the thing, except when in a hurry when a horse was used, to amble sedately along on a Bahrain donkey. They were quite expensive and were then as much a status symbol as Cadillacs are now.

Because of its extensive, rich pearling grounds, the Sheik of

113

Bahrain (and some local pearl dealers) had been extremely wealthy even before the advent of oil. The Bahrain pearl was prized for its size, shape and lustre.

Years later, when a prisoner-of-war in the Far East, I became friendly with a French Jew called Rosenthal. He had won the MC at Dunkirk and was one of the very few Frenchmen who had taken advantage of Churchill's offer of British citizenship made at that time. In addition to the MC he had won the Croix de Guerre in the First World War. He was a rare, indomitable character and an outstanding raconteur in French, Arabic, Spanish and broken English. He used to fascinate us by his accounts of strange experiences all over the world. For some time Rosie had been a pearl merchant at Bahrain and used to describe how very valuable parcels of pearls changed hands without a word being spoken. The dealers used to squat down in a close circle, with their hands under a sheet, offers were made and accepted by clutching the fingers of the person one was dealing with. There was a code whereby the numbers of fingers grasped at different knuckles for a different number of times signified the amount in question in units of hundreds or thousands of rupees as pre-arranged. He said that he had never heard of disputes but if a law case had occurred it is difficult to see how it could be decided whether the parties had been *ad idem*.

The next day we lay a little way off Bushire which in the distance looked much more Arab than Persian. At first the Passport Officer, an unshaven ruffian of a fellow, refused me permission to land. I learnt afterwards that I should have given him a set fee for his own personal enrichment. I did not realize this at the time. Eventually when he realized that he would get nothing from me he gave me permission to go ashore but by this time it was in the heat of a blistering day. I felt rather perverse and stayed on board. I regretted this as I always regret missing any place that I might possibly have seen. However, I was later to see more of Bushire than I wanted. We spent the whole day loading sacks of cement.

We sailed in the evening and by the morning of the following day we had ascended the estuary of the Jarrahi to Bandar Shahpur. The Jarrahi is one of the only two navigable rivers in the whole of

Persia, a country larger than France, Spain, Italy and Great Britain put together. The other navigable river is its neighbour the Karum, on which stands the oil town of Ahwaz.

The fact that there are only two such rivers in Persia is the key to most of its difficulty – insufficient rainfall leading to great sand and salt deserts. These two rivers are fed from the snows of the Zagros Mountains.

Bandar Shahpur, named after the great Persian Emperor, Shahpur, was destined to become the terminus of the railway which had been started at the port of Bandar Shah on the Caspian and had by then reached Tehran but no further.

We had to wait two hours for the lighters to be got ready and then another hour or so for the coolies to arrive to work the cargo. Finally a very large motor lighter came alongside and a long, tedious time was spent in getting another lighter adjusted for the after hold. At last we unloaded a large German-made cotton-spinning machine for the state-owned cotton mill at Malayer (Daulatabad), south of Hamadan. As there was no railway and only the most rudimentary road through formidable mountain country, it must have been a difficult task to transport it to its destination.

The next day we took on the pilot for the passage up the famous Shatt-al-Arab, the combined estuary of the Tigris and the Euphrates. We did not follow the normal Rooka Channel apparently because several dredgers were working in it.

As we went further up the Channel the shore on each side gradually became visible and eventually we were passing along the winding river between banks fringed with date palms. The flat-roofed mud houses looked clean and well-built and there were many irrigation channels leading from the river to the date groves and patches of cultivation growing rice and melons.

We passed Abadan which was then, I believe, the largest oil refinery in the world and we dropped anchor at Khorramshahr in the evening. Here we unloaded the cement and the coolies made a far quicker and smarter job of it than the loading.

As the sun set, the temperature dropped and a golden full moon rose to dapple the water with its dancing beams. Persia lay on the east side of the river and Iraq on the other. I liked the glimpses I

115

had so far seen of both countries and was full of contented anticipation.

We sailed at first light and had arrived at Basra by 6 a.m.

There was a very noticeable difference in the attitude of the passport and customs officers from those in Persia. Iraq had long been a British mandate. The RAF was still stationed in strength at Habbaniya as the chief agent of law and order in the country. I like to think that the friendliness shown by the officials was due to the example of courtesy set by British officials and because the Iraqis had learnt some liking for us which was, alas, to be altered later.

A Hindu taxi driver from Amritsar, 35 miles from Lahore, drove me to the Railway Rest House.

At the rest house there was a pleasant little manager who wanted to attend to my every need making the repeated suggestion, amongst others, that I should see the girls – 'Just for five minutes.' However, I decided it would be safer to see the town. So I got the fat Hindu taxi driver again and he showed me the town. There were some very fine public buildings and the post office was particularly impressive – being somewhat like a bureaucratic version of the Taj Mahal. British official architecture had obviously not predominated in the design of this building.

I spent an hour or so in the Overseas League Club House, came back to the rest house for a very reasonable dinner, again avoiding oriental *houris* as hors d'oeuvre or savoury.

After dinner I went for a walk in the bazaar and lost my fountain pen to a pickpocket. The bazaar had not been particularly crowded and I had no knowledge of being jostled or even touched. I was furious but had a certain admiration for the thief's consummate skill.

I then went to the station to catch the 10 p.m. train for Baghdad.

At the railway station there was still a vestige of the minor Indian functionaries that one saw here and there in Iraq, dependants of the former British administration. The ticket collector was a fat Madrassi, the last Indian, he told me, of many formerly employed by the Iraq railways. He apparently did not like Iraqis or the Congress Party in India and in a typically Indian way he immediately launched into a political statement.

116

It was a metre gauge railway but I found that the standard was far higher than in India. The general fittings and upholstery of the carriages, in particular comfortable leather bunks, were better than in India. There was a smart, efficient steward unlike India where one had to bring a servant or look after oneself. Clean comfortable bedding was supplied on the train – also unlike India where we brought our own. It was a corridor train, which was very unusual in India.

The morning found us still running through the dead flat sandy plains which seemed more truly desert than Sind. However, far less dust penetrated the train than on any run in the drier parts of India.

All the stations seemed to have some source of water which turned them into small oases. Smart looking soldiers were in evidence on most platforms.

On arrival at Baghdad I booked in at the Tigris Palace Hotel and the next day was joined by Bingham.

The hotel was old and conservative but the food and service were very good. My room was very hot in the day, as shade temperatures rose well above 120°F. I slept on the flat roof of the hotel and so rapidly did temperatures drop in this sandy area that a blanket was needed at night.

The Maude Bridge was not far from the hotel. Although Baghdad is such an ancient city it had never up to that time possessed a properly built bridge crossing the Tigris. The Maude Bridge was a rickety pontoon bridge and it was impossible for a vehicle and a loaded camel to pass each other on the bridge.

The next day or two I spent wandering round Baghdad. It had one main fairly modern street, New Street, running right through it. This had been built in Turkish times. They had ruthlessly torn down old houses and dynamited mosques and historical buildings in a way no infidel European power would have dared.

Away from New Street I found the streets so filthy as to make even the back streets of Lahore and Old Delhi appear hygienic. In places there were large encampments of buffalo and the streets were ankle deep in buffalo dung.

I found the old Arab houses very interesting. They lined the twisting lanes that led off New Street. As in the north of India there were blank walls on the street at ground level but second storey unglazed windows or balconies were shuttered with beautiful, intricate wood-carving like the marble arabesques of the Moghul buildings in India. One could imagine Haroon-ur-Rashid flitting down the streets in the guise of an ordinary citizen and keeping in touch with public opinion by gossiping through the lattice-work.

I had expected that the bazaars of Baghdad would be full of the most interesting merchandise from all over the East but found that, although they had a good range of silks, carpets and other oriental ware, they were disappointing compared with those of Lahore or Srinagar. There was one article of handicraft for which Baghdad was famous — that was silverware with a black design inlaid in it. This was on sale everywhere but was rather expensive and I confined my purchases to one cigarette case.

There was a fantastic night life in Baghdad and Bingham and I visited the cabarets. Some of the entertainers were local Arab and Armenian girls but most of them were eastern Europeans. Rumanians, Hungarians, White Russians, Bulgarians and Greeks appeared to predominate in that order. Most of them or their families were apparently political refugees of one kind or another.

After dark all the police used to go about in pairs with rifles and fixed bayonets. We did not know whether this was really necessary but it gave a slight touch of dramatic interest to our nocturnal expeditions.

The cabarets were nearly all open air and free as long as one had a drink and we used to spin ours out in a very frugal fashion. In addition to the normal European turns we saw the celebrated Arab *danse du ventre*.

After a day or two in Baghdad I decided to go out to see Babylon. I was up at 4 o'clock the next morning and on the road by five a.m. I had hired quite a good Buick taxi. The merest drop of Arab blood in a driver's veins seemed to impel him to drive a vehicle at top speed, irrespective of the alignment or surface of the road. We proceeded in a series of sickening bounds and lurches from pothole to pothole.

I was somehow disappointed by Babylon which was smaller and less impressive, to me, than I had imagined. However, the excavated ruins were quite extensive and the ancient brickwork of some of the walls looked as if it could have been built yesterday. There were some very realistic pieces of sculpture especially that of the lion trampling the man. The brick bas-reliefs of human and animal figures on the walls were clear, detailed and life-like. I gazed at Belshazzar's dining hall and tried to picture, without much success, the scene when the writing appeared on the wall as described in the Bible.

I had lunch with the American archaeologists doing the excavation and after lunch they showed me round explaining the plan and main buildings of this ancient city.

When I got back to the car I found that the two Iraqi dinars, equivalent to two pounds, that I had been foolish enough to leave in my coat had disappeared. The only people who had been on the scene were two young Arab boys isolated in hundreds of miles of desert but needless to say a search of them, each wearing an *abbiyah*, a long Arab night shirt as their sole garment, and the surrounding sand, did not reveal the missing notes.

On the way back I called to see the Great Hindiya barrage which irrigated and brought prosperity to a wide area of former desert. The irrigation engineer explained the set-up to me and gave me some delicious water melon and we stood watching the fish jumping the weir.

On my return to Baghdad I formally reported the theft of my money at the chief police station.

Bingham and I went out to drinks and dinner at the leading hotel in Baghdad, the Maude. After this we went to an Arab dancing place where the majority of the turns would have been unexceptional in London. I preferred the rather more exotic and frenzied type of Arab dances.

The next day I crossed the Tigris on a *gufa*. These are supposed to be some of the oldest craft in the world. They consist simply of a large round basket of plaited bulrushes made watertight by a coating of bitumen which has been used since early times in Iraq.

I spent the morning wandering around the administrative and diplomatic quarters with their graceful, cool white buildings set amidst welcome avenues of trees.

In the evening I saw off Bingham, and some French friends that we had made, on the Nairn bus to Damascus and Beirut. This route had originally been pioneered by two New Zealand brothers driving open American cars the 600 miles across the Syrian Desert, generally accepted as being one of the most fearsome deserts in the world. They worked out the route themselves and marked it at long intervals with crude cairns or oil drums. They had many exciting and dangerous experiences before they established the service and were more or less accepted by the desert Arabs. The solitary fort of Rutbah in the middle of the desert, set up to guard the pipe line, was the normal night stop.

By this time the buses were huge diesel semi-trailers, with lavatory and wash places and the last word in road transport.

The next day I started off to visit the famous Shia Shrine of Khadimain on the outskirts of Baghdad. I walked for some distance on the track of the horse-drawn tram. After a bit I got rather hot and tired and hailed the tram but although going at a slow jog trot it would not stop nor would the conductor let me jump on – apparently one could board only at set places.

I continued my walk getting hotter and somewhat irritated and soon found myself being plagued by a crowd of Arab boys trying to get a free English lesson from me. They were fairly friendly but rather teased me. After a bit I got completely fed up, as this was exactly what I was on holiday from. I was young and I suppose intolerant, certainly hot-tempered in a difficult climate, and I regret that I lost my temper, swung round and caught the nearest, a very unpleasant, precocious youngster, a terrific clip on the ear. They all immediately dispersed and I had a few moments of blissful calm to be broken by a brick bat whizzing past my ear. I turned round to find that they had been reinforced by fathers, uncles, cousins, and elder brothers all of whom were busily stoning me. It was an awkward situation. I felt that I could not let down the prestige of the British raj by running away – anyway they could probably run faster than I could; I could not walk all the way to Khadimain backwards and when I turned my back on them I didn't know if I was going to get half a brick on the back of my neck. There is a lot of ammunition in the streets of Baghdad. However, this battle was won on the playing fields of another

Myself looking like an Iraqi

My house at Aitchison College (Godley House)

College exhibition

Some of the boys at Drigh Road

Muslim boys in their gold braided Id dress

Muslim Mosque with corner of one boarding house

Id service at Mosque in Lahore

Hindu Temple at college

Sikh Gurdwara (place of worship) in college

Cricket field

Part of the college playing fields under irrigation

Sports day, cricket pavilion on the left (present college)

Hockey match at Aitchison College (present college)

Basket ball (present college)

On top of boulder we climbed in the dried-up bed of the valley at Ajanta

A group of Old Boys of the college listening to a lecture, several Rajas in front row, one of whom was ambassador to Brazil after independence

English school. Luckily these Arabs had never learnt cricket and their fire although rapid was inaccurate. I adopted the tactics of walking on slowly until things became too hot and then turning round and launching a counter-attack. My aim was much more accurate than theirs and I scored a few hits without being touched myself. Finally I achieved a *coup de main* as I managed to catch one stone as I swung round and hurled it back hitting one of the leading men full on the crown of the head as he ducked to avoid it. He himself dropped just like the stone and shortly after that the walking battle was broken off much to my relief.

I was right in the worst area of Baghdad, near a shrine noted for the fanaticism and anti-Christian bigotry of its worshippers, and was very lucky to get away with my foolish act.

I passed a huge herd of buffalo – half defecating in the streets, half cooling themselves in the river by the floating dock and train ferry.

At weary length the golden domes of Khadimain came into sight towering above the walls of the great quadrangular court-yard. Bazaars clustered round the walls of the shrine intent, as all shops near all shrines of all religions, on selling all the curios, souvenirs and general goods they possibly could to devout and credulous pilgrims. In the old days there was an unsavoury feature amongst the offerings to pilgrims. By a specious process of religious and legal sophistry, the Shias, who compose the chief minority sect of Islam and have their own school of law, including their own marriage laws and rites, recognised temporary mar-riages. The great Shia centres of pilgrimage were Karbala (near where the Prophet's sons-in-law Hassan, believed by the Shias to be the true *imam* or spiritual heir, and Hussein, met martyrs' deaths in battle at the hands of the rival party after the death of Mohammed), Najaf and Khadimain, all fairly close to Baghdad, and Meshed in the wastes of Khurasan in north-east Persia. These shrines were generally more revered by Shias than Mecca and attracted hundreds of thousands of pilgrims every year. A procedure for the temporary marriage of these pilgrims had been tolerated and practised by mullahs and qadis which was no more than a hypocritical formalisation of large scale prostitution. It was very noticeable that the merchandise at Khadimain included

121

none of the imported Western goods so common in the *suks* of Baghdad.

Khadimain seemed to preserve the old Shia atmosphere much better than any of the mosques or shrines of Baghdad. The large domes were placed on cylindrical columns and were more elongated than the vast, swelling domes of Moghul architecture. They were thickly covered with shimmering gold-leaf as was the upper flight of the four soaring minarets at each corner of the building. The buildings and precinct were clean and neatly kept and thus escaped that atmosphere of tawdriness and untidy neglect that is so often the fate of similar buildings in the East.

A tout got hold of me and for appropriate bakhshish took me up into a house from which I could overlook the courtyard of the mosque and the study cells of the adjoining Madrassah or theological college. Mullahs were everywhere at their prayers or studies and a religious hum filled the air. In spite of the shopkeepers and the demand for bakhshish from my guide I felt the air of intense devotion that permeated the place.

I caught a rickety local bus back to Baghdad and, never giving up hope, called at the police station to see how the enquiry into my loss was going.

I was met by a fat, jolly inspector who said the case was hopeless but that as a compensation he would, if I liked, take me round Baghdad that night as a guest of the police force and introduce me to 'our national theatre'.

We met as arranged after dinner and the first place we went to was the place that Bingham and I had visited the night before. After that we went to some more truly Arab places, at all of which the inspector was received as a guest of honour.

The pattern of the Arab places was all the same. There was a big square room with a small low stage at one end, spread with oriental carpets and straight backed, uncomfortable looking bent-seated chairs that looked as if they had been made in Birmingham. In front of the stage were the *fauteuils d'orchestre*, slightly less uncomfortable chairs in which we were seated. On each side of the room were wooden galleries furnished with benches. The top gallery always seemed to be occupied by the *hoi polloi* of Baghdad and the bottom by Bedouins from the deserts.

122

On the chairs were three or four girls, mostly Arabs with an occasional fair-skinned Armenian, and two or three male musicians usually with instruments like guitars.

There was a *maîtresse de cérémonie* in gold lamé evening dress. At irregular intervals she would make some announcement and one of the girls would get up and sing or dance. Performers and audience alike generally seemed bored. The girls were mostly dressed in the height of decorum and most dances would have passed the Cheltenham Watch Committee. One or two of the girls had a skirt that opened in front and as the climax of a stilted, stereotyped dance she would lift up her skirts sideways with her arms at shoulder level, do one or two languid pirouettes like a moth fluttering in the lamp light and finally collapse on the chair as if she had been singed.

The star turn was a colossally fat girl called Sachao Georgi who I learnt was a famous broadcaster throughout the Arabic world. She did a song and dance which brought the house down. I could see the dance but not understand the song which led me to believe that everything must have been in the song.

Occasionally one of the Bedouins would release a stentorian expectoration into one of the battery of spittoons and apparently depart in disgust to cleanse himself in the desert from the contamination of Kaffir-tainted civilization.

The next day I took a car out to see King Faisal's tomb towards the edge of the city. This was a barely finished building in the traditional Muslim style but less ornate than some of the older shrines. It achieved its effect largely by its beautiful proportions rather than its ornamentation although it had some graceful brick arabesques and the outside of the dome was set with beautiful faïence tiles.

The inside of the building was austere and the inner surface of the dome completely plain. However, the most beautiful effects were achieved by letting the brilliant sunshine into the darkened dome through a circle of clerestory windows only. The windows were divided by geometrically designed brick fretwork. These made a beautiful pattern of light against the vault of the sky and a corresponding pattern of sunlight and shadow danced an intricate minuet partnered by the design on the tiles of the floor.

123

I thought that I could not leave Iraq without seeing an Arab tribe in the desert and was advised to call on the Abu Tanin. I went on there by car from Faisal's tomb. We bumped over the desert in extreme heat and blinding glare for about 20 miles. As we approached the tents we had difficulty in crossing the irrigation runnels which bring water from the Tigris. A sandstorm blew up and for some time we had to remain stationary as visibility extended only to a few yards.

After the storm was over we got to the tents and were welcomed by a dirty but very tall, well-built and impressive *pater familias*. He immediately spread cushions and rugs for me in his tent which was an extremely crude affair. It was nothing like one sees in films, being made of strips of hessian, instead of camel-hair, spread on sticks to form a roof, back and sides, with an open front. There were two smaller, enclosed and obviously hotter tents for his womenfolk and kitchen and household utensils. There was a rough cane wind-break at the back.

The taxi driver acted as interpreter. I was asked to tell the old man a story. I thought up some feeble anecdote for which I was suitably recompensed with a cup of dirty water. He asked me to have a meal and stay for the night but we said we could not stop and went on to another tent where we were given Turkish coffee and examined some daggers with wooden sheaths and handles ornamented with chased silver. The owner of the tent produced one of the sorriest nags that I have ever seen, said it was a famous steed of an illustrious lineage and prodigious performance and asked me what I would offer for it.

I decided to return via Agarquf to see the remains of the ziggurat there. We lost the track once or twice in the desert but finally saw the massive column of our destination looming in the distance through the haze.

The eroded, remaining hard core of this ancient construction was a flat-topped massif looking more like a butte formed by nature in the Far West of the United States of America than the relics of the handicraft of ancient man. It was markedly striated; the protruding ridges appeared to be formed of the outer edges of less eroded, harder brick courses set between softer sunbaked mud. Halfway up was a sizable cave.

124

Months before leaving India I had applied to the Russian Legation in Simla for permission to cross the border at Julfa from Persian Azerbaijan into Soviet Nakhichevan as I was very keen to see the Caucasian regions because of their wonderful scenery, interesting history and fascinating racial mélange. I had given my proposed itinerary and was told to call at the Russian Embassy in Baghdad where I would get permission. The only result of several calls at this outpost of the Kremlin was the advice to call at the Russian Embassy at Tehran. I met a somewhat surly junior secretary who spoke good English to the Iraqis just in front of me but for an inscrutable Russian reason would speak nothing but French to me. All I could get was, '*à Tehran tout sera reglé et on vous donnera sans doute le visé.*'

I had seen enough of Baghdad – Persia was calling and I could wait no longer. At least I thought that I could wait no longer. The taxi agency at which I had enquired had told me that I could take a taxi to Tehran at an hour's notice but when I asked to go the next morning I got evasive replies. It was the same the next morning and I went out for a walk to be met on my return by a man who said that they were ready to go. I got ready in a hurry and we left after lunch in a big Buick.

I had three fellow passengers. The first presented me with his card on which was inscribed 'Abbas Seyghal, Chancellor of the Imperial Legation of Iran, Baghdad'. He wore a very crumpled suit, Persian type canvas shoes with rope soles and three days' growth of beard – apparently prescribed in General Orders for all Persian officials appearing in public. The second was a fat, swashbuckling Iraqi who said he was an Army officer but wore *mufti* – perhaps necessary or expedient when visiting Persia as there was at that time no love lost between these two countries. Both of them could make themselves understood in English. The third was a sinister looking Syrian. He eventually unbuttoned to reveal that he had kept a Muslim eating house for years in New York. He gave me the address and invited me to call if ever I was in New York. When I asked him what he was doing he said that he had a blood feud on his hands and the object of his return to the Middle East was to kill the murderer of his brother in Damascus but that he had to go to Tehran first of all to gather evidence.

The afternoon's journey across the desert was so hot that it seemed that the heat and glare were belabouring us with physical blows. The glare made one's eyes ache even through dark glasses; the quivering, radiant heat was like hot thumbs pressed on one's eyeballs.

We ran down the stony, dusty streets of Khanaquin about 9.30 at night. My companions left me to take up the lodgings they had for the night and I went off in a rickety *arabana* to the railway Rest House. This was the first *arabana* I had met. These vehicles are made entirely of leather except for the wooden wheels and steel axles. The body is made of stiff leather panels and it is suspended on the axles by stout leather straps. The vehicle swayed sickeningly from side to side on the rough cobbled streets and I felt that if I had gone very far on it, I would have been seasick.

At the Rest House I encountered two signs of British Indian influence in ascending order of welcome – a Hindustani-speaking Iraqi waiter and iced Allsop's beer. I was very dehydrated and drank two large bottles straight off and wolfed down with them the cold supper I had brought from Baghdad. It was just as well that I had brought food as the twice weekly provision train had been delayed and the Rest House was as bare as Mother Hubbard's cupboard.

I was up at 5 a.m. and breakfasted off three eggs, tea and last week's fermenting bread. When I had asked if it were possible to have some hot water for shaving I was told that that also depended on the train.

We set off soon after breakfast first of all passing the Iraqi customs and then the Persian customs. The latter customs house had not been completed and I was fascinated as I watched Persian artisans making an ornamented, stucco ceiling. This was not made by a moulded form as I had imagined. They simply threw the white plaster on to the ceiling and with a few rough tools and incredible skill and speed shaped out intricate flowers, rosettes, knobs and curlicues on the ceiling. They did not seem to spill any nor did any drop off. There were lovely Persian rugs spread all over the customs house and in particular in the office to which we were ushered to have tea.

Tea drinking in Persia is almost as much a ceremony as it is in

Japan. Tea in Persia is universally milkless and commercially sugarless unless one pays extra for the sugar. It is also always served in glasses, usually in metal holders, which are made of filigree silver in the case of the well-to-do. Each person has an individual tray. If sugar is taken it is usually broken off in irregular knobs from a cone of sugar and a lump is often held in the teeth whilst the tea is sucked vigorously and noisily through it. This habit is possibly based on the scarcity of spoons. I was told that sugar became seven times the price after it had passed the Persian customs on being imported from Russia. This led to a great deal of smuggling. Sugar was often buried on the beaches and dug up when the coast was clear. It was therefore quite common to have sand in one's mouth after taking Persian sugar. After drinking tea and chatting with the senior customs officer we went on with no examination of our baggage. This I suppose was out of deference to Seyghal in whose protection we basked.

I must confess that I was guilty of smuggling. At that time Persia was a police state under the dictatorial Reza Shah Pahlavi who personally and rigidly controlled every aspect of the country's life – including the economic and fiscal life. There was a strict currency control in Persia. Although this is common these days, this was the first example of which I had ever heard. The official rate of exchange was laid down between the pound sterling, or its equivalent the Iraqi dinar, and the Persian toman. This was followed by the State bank in Persia, the only legal agency for changing foreign currency. However, on the black market in Persia and everywhere in Iraq one could get exactly 50% more tomans to the pound. I regret to say that I changed some of my sterling travellers' cheques into tomans in Iraq and smuggled them across the frontier. I got the impression that our driver's cushion was stuffed with Persian currency and that the customs officials were turning a blind eye to it. The value of the travellers' cheques that I retained unchanged and declared was carefully entered on my passport in Persian that I could not read.

Leaving the Customs House we passed through desolate, undulating sulphurous sandhills which might have borne oil but certainly bore not a single blade of vegetation of any description. All we met on the road were a few dyspeptic, eructating camels and their misanthropic drivers also looked similarly dyspeptic for a similar cause – swallowing dust from the road as they plodded wearily along in the oppressive heat.

It was a gloriously welcome sight on topping a long hill to see before us the green trees, blooming orchards and silver streams of Qasr-i-Shirin. This is the surpassing delight of travel in Persia – to come suddenly upon a green oasis after hours in the desert and to slip from a hot dusty *kuché*, or town street lined with mud walls, into the cool of a Persian rose garden with its pool, fountain, runnels, beds of brilliant flowers and walls lined by the ordered soothing formality of stately cypresses. The dramatic transition from desert on one side of a mud wall to rose bowl on the other heightens the delight. The tall walls shut out the heat and worries of the outer world and led one to understand how Saadi was inspired to write his mellifluous verses in praise of accepting the joys of the world and shutting out the cares from the mind.

Qasr-i-Shirin, often pictured in Persian literature and miniature paintings, was like an illustration from a fairy tale. The long, wide, main street ran perfectly straight down a gentle hill. It was flanked by lovely gardens enclosed in walls or wrought iron railings periodically pierced by pillared gateways. The upper end of the street was surmounted by a waterfall flowing over an ornamental arch of masonry and the water was led by channels to either side of the street down which it flowed in *jubes* or brick-lined runnels which gave life to a graceful avenue of trees.

The altitude there is 1,655 feet and the provincial governor had a house set in a garden shaded with trees on which, as the sun caught them, gleamed clusters of figs, oranges, apricots and pomegranates. He invited us to tea and was very courteous and gracious to me.

The next stage was the village of Pai Taq and by then we had reached 3,350 feet. The nature of the country had been the same – arid and inhospitable. The road wound its way over the dry hills in a series of persistent loops. In the few spots where there was water there was vegetation. Pai Taq was typical of such a resting place – a clump of trees sheltering a tea house on the road and a stream in the little valley below the road, with a village embowered in the wood to which the stream had given birth and which followed the line of the stream. At Pai Taq, Abbas Seyghal took us to a large house where he said His Excellency the Consul-General for Iran at Baghdad, and presumably his boss, was on a holiday to enjoy the cool of the hills. He told me that the Consul-General spoke French and introduced me to him in that language and I therefore made some remarks in French. As I had taken an honours degree in French and had had several trips in France I knew that my command of French was adequate and my accent at least intelligible to French people. However, it was not intelligible to the Consul-General and there was a somewhat embarrassed pause until Abbas stepped into the breach and suggested that it would be easier for me to speak English which he would translate. The representative of the Iranian Empire wore broken canvas shoes, darned socks and no tie. I thought therefore that he was neither sartorially or linguistically the perfect pattern of a diplomat. In fact the stilted three-cornered conversation that we carried on showed him to be rather a pompous bore with practically no knowledge of world affairs or appreciation of Persia's position in world power politics.

After Pai Taq the road really began to climb as we crossed the barren, brown, completely grassless hills that formed the outlying flank of the great Zagros Mountains. Karind, at a height of 5,380 feet was the next town we reached. This town was chosen as a hill station for British and Indian troops in Iraq and Persia in and after the First World War. I saw many truly lovely sights in Persia but this modest, quaint hill town was one of the most delightful. The whole town is built on crags and crannies in a defile through imposing hills. Houses clung to every available eyrie and struggled up and down the long street in chaotic but pleasing confusion so that one stepped from the threshold of one on to the roof of the next. Springs, fountains, cascades, artificial pools and natural streams sparkled in the sun on every side. The sombre, mud-brick walls and roofs enhanced the brilliant splashes of roses, marigolds, scarlet pomegranate blossoms growing by the sides of the houses and the red chillies drying on the roofs. The street here was also lined by a turbulent *jube* and flowering creepers grew over many of the homes.

We all had a tasty pillau as an early supper and then called on a 'noble of Kermanshah' who was a delightful fellow living in a pretty flower bedecked plaisance down by the river.

I left the others there and climbed up the hill just outside the town to see some tents where some English employees of the Anglo-Iranian Oil Company were said to be living whilst on a survey. However, only the servants were there.

I then came back and went for a walk in the town. Many of the courtyards had massive, beautifully carved and studded wooden doors and if they were open one could see into some of the small rooms of a caravanserai lining the courtyard and opening onto it through domed arches. In others one looked onto the verandas and upper wooden galleries of substantial private houses.

There are in Persia many minority races of which the chief division is those of Turkic origin who made these parts the destination of their great migration from central Asia long before the Osmanli and Seljuk Turks went on to form the state of modern Turkey. The broad, steppe province of Khurusan in north-east Persia is peopled by Turkoman tribes. Other Turkic tribes of a different type – such as the Qashgai, Bakhtiari, Lurs and Kurds, inhabit the great mountain barrier running up south-west Persia and the borderland between Persia and Iraq and Turkey. The oak-covered mountain ranges of Pasht-i-Kuh, Kabirkuh and Zagros in Persia which go up to peaks of 14,000 feet, had been the unchallenged range of free, proud nomadic tribes for centuries. These tribes were possibly second only in their fierce, proud independence and fighting ability to the Pathans of the north-west frontier of Pakistan. They depended very largely on their vast flocks of sheep, horses and cattle which they took up to the high mountain pastures in summer by tracks known to them and them alone. Sometimes they planted a grain crop on their way up and harvested it on the descent. Sometimes they grew a few simple vegetables when the mountain camps were sufficiently static. Here in the upland meadows they lived a life of idyllic, pastoral simplicity, subsisting chiefly on milk, milk products and meat. They spun wool for their clothing or for making beautiful rugs which they dyed with vegetable stains and fulled in the mountain streams. For their simple cash needs they sold rugs, wool, ghee, butter and cheese usually sent out by special horsemen to the nearest Persian town. Most of the ordinary tribesmen were illiterate and could speak only their own Turkic dialect. Although simple, they had a native shrewdness and a highly developed and mystical sense of communion with nature and of the unity of the tribe. This was very necessary when their life depended on a delicate balance between stock and pasture and the latter depended on unreliable rainfall or melting snow. The women had a freedom and equality with men most uncommon in Muslim races.

The annual migrations were rigidly controlled by the chiefs or *ilkhans* who decided when it was appropriate to leave the *garmsir*, the hot lowlands of the Persian Gulf, for the *sardsir*, or cool uplands. Upon their sense of timing, weather wisdom and choice of mountain tracks depended the difference between flocks reduced to a size that made existence a struggle or maintained at a level that brought a rude comfort.

Some of their chiefs were men of wealth and maintained fine town houses in such places as Kermanshah, Khurramabad and Shiraz where they spent some of the winter months. Occasionally such chiefs married Persian women. A sprinkling of them had been educated at universities in England, France and Switzerland and I played tennis in Tehran with a young Bakhtiari chief who had been to Oxford.

Such chiefs, even when they became, as they sometimes did, leading social figures in the highly sophisticated and highly artificial society revolving round the Shah's court at Tehran, never seemed to lose their innate toughness and love of the simple joys of a nomad's life. They led their people in hunting the fierce snow leopard, found only in the most inaccessible places, and the cunning wild boar for sport but not food, of course, as they were all Muslims of a sort. They hunted the wild mountain partridge, capercailzie and grouse on horse, giving them no rest until they were so exhausted they could fly no more or, unbelievably, they sometimes even shot them from the saddle at a canter.

These same chiefs could be at a diplomatic levée or cocktail party one night and a few nights later, back in their beloved mountains, would be quite happy in their tents or even sleeping on the ground whilst on a journey between tent and town house.

Most of the Persians despised the Turkic tribes because they

131

were illiterate, could not speak Persian and had no learning or literature and because of their nomadic way of life which always seems to be despised by settled farmers and townspeople in every country. On the other hand the tribesmen despised the farmers and shopkeepers and thought that in any battle they could take on ten to one – in their own hills at least.

When Reza Shah Pahlavi had established his dictatorship in Persia he set out on a programme of modernisation of the country. Some aspects of the programme were well conceived and I suppose that all were intended for the ultimate improvement of this ancient power that had fallen onto evil days. He brooked no opposition and carried through his projects with great ruthlessness. One project was the breaking of the power and the settling of the nomadic tribes. The chief of the Bakhtiari was called to Tehran to be made Minister of War. It is doubtful if he would have gone without some such pretext. After a period in this office he was thrown into prison.

Measures of such a nature were taken against other chiefs which led in some cases to guerilla war between the tribe and the Persian Army. Expeditions against the tribes in the hills were seldom effective because of the much greater mobility of the tribesmen but they suffered considerable losses to their stock. Major operations entailing several divisions and armour were undertaken against some of the tribes at places where they had to cross main roads with their stock in the course of their annual migrations. Some suffered heavy losses in this way and these usually included their leaders. They were forced to live in settlements in the lowlands. It was then discovered that many of them died from malaria; the land and the rainfall where they were settled were not suitable for permanent cultivation, and the nice balance that they had worked out from experience between stock and shifting pasture was just about the best way to use the land with the scientific and financial resources then available.

Reza Shah had ordered Persians to wear modern European dress and the women to discard the veil (it was never worn by the tribeswomen). The *Turki topi* or fez was forbidden, the flat cap was encouraged. It was said that the Shah encouraged the latter, as did Mustafa Kemal Ataturk of Turkey, on whom he seemed to model himself, because the projecting peak would make difficult the Muslim brow-to-earth prostration in prayer and both dictators seemed to wish to discourage religion or at least religiosity. This was probably the reason why the cap was commonly worn back to front in Persia making the wearers look like old-fashioned motor cyclists, or current American baseball players.

In particular, tribal dress was forbidden and I was therefore surprised on walking round Karind and peeping into all the court-yards to see in one a beautiful, young Kurdish woman openly sitting down in the tribal dress of long yellow robes and flat, pill-box-like, saucy-looking hat. She was swinging her baby in a big wooden cradle slung from a framework.

Some of the little shops had a fine display of rugs and some of their neighbours were busy at treadle sewing machines making peaked caps. I had a glass of the ubiquitous *chai* or tea on the veranda of a little cafe with potted flowers all round it. Immediately opposite was a building with the strange combination of police station on the second storey and a busy inn on the ground floor. A pretty flowering creeper grew all over this building but a jarring note was struck by the rusty old petrol tins in which the creeper was rooted.

Butchers' shops are usually noisome places in the east owing to the lack of refrigeration or fly-proofing. The shop in Karind was no exception. Livid, fly-covered gobbets of meat hung on any pro-tuberance in the open front of the shop; a few were suspended from the branches of a nearby tree and receiving the attention of a couple of pi dogs which were only perfunctorily shooed away occasionally by the butcher. In addition to the meat, the butcher offered for sale the hides and fleeces of the animals he had apparently slaughtered on the blood-sodden sand just near the shop.

Small boys were bringing in trains of two or three donkeys carrying paniers full of wheat grown in the neighbouring pocket handkerchief-sized fields and spreading it out to dry on the flat roofs of the houses. This hardly seemed necessary in a climate with so low a humidity.

I wandered to the end of the little town where I found another small waterfall spurting out from an opening made in a small dam blocking a mountain stream.

All in all Karind made an impression of quaint beauty that I still retain.

After the long lunch break we pressed on to Kermanshah which we reached about 5.30 after a series of punctures. In places where water was obtainable the road ran through poplar-lined fields.

I went for a walk around the town before the evening meal. It seemed drab and unattractive. There was considerable evidence of the emancipation of women in Kermanshah as I was to find later in other Persian cities. Kermanshah, a city of about 70,000 people, appeared to be an army centre of some importance and the streets were full of women trying to pick up the Persian officers who looked quite smart – the first examples of smart uniform I had so far seen in Persia. A troop of soldiers marched down the street – ragged in every sense. It was noticeable that the women completely ignored the common soldiers walking on the streets which suggested that, as usual, their pay was greatly in arrears.

The hotel was a fine modern building set in the type of lovely garden in which the Persians excel. They must be some of the world's best and most industrious gardeners. It is common to see an illiterate Persian labourer toiling from dawn to dusk through the fierce heat, tending, watering, budding, transplanting and designing flower beds, with an eye not only to the shape of the bed but to the combined effect of the different coloured flowers, with an inbred skill and a devotion which must be based on more than the mere desire to keep his job in a hard world.

I was offered a pretentious bedroom at a pretty stiff rate. I found that the electric light would not work, that there was no water in the wash-basin, bath or lavatory and no mosquito net. It is fairly common for there to be no water supply in the single lavatory in country hotels in Persia and it was therefore never necessary to ask where the lavatory was. However, as the Manager had boasted that his hotel was up to the best European standards, and as I was indeed paying for such a standard, I went to consult my fellow passengers sitting in the garden. They advised me not to pay for the room but to eat at the hotel and sleep in the garden as they intended to do. I had brought a light camp bed for such circumstances and I managed to persuade the driver to get it from the boot of the car. He was very surly and reluctant and said that as we would have to be up by 4 a.m. a bed was hardly necessary.

However, the evening developed into a roaring success. After quite a pleasant dinner in the garden listening to the orchestra, a young fellow came up to us. He had heard me speaking in English to Abbas Seyghal. He introduced himself as Ahmad Bey, a Kurdish chieftain, who had been on a course for a year or two in Lancashire to learn all about the manufacture of cotton. He, of course, had a marked Lancashire accent. He turned out to be very pro-English and anti-Persian and said that he intended to get drunk himself and get us all drunk. (Most of the Persians are Shias. The Kurds and Baluchis are Sunnis but the former are rarely so orthodox that they do not drink alcohol.) He pressed bottle after bottle of beer on us and took his own share. He would not let us pay a penny saying that we were guests in his country which was *Kurdistan – Kurdistan* not Persia – which he kept emphasising. The more he drank the louder became his voice and his denunciation of the Persians. This was rather strange when a Persian official was one of his guests.

Strangely enough three young English fellows came up to the next table – they were already drunk. The whole evening struck me as most bizarre. After we had finished a lot of beer, Ahmad Bey insisted that we should have a bottle of the thick, rather sickly local red wine. I think by the end of the evening he had succeeded in his objective. I tottered down the garden path to my camp bed where I slept in my clothes under a cypress tree for what was left of the night. There was a pleasant nip in the air.

We were up, as insisted upon by the driver, by 4 a.m. Breakfast consisted of two boiled eggs each, both bad in my case, bread, butter, honey, cherry jam and cheese. We set off immediately after breakfast and that day I was like my companions – unshaven.

The country was a succession of wide depressions, something like the *margs* of Kashmir or the *cuencas* of Spain, each separated from the next by a line of hills. These features were repeated mile after mile until we got to Hamadan.

Hamadan was the Roman Ectabana. It was a city of over 100,000 but it showed little of its ancient glory. It was surprising to learn that it had a population of this size. One would have estimated the population of a European town of its extent to be at the most 20,000 – such is the overcrowding in the East. It was typical of the modernised Persian provincial centres. The focus and centre of the town was a large circus consisting of a fine, wide street with a railed garden in the centre of the circus and the *shahr bani* on one side of the circus. *Shahr bani* means roughly 'Head of the city' in Persian and is a building which combines under one roof police, municipal and provincial administration, tax and licence offices and every other function of government. This is an example that could well be followed in many British colonies or indeed country towns in England where buildings are normally built or acquired in a haphazard fashion all over the town as the various needs arise. In this, as in other aspects of town planning, as I hope to show later, Persia had a good example to set.

A few streets radiated from the central circus at Hamadan but did not seem to go very far until they merged into the dusty countryside. It struck me as a smug and dingy place and it seemed incongruous that its chief industry from Roman times has been the production of rugs of outstanding beauty.

After leaving Hamadan the road climbed to nearly 6,000 feet and offered some magnificent views of successive chains of hills. For some time we wound along a narrow ledge through a grim gorge.

We stopped at a *chai khana* or tea house for lunch. These were found along all the main roads in Persia. The main design of all was fairly similar. They were square, flat roofed buildings divided roughly into kitchen and dining room. The more pretentious were built of rough brick; the smaller were merely very thick baked mud walls with branches of trees laid across the top plastered with sun-baked mud. The seating in many of them consisted of mud benches lining the wall covered with several layers of beautiful Persian rugs which were more sat on than walked on in their country of origin. On the rugs usually sprawled drivers sodden with sleep and opium. Floors were paved with flagstones. Invariably, large photographs of the Shah and Crown Prince faced the doorway. The remaining space on the walls was usually taken up with faded oleographs of tight-waisted Victorian beauties and a few horns of mountain sheep.

136

Our lunch consisted of a good mutton pillau accompanied by stewed green figs; delicious wafer thin charcoal-grilled beef steak spread with mint and cucumber, the unleavened flat Persian bread (*nan*) and *mast*. This is a drink made of salted milk common all over Persia to the almost complete exclusion of fresh milk. An alternative drink in the heat of the day is water cooled by the addition of ice and snow deeply buried in winter and protected from the sun by mud enclosures. However, with the ice come vestiges of mud and gravel and other additives. On my return to India I developed a very persistent attack of amoebic dysentery which I think must have been caused by drinking water cooled by this means.

After lunch we pressed on through the semi-desert country. At one place the road was completely blocked by two petrol lorries whose drivers were having an argument. It was only our superior numbers that persuaded them to let us through before they had had it out.

We arrived at Tehran in the evening. I had been advised to stay at the Palace Hotel. There were one or two hotels in Tehran that were supposed to be better but this was said to be the most reasonably priced of the reliable European style hotels. I found the tariff rather high but when I left I found that they had cheaper rooms which had not been disclosed to me. The food was good – a Persianised version of the French cuisine and as the menus were in French as well as Persian I more or less knew what I was going to get. I recall a fine range of hors d'oeuvres including the smallish black Persian olive, the most delicious I have ever had. The Manageress/Reception Clerk was a raven-tressed alabaster-skinned Armenian beauty who spoke good French. I was still hoping to get into Caucasian Russia and asked her what she knew about the region. However, she came from one of the Armenian colonies in north-west Persia and could tell me nothing except that there was an Intourist office in Tehran which could advise me.

I thought that the first things that I should do the next morning before seeing the sights of Tehran were to clear up all necessary formalities and make onward travel arrangements. I have mentioned the dictatorial nature of the regime. It seems that two aspects of a dictatorship are often xenophobia and extreme sensitivity to criticism. One manifestation of this was that every-one, and in particular foreigners, had to have permits for a camera and to take photographs. Even after these permits had been given, photographs which the unsuspecting foreigner would think were of objects of historical interest or beauty were sometimes not allowed if the authorities thought that they might tend to show the outside world that Persia was backward. In some such cases the camera was confiscated or the entire film destroyed.

I therefore went to the Government department concerned and was interminably passed from office to office. None of the clerks or officials seemed to have the slightest interest in me. Finally I found a business-like messenger who spoke English and led me along corridors and up and downstairs past offices where officials drank glasses of tea behind tall stacks of files covered with dust. As these were on occupied desks, they were not apparently archives but current files and it led me to wonder what the dust/day ratio was in Persian offices. At last we got to the right office and I was given a long form to fill in. Filling in this form amounted to a potted autobiography, including a declaration of religious and political faith and reason for visiting Persia. There were some linguistic obstacles including considerable confusion over camera number and passport number. After a trying triangular conversation between the official, the messenger and myself I thought the business was finished. I then learnt that I had to produce three passport sized photos of myself before I could take a photo of anything. I was told that after I had produced the photos I might have to wait a few days for permission.

I eventually got the permit after about a fortnight but was never asked to produce it although I took photos openly all over the country in front of soldiers and policemen. I believe that outside of Tehran the formality was ignored and I had taken a number of photos on my way to Tehran.

There was a system of *jahwaz* or cartes d'identité for Persians and foreign residents and all foreign visitors had to carry their passports. These were examined on passing through every municipality – both on entry and exit – even if they were within sight of each other. It seemed to take an interminable time on occasions to examine a bus load of people and I was constantly told that the time taken by the police was in indirect proportion to the size of the note enclosed by the driver in his *jahwaz* or in his driving licence. The Persian script, of course, reads from right to left and therefore all books in Persian open the opposite way to European books. I used to find it extremely exasperating to wait up to ten minutes or more whilst a Persian policeman, probably only barely literate in his own language, went through my passport page by page solemnly pretending to read English, French, German and Italian entries as he held it upside down. Continually repeating the number of my passport at least helped me to learn the Persian numerals and I can to this day immediately recall in Persian the number of my first passport whereas I cannot remember the number of subsequent passports even in English.

It was also necessary to fill in an elaborate form everywhere one stayed the night. This consisted of about 10 major questions, some of which had three subsidiaries, enquiring into every aspect of one's place of birth, family, occupation and religious and political beliefs. On one of the first occasions that I answered this I automatically put down 'Church of England' as my religion. I was sharply told not to prevaricate and state clearly whether I was Muslim, Christian or of some other faith.

The questions were in Persian and French and could be answered in no other languages. Some foreign travellers might have been in difficulties. I naturally answered in French. The last cage on the form was for any remarks. Day after day I filled in this form and it was taken away and studied by officials I was sure could not speak French. One night at a little village in the mountains I relieved my feelings by writing something in French to the effect that I considered it was rather pointless to have to fill this in every night. It was a small village with no senior officials and I felt sure that no one there could speak French. However, the police dug up the village schoolmaster who translated my remarks and I was given a lecture, as I suppose was only fitting, on the right respect that should be accorded to Persian official forms.

I am afraid that I found the Persian officials always seeking to put up some obstacle, irrelevancy or delay in the hope of extracting some *bakhshish* to waive the contrived difficulty. This was in marked contrast to my experience in Iraq and again I hoped that

139

this was the British influence in Iraq. One could hardly blame the Persians as their salaries were miserable and often long in arrears due to some senior officer trying on them the tactics they tried on the general public.

There was also a very common habit of trying to pull a fast one in any deal. On the other hand I met a great deal of kindness, charming courtesy and hospitality from rich and poor, peasant and townsman.

There was quite a strong anti-American feeling in Persia at the time, especially amongst officials. This was extended to anyone speaking English, as they could not distinguish the accents, until one made it clear that one was English when the atmosphere usually but not always became much more cordial.

The anti-American feeling had arisen from the following trivial cause. The Persian Minister in the United States, who was married to an Englishwoman, was motoring in the southern States. He was stopped by an Irish-American cop and accused of exceeding the speed limit. He said 'I am the Minister for Iran', as the Persians then officially called the country. This was introduced by Reza Shah to signify a break with the past. The policeman had never heard of Iran and thought he was addressing the Minister of some strange religious sect. An argument ensued. The Minister's wife threatened the policeman with her umbrella. They were both arrested and put behind bars. Eventually he established his identity and they were released.

About this time the Persians had just launched a small armed vessel on the Caspian as what the Shah said would be the foundation of Persian naval might. A big American paper got hold of the incident about the Persian Minister, wrote it up in a tactless way and finished the article by asking, 'Will Reza Shah Pahlavi send his navy to bombard New York?'

The Persians, a proud, ancient and sensitive race were very hurt. There were diplomatic protests and demands that the paper should apologise. I was told that the paper printed a few special copies with apologies which were sent to Persia but that the apologies did not go into the normal circulation. This also came to the ears of the Persians and made the feeling even worse. As a result, all Americans in Persia were being subjected to as much annoy-

140

ance as possible by Persian officials. Some of the feeling engendered by this seemed to spread over to other foreigners – especially if they spoke English. Occasionally I suffered from it.

I went to the Russian Legation and Intourist about permission and arrangements to visit Nakhichevan, Armenia, Georgia, Russian Azerbaijan and Daghestan. I was told that as I would have to go through Tabriz I should call at the Russian consulate there where everything would be finalised and I would be given permission.

I had a letter of introduction to the Groveses – American missionaries who ran the Elburz College in Tehran. This was an institution teaching English and western academic subjects up to what appeared to be the equivalent of first year University standard in Europe. It was largely run by American missionaries and other European staff engaged by them and almost entirely financed by American funds. It was somewhat condescendingly tolerated by the Government.

I called on the Groveses. They took me to swim in the pool at the American Legation. This was a delightful stone-lined pool fed by a cool mountain stream and surrounded by rose plots.

In the evening we went to the British Legation, wandered round the delightful gardens and met some of the interesting and charming British staff.

The Groveses had a young American artist staying with them who had travelled round India and was going on to Russia. After a few days they asked me if I would also like to be their guest, paying for the cost of my food. As the hotel was really more than I could afford and as they were the most delightful people I gladly accepted this generous offer.

I found Tehran a fascinating and exhilarating city. It has a fairly reasonable climate as it stands at a height of 3,700 feet pleasantly placed on a gravel fan skirting the southern foothills of the Elburz Range and in the centre of a fertile plain. Even in the hot weather the temperature is not too extreme and the nights are fairly cool. The dryness of the atmosphere reduces the effect of the heat. At the same time those who can are glad to go to the satellite summer colony at Shimran in the foothills of the Elburz.

The mighty peaks of the Elburz dominated by Mount Demavend, 18,530 feet high and 5,000 feet above the mean height

141

of the range, formed a dramatic background as one looked down some of the broad new avenues in Tehran.

Tehran is relatively modern by Persian standards as it was founded in the 13th century. It slowly grew until it was sacked by the Afghans in 1721 and started its real growth when it was chosen as the capital by Shah Agha Mohammed in 1788. The real reason for the choice was that it was protected by the mountains against invasion (by the Russians) from the north. Shahs of the Kajar dynasty, in particular Nasir-ud-Din, beautified and walled the city.

Reza Shah Pahlavi planned a modern city there and began to put his plan into effect in 1925. With the speed and ruthlessness possible only for a dictator he cut wide modern avenues through old slums, lined them with graceful, shade-giving trees and constructed a number of fine new squares chief of which was the Maidan-i-Sepahsalar. This was the administrative and business centre of the city and was surrounded by a number of imposing official and commercial buildings of which one of the most magnificent was the State Bank.

Reza Shah built a fine new royal residence called the Pahlavi Palace on the outskirts of the city. Marble and onyx from Yezd were used in its construction and the main motif in the decorations was sculptures copied from Persepolis. He also built a university.

I was frequently asked if I did not think that Tehran was like Paris, or as beautiful as Paris. In spite of the fine town planning and buildings I could not agree with that although somehow there was a very French air about the city. For example, one saw confiseries and patisseries all over the place – frequently called by these names – and wayside cafes with seats and tables on the pavement as in France. On the other hand, one saw much that was definitely oriental such as the tiny little shops of craftsmen and Persian style bakeries with unleavened native bread hanging up in the open windows looking like the seats of those hard, round wooden chairs.

Under the modernisation campaign the Persians had come to despise the marvellous glories of old Persian art that had adorned Tehran. For example, the twelve gates of the city decorated with exquisite porcelain tiles and graceful minarets had been knocked down to make way for new roads.

Although great progress was being made in modernising Tehran there was still a lot to be done. For example, there was no piped water supply and ordinary people drank the water in the *jubes* at the side of the street. Diplomatic missions and certain major buildings and hotels had supplies from their own springs. The electricity supply was also very weak and uncertain.

The old glory of the Gulistan (Rose Garden) Palace famous in Persian history and literature was still maintained as far as possible. The Shah's Throne Room therein was kept up and used on occasions for diplomatic receptions and in a nearby museum was the historic gold-studded Peacock Throne from which a Persian Emperor once ruled India as well as Iran.

One evening we went to the *Danish Serai Ali* − beautiful gardens which formed a cool, sweet-smelling oasis in the midst of dusty, stinking refuse-strewn lanes. Another evening we had dinner at a delightful open air restaurant in a lovely pooled garden and went on to an open air cinema where we sat on comfortable armchairs amid rose bushes and were served with snacks and drinks in the interval.

One day the Groves took the American artist and myself to the library where we examined some beautiful old illuminated Persian manuscripts including one which had recently returned from an exhibition at Leningrad. It had been much photographed and internationally publicised and was said to be worth 2,000,000 tomans.

One day we went up to Shimran in the foothills and met the diplomats and rich business people taking refuge there from Tehran. Some had lovely houses, some were living in elaborate tents but all − houses and tents − were set in beautiful gardens.

I heard many stories of corrupt officials and of the tyranny of the Shah − even that he shot people in public himself as a punishment for inefficiency, corruption or disobedience. However, in spite of his methods and his love of personal power, glory and wealth, he did seem to be striving to break the age-old bonds of corruption, nepotism, conservatism and inefficiency which were holding back his ancient Kingdom.

One of the great points in the Shah's modernisation campaign was the emancipation of women and he had succeeded in this but there was one result of his campaign which had probably not been foreseen. When he ascended the throne Persian women had been in *purdah* and could only appear in public when heavily veiled. He decreed that men and women should wear European dress and that the veil should be discarded. There were public unveiling ceremonies to start the campaign in which the leading ladies in each locality unveiled on public platforms. On the whole, although there were some strange incidents, this campaign of unveiling went forward with little opposition from men or women, except the most conservative, usually *mujtahids* or other religious leaders. Simultaneously there was a campaign to break the power of the religious courts.

By the time I got to Tehran the pendulum had swung to such an extent that the city was thronged with prostitutes. They drove up and down the avenues in *droshkies* plying for trade and one had literally to run a gauntlet of them to get into the hotel.

One night I went out to a party with some of the junior staff of the Elburz College, including some Swiss teachers. We had a merry evening and when I got back to the hotel not excessively late I found it locked up. Apparently, they made no provision for late revellers. I was somewhat under the influence of the drinks we had consumed and without a second thought I climbed up a rickety drain pipe to my room. The next day when I was in the street and saw where I had gone my blood ran cold.

I played exhilarating tennis on very fast dried earth courts and had a few games of golf on the dried up course with 'browns' made of sand. One hole was a dog-leg passing round the high mud walls of a Persian nobleman's garden with a tall brick dovecote at the corner. I managed to clear the walls on occasions but once disturbed the peace of the dovecote and on another occasion that of the nobleman himself as my ball plonked in the pool near where he was taking his ease. He was extremely enraged, rushed to the gate threatening to shoot me and refused to give up my ball. Apparently no one had ever landed a ball in his pool before which was surprising.

The pleasant days passed and it was time to pass on and take leave of my charming hosts. They gave me a letter to another

American missionary in Tabriz who they said would be pleased to put me up on similar terms.

The bus for Tabriz was supposed to start at 4 o'clock. There was also a law in Persia stipulating deductions to the fare according to the delay in starting – a most welcome innovation brought in by the Shah. When I arrived at the bus station the man in charge coolly said that the Tabriz bus would start at 6 o'clock. It actually left at 8.45 by which time I was annoyed. I pointed out the delay to the functionary and asked about the legal deductions. He flew into a rage and screamed at me '*C'est rien, c'est rien*' but I thought that, even in Persia, $4\frac{3}{4}$ hours behind the timetable was something. I never found out what I should legally have paid but in the end I paid the full fare – only 5 tomans, the equivalent of 12 shillings, and nothing for my luggage. I thought this was very cheap for a journey of well over 400 miles and taking 48 hours.

When I boarded the bus I saw some of the reasons for the low fare. It was a 22-seater Chevrolet bus. Every bus that I saw in Persia was a Chevrolet. In the bus, counting myself, were 32 passengers, a big sack of wheat and a live sheep. The seats were narrow, uncushioned wooden benches. As a foreigner, and rightly considered not so inured to Persian travel conditions as a native, I was courteously offered the place of honour behind the driver. This was a seat designed for two and had the great advantage of an inch or two more leg room than the other places. It was still very cramped. However, it soon became apparent that the only possible place to put the wheat and the sheep was next to me. I could not grumble as I still had more room than anyone else. As we proceeded on our long, weary journey the atrocious roads threw the sheep or the wheat or both into my lap and it was very trying.

Before we got to the outskirts of Tehran the sealed roads finished and we started on a gravel road. At first, in my naivety, I thought that the road must have been broken up for laying sewers or some other purpose but as mile after mile and hour after hour passed I came to realize it was the normal condition of the road.

There were a lot of students from the Ecole Militaire in Tehran going home to Tabriz for the holidays. One of them could speak French and we entered into a long discussion through him as an interpreter. The chief topic was the evils of Iran. They were lively, intelligent fellows and eagerly asked a multitude of questions about conditions in England and other countries I had visited, my education, work and pay. I was rather embarrassed by the last question as my modest salary must have seemed a fortune to them.

We had supper together at a wayside inn and continued our discussions. After supper the bus drove right through the night without a stop and by morning we had arrived at Kazvin where the road branches for Hamadan and Baghdad and through which we had driven on my journey to Tehran.

It was very cold and I was very glad of some glasses of hot, sweet tea, after which I freshened myself up with a wash in the wayside *jube*.

From Kazvin the road began to climb steadily. By midday we had reached Zenjan where we had lunch. We spent the night at Mianeh widely reported to be the home of a strange, poisonous bug whose bite carries a serious illness. The great administrator, traveller, antiquarian and writer Curzon spent the night here during his travels and pronounced the bug to be a humbug as he did not see it. The journey had been very trying until the constant severe jolting, the heat, haze and dust of midday and the cold of night finally reduced one to a semi-coma – as on a long train journey in India.

Everyone was very glad of a relief. To the driver and a number of the older passengers this took the form of going straight to the benches on the side of one of the rooms in the inn and without food or drink starting to smoke pipe after pipe of opium just as the driver had smoked cigarette after cigarette whilst driving.

The Persian opium looked like a brownish lipstick and seemed to have the same consistency. The opium poppy was grown all over the country where soil and climate permitted and we had passed many fields on the way. A piece about the size of a pea is cut off the plug, held in tweezers and rolled and roasted in a flame. It is then placed with a tiny glowing ember of charcoal near a hole on a porcelain tube at the end of a straight wooden pipe. The pipe is sucked and the fumes inhaled. They invited me to join them but I do not even smoke tobacco and I found the dense, sickening fumes of the opium quite nauseating. In fact I think that I would have been sick if I had stayed very long in the smoking room. I had my supper in another room and slept on my camp bed in the courtyard.

In the morning we were in really difficult mountain country and I was rather apprehensive of the driver's fitness after his night's debauch. No one else seemed to give it the slightest attention but it seemed later that my anxiety was not unwarranted.

We ground up and down several fearsome passes from one of which there was a pretty view of a lake. We then came out onto a long mountain slope along which the narrow road snaked its way with a drop of several thousand feet on one side – usually the side on which we were driving.

I noticed a blanket-wrapped object on the side of the road. Then after a few hundred yards, another. I had an ominous foreboding and then round a corner we came to a group of people and a couple of gendarmes at the place where the previous bus had gone over the side with the loss of everyone on board. The bodies had been scattered far and wide down the mountainside and people were struggling up with them and depositing them on the roadside where they reached the road. The general theory was the driver had fallen asleep due to too much opium smoking. After a short pause we drove on and apparently no one gave the matter a second thought or remotely entertained the idea that it might happen to us.

A final pass near Shibli and a fantastic zigzag descent and Tabriz, a city of 214,000, was visible below us on a fertile terrace at the foot of the Sahand volcano.

My passport was taken away from me at the police check post and when the bus got to the garage I could not find my ticket and they made a great fuss over that but I did not pay again.

I took a 'phaeton' as they called it to the British Consulate. I was met by the very charming Consul, Urquhart, in the garden. From him I went on to Christy Wilson, the American missionary who ran a hospital at Tabriz and with whom the Groveses had arranged that I should stay. This time the drive was in a *droshky* which was an example of the cosmopolitan nature of Tabriz. The main *khiabin* at Tabriz was quite an imposing well-surfaced modern-looking street, but to get to the Mariz Khana-i-Amerikani or American Hospital we cut through a maze of narrow cobbled twisting streets. By this time it was dark and the occasional fitful

147

street lamp cast the moving shadow of the *droshky* on the blank mud walls of the street. I was slightly dizzy from travel and insufficient sleep by then and I found the whole effect rather macabre.

There was quite an American colony at the hospital and they had numerous Persian and some Assyrian friends. We had several delightful evenings talking to these interesting people and a very good party at the British consulate.

One night we all went out to dinner – literally out to dinner – in the courtyard of a hotel. The courtyard was paved with flagstones with flowers growing between them; in the centre was a pool and fountain and as always in Persia a border of roses round the pool. The courtyard was flanked by the high buildings of the hotel and some of the party had been dining there the year before when an earthquake shook the buildings and gave everyone a fright – one person dived into the pool. (Tabriz is an earthquake centre and has suffered many shocks.)

The path to the courtyard was lined with a trellis on which grapes clustered. Tabriz is reputed to grow over 50 varieties of grape and one sees grapes everywhere. The vines frequently grow up high mud walls and the plant and clusters of grapes are supported by long strings thrown over the wall and counterbalanced by stones tied on to them on the other side.

Tabriz is a very beautiful town with poplar, mango, almond, fig, apricot, peach and quince trees growing everywhere and because of the greater rainfall a generally greener air than the other parts of Persia I had so far seen. The view from one of the flat rooms was one of delightful verdure. It was more modern in its buildings and public services than other provincial cities, although nearly all the buildings were single storeyed because of the earthquake menace. It was a polyglot city. Persian, Russian, Armenian, Kurdish, Assyrian and Turkish were all spoken but the last appeared to be predominant. Publications were on sale in the shops in all these languages. This was possibly why there was a British Consulate there as it must have been an excellent listening post. In the past it had been fought over by Russians, Turks and Persians. There was a railway, built by the Russians for obvious reasons, from Tabriz through Julfa to Russia. Then, as now, the bridge over the Araxes, the middle of which was the boundary between Persia and Russia, was barricaded and guarded and no trains ever crossed the border.

I was told that Tabriz once had 28 miles of bazaars or *suks* all covered by a complex multi-domed roof system. Most of these had been cleared away to make the modern streets.

From the roof of Wilson's house I could catch a glimpse of Lake Urmia and, in the distance when the sun was shining right, the pass in the mountains, leading towards Mount Ararat and the route in the mountains by which Alexander the Great was supposed to have retreated from the Parthians.

There were many relics of Alexander all around Tabriz. I bought an Alexander tetradrachma (confirmed as genuine by the British Museum) for one Indian rupee in the bazaar.

Like so many hills in really dry climates those around Tabriz took on the most wonderful colours in the evening sun – shading from primrose, pink and red through to green and purple.

At night the lights of Tabriz twinkling over its various hills were a spectacular sight and unlike most Persian towns it had a 24 hour electrical service.

Some of the old Muslim cemeteries had been converted into beautiful parks and in one there was a bust of the four great emperors of Persia – Darius, Shahpur and Shah Abbas at each corner and a full figure of Reza Shah dominated the centre!

The Ark or citadel at Tabriz had an even larger arch than that at Ctesiphon but stood only 20 years before it was destroyed by an earthquake. The noted Blue Mosque, one of the finest Arab mosques in Persia, was similarly damaged but the beautiful inlaid tile work still remaining on its ruins, and its name, give a good idea of its former glory.

At the beginning of the Pahlavi regime the local Swedish-trained gendarmerie mutinied as they wanted provincial autonomy and were attacked by the Persian Cossacks recruited from the Turkoman tribes of Khurusan, in which the Shah himself formerly served. It is said that the Cossacks fired 300 rounds of artillery fire at the gendarmerie in the Ark of which 3 found their mark. Backed by an indiscriminate hail of machine gun fire this was enough to dislodge the gendarmerie, who retreated in the night, looting the bazaars as they went before scattering to their native hills. The

Cossacks occupied the town the next morning and looted what was left. Bullet marks were to be seen everywhere.

One morning I climbed up to a mosque on a hill above the town with an English speaking boy from the Mission school. The whole city was spread out before us. Once again it was difficult to believe that it was as big as its known population.

By this time the Russians had to give me a definite answer and, of course, it was 'No'. This time they told me, in English, that unfortunately a message had just been received from Moscow that I was not to be allowed to enter Russia. I realize now that there must have been an Iron Curtain even in those days – at least in sensitive, strategic regions such as Caucasia.

I suppose that the Russians did not let me in as they thought that I was anti-Communist. However, the Persian police must have noticed me going to the Russians in Tehran and Tabriz and decided that I must be a person to be watched. A little man in a grey felt hat and big boots seemed to turn up in future at most of the places where I stayed and sometimes where I ate. It seemed to be more than a coincidence. I got heartily sick of him and some-times thought of approaching him or pulling his leg but thought better of it.

The only reason I had come to Tabriz was to try to get into Russia but I did not regret my visit.

I played tennis with the Urquharts and some of the Americans in the evenings. I corrected the English of a guide-book to Persia written by a German staying with some of the Americans and I translated some passages of the French version of Attar-e-Iran for Christy Wilson who was writing a history of Persian art.

When I went to regain my passport from the Persian officials I met with great and provocative insolence and a hybrid Persian-French demand for 'char photographies' or four photos of myself before they would release it. I quarrelled with the lout. He accused me of trying to regain the passport by force and wrote this down in Persian in the passport. We came to an angry impasse and I left in a fury saying I would go to the British Consulate at whose power and influence he jeered.

The next day, Urquhart's *munshi* took three reserve photos that I had, got my passport and got a senior official to endorse that my alleged insult to Persian officialdom was the fault of the officer concerned.

I left Tabriz for Kazvin at 9.45 a.m. in a terrifically over-crowded bus which was stopped at the police post outside the town and told to go back to Tabriz and unload some passengers. We went back a mile or so to a tea house and waited there about an hour and a half and then drove back towards the police post again. At a strategic point five of the passengers got out and walked down the hillside to detour the control post. We then went on, got our *jahwaz* passed and waited for the others on the other side of the village. We finally got going at 2.15 having made an effective distance of 4–5 miles in $4\frac{1}{2}$ hours.

We arrived at Kazvin at 1.30 a.m. Two men carried my baggage until we found a *droshky* in which I drove through the streets to the Grand Hotel. The streets were lit by hurricane lanterns suspended on posts and patrolled by pairs of policemen with the inevitable rifles and fixed bayonets. The hotel appeared to be more grand by name than by nature but it was fairly comfortable, rather more in the Persian than the European style. The entrance was flanked by tiny bazaar-style shops – one of which was a little tinker's shop and workshop. He was still industriously hammering away.

The main public room of the hotel was like a covered courtyard (this was full of animated groups of Persians, chiefly army officers, drinking at tables and continually shouting at the top of their voices for waiters). From this room covered stairs on two sides gave access to a rectangular wooden gallery from which the bedrooms opened. The dining room was on the same level as the bedrooms. I discovered what was apparently the only lavatory by the normal olfactory directional aids. When I went there I found that it lacked a seat or a flush and I was considered a tiresome eccentric by insisting on water to flush it.

The whole building was lit by a few dim oil lamps. Next evening I found that there was a fitful electric system in the town which finished at 11.30 p.m.

The town was not very impressive for a former capital of Imperial Persia but the streets were pleasant and tree-lined and converged on the *shahr bani* which had a fine arched gateway and, as usual, a well-painted impressive Persian coat-of-arms.

151

There was a rectangular *maidan* or *place* in the middle of the town which was the usual centre of social activities. The Persians, since the emancipation of women, seem to have adopted a habit similar to the Spanish *paseo* as the younger women and men were strolling up and down in pairs – the sexes segregated but ogling each other as they passed.

I had a strange experience at dinner that night in the hotel when I was joined by a Dr G–. The radio was blaring out a Nazi speech from a Nürnberg party anniversary festival. My companion asked me in German, which I did not speak, if I was a German. When he learnt that I was English he said that he was a Czechoslovakian. As he had a German name I asked him if he was Sudeten Deutch and he said that he was but added an anti-Nazi outburst.

He said that he had spent three years in a concentration camp in Germany for pacifist propaganda even before Hitler really came to power. He had managed to escape back to Czechoslovakia but found things too hot for him there and finally landed up in Iraq, where he established a small practice. However, at that time the German Ambassador had considerable influence and put the police on to him as a Communist which I should imagine he was. He decided that he must leave quickly and fled to Tehran in a car without any money. He showed me injuries on his hands which he said had been caused by torture. I believed his story and as he was short of money gave him some.

My next objective was the Caspian shore of Persia. As I could find no bus going there I had to hire a taxi and left in the morning for Resht in a big Dodge.

For the first hour or so the countryside was undulating semi-desert, supporting patches of tussocky grass with a few stunted, drought-resistant trees and fortified villages where the presence of water made cultivation possible – typical of most of the Persian scenery.

The road then began to climb up and up, following all the time the valley of a reddish-chocolate river, until we reached a great height with magnificent views of the Elburz Mountains. We reached the pass somewhere in the neighbourhood of Rudbar. When we got into the narrow gorges of the pass there was a wind so violent that not only sand but gravel was hurled against the car. It is said that there is invariably a fierce wind in the gorge.

Upon gaining the slopes facing the Caspian a dramatic change occurred. We had left the desert to enter a region where the rain-bearing winds from the Caspian caused extremely high fertility and luxuriant vegetation. It was the most dramatically sudden transition between climatic and vegetative zones that I have ever seen. Behind: dry sun-scorched rock and sand and only the hardiest scattered desert vegetation struggling to exist – in front: oppressive humidity and overwhelmingly luxuriant growth.

The highest slopes on the seaward side were covered with a wide range of conifers which as we descended were soon succeeded by forest and fruit trees of all descriptions among which apricots, peaches, figs and almonds predominated. There were also large fields of opium poppies.

Instead of flat-roofed mud houses there were wooden cottages with conical or pyramidal roofs of thatch or wooden shingles usually covered with trailing vines, creepers or melons. The people as well as the landscape smiled and offered a marked contrast to the usually austere aspect of the Persian people and countryside.

We had now entered what was then called the province of Gilan but is now the First Province. It was largely the personal estate of the Shah. His son subsequently gave most of it away to formerly landless tenants.

We descended the course of the Sefid Rud river, which separates the Talish Hills of Gilan from the Elburz Mountains proper of Mazanderan, through really lovely countryside, passing sleek herds of well-fed cattle grazing on the grass which had grown up on the flood terraces of the river. We went through one outstandingly lovely village with its street lined with graceful trees and lovely red flowers. There was a walled park surrounding what was I suppose a nobleman's country mansion and along the outer side of the wall was a row of bazaar shops – somewhat similar to an estate and small country town in England.

We passed lots of charcoal burners at work. A great deal of charcoal was produced in Gilan and sent by caravan or lorry to other parts of Persia. On the coastal flats we came to sugar-cane, tea, tobacco, rice and a wide variety of vegetables.

153

At Resht I stayed at the Hotel Iran which was very clean and pleasant and where the manageress spoke French. There was a notice in my bedroom in Persian and French which said that hot baths were available on the payment of a slight extra charge. It was quite an event to be able to get a bath at all – let alone a hot bath – in a Persian hotel and so I made the mistake of telling the manageress that I would like a hot bath. She seemed rather surprised but said that it would not take long. I waited what seemed an interminable time and then went to the bathroom to find that it had obviously been used as a store room and a harassed maid was emptying it of accumulated junk. There was a large tiled bath with something that looked like a cross between a giant samovar and a giant hookah at one end. This was the water-heating apparatus. I then told the manageress that I really did not mind whether I had a hot bath or any bath at all. However, her professional and national pride had been roused by then and she insisted that I had a bath and a hot one too. The apparatus was lit and eventually the manageress called me and conducted me personally to the bathroom. The central pipe of the apparatus was red hot, steam issued from cracks and the whole rickety contraption wheezed, bubbled and hissed in a manner which quite frightened me. The manageress was bursting with pride. I thought at one stage that she was going to stay to see that I really did have a bath but eventually she left. I then found that there was inadequate cold water to cool the hot and all in all the experience consumed a lot of time and patience.

I went to the *shahr bani* to try to get my *jahwaz* to go to Pahlavi. This town was originally called Enzeli but was renamed in honour of the Shah.

There was a great deal of discussion about my request which I could not follow nor could I make myself fully understood in the smattering of Persian I had by then acquired. I was asked to come back in an hour. When I did so there were more gesticulations but finally a French-speaking European, who appeared to me to be a Russian, was produced and he explained to me that no permit was necessary to go to Pahlavi.

I therefore arranged for a car to take me to Pahlavi and wandered around the bazaar for an hour or so until the time arranged for departure. I found the cobbled streets very clean and the shops very well stocked. As elsewhere in Persia, stationery seemed to be an item very much on display. In general this area of Persia seemed to be much more European in atmosphere and outlook than elsewhere. Although Resht had a population of 122,000 it had the air of a small peaceful country town.

I found the hotel at Pahlavi very pleasant and the food good. It was built around a red-tiled central courtyard. The manager was a Russian.

After a meal I went to look at the sea and was surprised to find very heavy waves dashing on the beach. Somehow I had always thought that inland seas should be placid. There was a little dock and wharves surrounded by expanses of exposed mud up a small river guarded by two breakwaters. There were some small groups of Persian sailors lounging around and one naval launch. They looked even more ragged than the soldiers I had so far seen. However, some of them were kind enough to row me over the estuary to see Pahlavi proper – the Resht side of the water is called Ghezjan. Both ports are on the extensive delta of the Sufid Rud.

An attempt was being made to develop the town as a port and pleasure resort and some pretty gardens had been laid out. However, the place seemed quite dead. It appeared to consist mainly of one street of fairly good shops and a few holiday houses.

A new but empty casino stood in melancholy solitude at one end of the beach. At the other, as if to point the contrast between old and new in Persia, stood an ancient whitewashed lighthouse with a quaint, antique clock, one face of which showed the hours in Persian characters and the other in Roman. The only people on the beach were an English family struggling to erect a couple of tents in the shelter of the sand-dunes and a party of boisterous young Russians being rewarded, I suppose, for having exceeded some norm. The girls were blonde and pretty and wore what was then the latest in one-piece bathing costumes. There was one drawback to bathing in the Caspian. The first yard or so of water as one entered the sea from the very shallowly sloping beach was swarming with unpleasant lice-like insects and it was necessary to jump over them when entering or leaving the water.

The next day I arranged to go back to Resht by bus. It was very late starting and took a long time on the way. When we arrived I popped into the Hotel Iran and had a quick lunch whilst they arranged a car for me to go on to Ramsar.

I shared the car and the fare with an extremely attractive young Persian woman. We carried on a strange conversation in my few words of Persian and her few words of French from which I gathered that she was born in Tabriz and had learnt Persian, Turkish and Russian as she grew up. She married a German from whom she learnt German. Her husband had gone to work successively in Iraq and Italy where she learnt Arabic and Italian. She said that although she could speak six languages fluently she was barely literate in any of them. I have come across other similar instances amongst Orientals which seem strange by European standards. Illiterates, who cannot make notes, often develop the most amazing verbal memories.

The drive along the Caspian coast to Ramsar was magnificent. The road ran along the gentle, lower slopes of the hills. On the left-hand side, to the north, were fields growing the fine feathery Caspian rice, sugar-cane, tobacco and opium poppies, and scrub-covered beaches stretching down to the coves and thundering blue water of the sea. To the south were tea-gardens on the lower slopes of the towering mountains followed by fir-clad heights dominated by the snowy summit of Mount Demavend, peeping in virginal shyness at a height of 18,530 feet from behind an almost constant veil of clouds.

At one place we passed through a crowded country fair. There were side-shows everywhere, stalls of cattle for sale, vegetables and fruit laid out on the ground, piles of sickly, fly-covered sweet-meats and women busily making *roti*, the unleavened bread, from small lumps of dough patted into thin rounds between the hands and baked on hot iron plates. The chief attraction was a religious maniac posturing and raving surrounded by a jeering crowd.

This district is noted for its spas and at Ramsar we came to a magnificent hotel owned by the Shah. It was extremely expensive but I decided to stay for one night for the experience. I found that it was so far above the purse of most Persians that apart from myself one Persian couple comprised the guests.

It was a most impressive white building on a hill above the sea. The gardens proper of the hotel were beautifully laid out and a

156

series of formal terraced gardens embellished with statuary and laid out with conifers, orange, lemon, apricot and pomegranate trees in formal designs lay between the hotel and the sea. The public rooms and bedrooms were on a palatial scale and all carpeted with lovely Persian rugs.

The maître d'hôtel, the chef and head waiter were Swiss. Guests were so few and far between, particularly those who could speak a western European language, that the head waiter was in a state approaching a nervous breakdown when I arrived. He was extremely pleased to unburden himself to me.

Enjoyment of the scenery on the Caspian shore was lessened by the intense humidity, although the temperatures were not high. I found the people in this region very friendly and I invariably received a 'salaam' when I was out walking.

I went down to the town to enquire about transport to Chalus. I found a very clean, pleasant tea-house run by an English-speaking man who told me that a bus should leave at 4 p.m. I walked around the town whilst waiting for the bus and came across a French-speaking Persian engineer with whom I exchanged the usual potted autobiographies.

The bus arrived and left at 7.30 p.m. At 7.45 p.m. it stopped for the driver to eat at a little tea-shop. This took till 8.20 p.m. Then, 20 minutes after we started, the lights failed. After a bit the driver got them going again. They then failed twice more before he decided to stop for the night at a small village perched on a ledge between the mountains and the booming surf.

There was one absolutely filthy little inn in the village. They offered me their best room for 30 rials but I got a smaller one for 15. The sordidness of the inside of the hotel was compensated for by the pleasant view of the hills and mountains revealed from the balcony at the back when the sun rose and the pleasantly murmuring stream which bubbled along the edge of the courtyard.

The place appeared so dirty that I refused an evening meal or breakfast.

We set off at 7.30 a.m. for Chalus and stopped at a small village for an early lunch. As it was then 24 hours since I had eaten I consumed an entire small chicken and a large mound of pillau. I ate in the open surrounded by a group of admiring spectators of all ages.

I had agreed to pay the bus driver 30 tomans before we started but I said that I wanted a reduction for the great delay. After a discussion with the police, 20 tomans was decided as reasonable.

The European-style hotel at Chalus was very pleasant but again almost empty. It was set at the mouth of a lovely little valley leading up to the mountains and the whole set-up of hotel and spa and mountain scenery seemed quite like Switzerland. There were cotton fields in the region and a cotton factory on the outskirts of the town.

In the evening I went for a walk along the then deserted Tehran road from which there were magnificent views. I had been warned that there were wild boars in the jungle that sometimes attacked people and that even the Hyrcanian tiger was occasionally seen in that region. I walked on for some time and was quite alone. I got quite a fright when there was a rustling in the undergrowth and a dark shape broke cover on to the road but it turned out to be a harmless domestic bullock.

Early the next morning I went for a walk along the road to Meshadsar, my next destination. The roadside trees were full of magpies, jays, crested hoopoes and other brightly coloured birds.

The hotel management had booked me a seat on the bus for Meshadsar which they said would leave any time from the morning to 4 p.m. I felt that I could not go very far for fear of losing the bus. Finally, when it had not arrived by 6.15 p.m. I went out to walk off my temper and to be soothed by the sound of the surf. I thought I would walk back towards Ramsar from where the bus was coming so that I would not miss it. I walked for about an hour and saw some dim lights approaching. At the last moment I could see it was a bus. I stopped it and found it was the Meshadsar bus. I almost decided to let it go on but came back in it to the hotel to pay my account and collect my luggage.

When it came to the paying an awkward incident arose. I found the bill was exactly twice what I had expected. When I had inquired the price on arrival, I thought the manager had said 'see toman', the Persian for three tomans but he had intended the French 'six tomans' which sounds almost exactly the same. This made the hotel very expensive and I protested. He was extremely good and agreed that because of the misunderstanding I need pay only 3 tomans a day. There was a rule at the hotel that the staff should not accept tips. The hall porter and chambermaid would not take anything in the hotel but intercepted me on the way to the bus – I gave them one and half tomans each.

The bus was stopped at Noshahr on the way to Meshadsar by the police. An officer got very excited and said that I had overstayed the period permitted in my visa for me to stay in Persia. This was quite correct but I pretended unintelligent ignorance. He said that I would suffer 'grande peine' unless I returned to Tehran as soon as possible. I said that was exactly what I was trying to do but was handicapped by the unreliability of the buses. He said that there were trains every day from Shahi but a helpful student from the Ecole Militaire said that they went only on Saturdays and Tuesdays which I later confirmed as correct. I said that I would make my way to Shahi as best I could and then catch the first train to Tehran. Honour was thus satisfied but only just.

I arrived at Meshadsar at about 1.30 and there was a long argument about the fare before I got off the bus. I objected to the constant attempts to make me pay more than the normal fare but all in all I suppose I was at that time quite often the typical, arrogant Englishman in the East and it was lucky that I did not get into more trouble.

The place where I got off the bus was on the outskirts of the town. I got a *hamal* to carry my luggage and he said that we would have to walk 3 kilometres to the hotel. We finally arrived at the pension to which I had been directed by Hussain Agha, a friendly fellow traveller on the bus. There were several fierce dogs that rushed at us as we entered the courtyard. The porter jumped behind me. We finally managed to wake up the landlady and the *hamal* told her that I was a '*Rais-i-Allemani*' or a German nobleman. This was a typical Oriental exaggeration but it was a significant tribute to the power of Nazi propaganda that he should think that the door would be opened more readily to a German than an Englishman. I speculated as to when the change could have taken place as a few years earlier there would have been no doubt that of all Europeans the English had the most prestige in Persia. However, even the grandiloquent introduction of my herald drew only a sneering repetition as she slammed the bedroom window shut.

We then found an unpretentious little Persian-style hotel elsewhere in the town which had a carpenter's shop on one side of the
front veranda. I was welcomed by a shy, kind-faced old lady
dressed in black. She had no empty room but I thankfully spent the
rest of the night on my camp-bed on the unoccupied part of the
veranda. I found the place scrupulously clean.

In the morning I had a breakfast of four fried eggs, some Persian style bread, butter and powdery cheese and tea. Just as I had
finished Hussain Agha passed on his way to call on me at the pension. He introduced me to the taxi-driver for my onward journey
and a boatman for me to go swimming.

After I had had my swim, I arranged with the driver to take me
to Shahi. It was understood that I would have to pay for the whole
car, as he had no other passengers, and that the fare would be 35
rials unless he picked up other passengers whereupon the fare
would be proportionately reduced. We had barely got to the outskirts of the town when we stopped to pick up an old woman and
her granddaughter waiting by obvious arrangement at the side of
the road. He said that they were very poor and asked if I would let
them travel for nothing. I agreed to this but thought that he must
have got something from them. We then went on about another
mile and came to a very dandified Persian major, in a smart
uniform, complete with gloves, waiting by the side of the road
also fairly obviously by arrangement. The driver again asked if I
would let him travel for nothing. I said that he must have at least as
much money as I had and that he ought to pay half the cost. After
some argument it was agreed that he would pay 15 rials and I
would pay 20.

The driver calmly stopped when we arrived at the small market
town of Babolsar less than half the way to Shahi. My luggage was
transferred to a broken down Chevrolet station wagon which was
already over-crowded with passengers. There was then considerable delay and I did not know what was happening but thought
that he had arranged for the other chauffeur to take me on. I
thought that this was rather sharp practice but was prepared to
accept it on a reasonable financial adjustment. However, the
first driver then approached me and asked for the original 35 rials.
I offered him 5 because of the shorter journey and the other

passengers. We had a fierce argument and he finally agreed to take me on to Shahi for the original 35 rials. He loaded my baggage back on his car and I got in. No sooner was I seated than 3 other passengers clambered in. I then said that I wanted a reduction. He refused. The other passengers and a policeman tried to persuade me to agree but I was 'as fixed and constant as the northern star'. He then threw my baggage off. He finally coughed up 15 rials and I was under the impression that he would take me on to Shahi for the 20 rials – with the 3 other passengers – which was similar to the arrangement after the major had got in. However, he left my baggage on the market place, jumped into the car, reversed it and was about to return to Meshadsar. I was so furious by that time that I jumped on to the running board of the car and gave him a pretty good left hook. He stopped the car with a bang, jumped out and rushed at me kicking. Luckily a couple of armed policemen jumped in between us as by that time I was in a mood to beat him up. As he struggled to get away from the policemen and at me, I stood in front of him shouting, 'You want a fight, do you? You want a fight, do you?'

The policemen very tactfully led me aside and we all went off to the *shahr bani*. I was not certain whether I was under arrest and on the way I had depressing visions of filthy cells and dysentery. I was surprised when I was treated very respectfully and politely. They said '*Be ferme*' (a courteous Persian phrase) and I sat down to await developments. After some time a pleasant blond European appeared who could speak English and Persian. I thought he was a Russian. The first question he asked me was: 'Is there no law about hitting people in England?' I found this very embarrassing but luckily he did not wait for an answer. After I had given my version of what happened, which was apparently accepted without question as the truth, a very long discussion ensued amongst the Persian police and officials. Finally, it was decided that I should apologise to the driver for having struck him, and give him 5 rials compensation to salve his wounded pride; he was reprimanded for having tried to cheat me and told to take me on to Shahi by myself for the original agreement of 35 rials. I expected an unpleasant journey but he was very chastened and polite and we parted on fairly good terms after a smooth journey to Shahi.

161

Shahi showed more promise of development than any other of the much vaunted Caspian towns. There were a good hospital, a well built *shahr bani*, a post and telegraph office, factories, shops and private houses, and a fine modern hotel in the course of construction. However, I could not buy a film for my camera.

I decided to send a telegram to the Groveses to let them know that I was returning and had the following conversation with the man in charge.

'Do you speak English?'

'Ah yes English.'

'Can I send a telegram to Tehran?'

'Yes.'

'Can I send it in English?'

'Yes.'

'Will it get there today?'

'Yes.'

'How much will it cost?'

'Yes.'

I then started again and by a mixture of French, pidgin Persian and mime managed to conclude my business.

I later met the same official on the street and we had a short, sharp, friendly and mutually unintelligible conversation.

I left on the train for Tehran at 10.30 the next morning. As this was only 23 minutes behind the scheduled time it was a relatively good performance especially as the train had started at Bandar Shah some 80 miles up the line at rail head on the Caspian – by now the road had come a little way inland.

The section of the railway from Bandar Shah to Tehran had only recently been opened. The line was eventually destined to link the Caspian and the Persian Gulf along a route of some 850 miles. Later routes were to branch out from Tehran to Tabriz and from Tehran to the great city and shrine of Meshed in the Turko-man steppes of north-east Persia and from Tehran to Yezd. There were many criticisms of the railway voiced to me in private but not publicly. The gist of most of them was that it was a personal whim of the Shah (as he thought that all modern states had to have railways) and that if the same amount of money had been spent on roads the country would have had a far better system of communications.

These criticisms were probably well founded but I found it a magnificent and spectacular engineering feat.

Different sections had been constructed by engineering contractors from various European countries and near one lonely station I noticed several graves with Italian names. The men had been killed in an accident while building a bridge.

There was a crowd of about 40 people madly struggling to get their tickets at the ticket office. Watching them were five policemen and a police officer. The only attempt at control was when periodically one of the policemen would dive into the crowd in the best rugger style and pull out a few people, usually including one who had reached the ticket window. There would be a violent struggle to gain the vacated place but no improvement in the general position. After a few minutes the police would then repeat their tour de force. Women were roughly handled by the crowd and the police and indeed some of the policemen very roughly tore the *chaddar* off an old woman who had not fallen in with the order to appear unveiled and wear European clothes in public.

I suggested to the police officer, who spoke French, that the crowd should be formed into a queue but he regarded me as a slightly offensive eccentric. However, he did kindly send one of his men into the office to buy a ticket. Without that I should never have got it in time to catch the train. Some people had not got their ticket by the time the train had left although they had been struggling for over half an hour and everyone could easily have got a ticket in time if there had been a little order.

There was also a great deal of fuss and running about by a clerk in charge of baggage who travelled with the train, although he had only 3 or 4 pieces to look after. He saw the luggage on and off the train at each station.

At the wayside stations, at all of which we had considerable stops, the engine-driver blew his whistle as a preliminary warning, then a second whistle a few minutes later. The guard would then emerge from where he had been having a glass of tea or a pipe of opium and produce a kind of hunting horn. He then proceeded to

163

rival Roland in the winding thereof. Everyone would rush madly for their seats and get settled. A long pause would then ensue and the most enterprising third-class passengers would enter into impassioned haggling for fruit, eggs, *mast* or bread. Finally, a last trump would send everyone rushing back again to the Gospel train where unfortunately there was not room for many a more. Usually the deals were cut short with either payment, change or produce not handed over properly.

I was one of the first Europeans, except construction engineers, to make the journey to Tehran after the railway was opened. I found the scenery absolutely fascinating. I believe that it was one of the highest broad gauge railways in the world. The specially designed engines were made in England but the rest of the rolling stock, on the Swiss pattern, was made on the Continent. We zigzagged by very steep gradients right across the Elburz Range. There were a number of breath-taking viaducts with silvery mountain streams in the valleys far below. Some of the mountains were pierced by long tunnels.

I took a walk through the third-class carriages and although they could not rival the overcrowdedness, heat, stench and filth of third-class carriages in India they were fairly bad. They were jammed tight with opium smokers, mothers suckling babies, babies vomiting, children performing other natural functions everywhere with all the unself-consciousness of the East, soldiers and gendarmes airing their sockless, stinking feet, vast families of peasants trying to eat and here and there young people, clean and dressed in European clothes. There was debris of all kinds thick on the floor chiefly melon skin and pips. The last was a sign that the eaters were people of some financial position, as they had to be to afford even the third-class fare, as the poor in Persia do not throw away melon seeds but dry them and eat the kernels. Indeed it is with some reluctance that they part with the skins.

Back in my own section of the train I had a talk with an Austrian engineer working on the railway and a Persian student who had spent nine years in France. When he learnt that I had been in Iraq and Baghdad he tried to draw me out on a comparison of Iraq and Persia. Feeling was fairly strained between the two countries at the time chiefly over some dispute concerning the Khuzistan border, rendered more acute because it was a rich oil-bearing region. I found that the Iraqis and Persians despised each other.

This student told me that the Arabs were very dirty and unprogressive, not like the Persians. I did not say much but thought that although the side street of Baghdad were undoubtedly filthy, it had a piped water supply, modern sanitation and machine-washed main streets – none of which existed in Tehran. He must have read my thoughts for he said 'C'est la nature des Arabes d'être sales et les Persans ont pris des habitudes sales des Arabes. Les Arabes leur ont appris d'être sales.' I thought to myself that they had been good pupils. He continued, 'Baghdad est la ville la plus infestée du monde.' I agreed with him there as far as my experience went. Later on I think that of all the places that I had visited I would perhaps give the title for dirtiness to Harar in Abyssinia.

We arrived at Tehran at 11.40 p.m. Everyone except the Austrian and myself got off quickly. By then we were the only two on the train with luggage. The Austrian had bought 40 hens with him from the Caspian region where they were very cheap. The luggage clerk said they would have to stay in the van all night. This didn't suit the Austrian. They had a long argument while I had to wait. Finally the Austrian was allowed to take his chickens. By then my suitcase and camp-bed were the only articles left and the whole station was deserted except for the two of us. I had to produce the tickets to claim these two articles, although the same man had given them to me in the morning. He made a great show of checking them against the numbers on the articles which he finally released obviously with reluctance as he had thought of no way of putting the squeeze on me.

At long last I got myself and luggage into a *droshky* and began the slow clop-clop to the other side of Tehran. We arrived at the Groveses' place at 1.15 a.m. I asked the driver to be quiet so as not to wake everyone up. He responded by asking for four times the correct fare and being as offensive and noisy as he could when I refused. He shouted and sang and did his best to wake everyone up.

I had another very delightful stay in Tehran and then started for Bushire to catch the ship back to Karachi. My original intention had been to return overland to India via Meshed skirting the

Dasht-i-Kavir, the Great Salt Desert of Persia, and going on through Herat and Kabul in Afghanistan to Peshawar but transport was uncertain and the road very difficult and I was afraid of overstaying my leave. The other overland route, turning south at Meshed and running along the edge of the Dasht-i-Lut or Great Sand Desert, was more certain, provided one connected with the weekly train at Zahidan to Quetta, but not as interesting as through Afghanistan. I therefore decided to return by ship.

The journey from Tehran to Qum was not particularly interesting – running through flat, arid country. At Qum I saw the tomb of Fatima, the daughter of Mohammed. Because she was the wife of Hussain it was a very important Shia shrine and only lately opened to non-Shias. I watched rows of pilgrims queuing up to kiss the brass rail surrounding the tomb where the sacred remains were supposed to lie.

Between Qum and Isfahan we ran through a desert area irrigated by underground channels which are unique to Persia and Baluchistan where they are known as *qanats* and *karizes* respectively. They are started by deep tunnels that penetrate into detritus or water-bearing gravel at the foot of a mountain. A series of perpendicular shafts are then bored and connected by tunnelling from the bottom of one to the bottom of another. The channel thus formed falls less steeply than the surface of the ground. It thus gradually approaches the surface and when it meets the surface, if the soil is cultivable, it irrigates cultivation. If the soil is unsuitable the water is led in surface channels until it meets cultivable soil. The channel is kept underground as long as possible in order to reduce loss of water by evaporation.

The building of *qanats*, as can be imagined, is a highly skilled and highly dangerous occupation as it is not uncommon for the tunnels or shafts to collapse burying the men working in them.

A *qanat* may yield only enough to irrigate one farm or garden; on the other hand some are so large and abounding in water that a few keep a whole city in being – for example, the desert city of Kerman with a population of 50,000.

Unfortunately the *qanat* also was often owned by the landowner and between rent for the land and *abiana*, or water

166

dues, the slave-like peasant would often have to pay up to three quarters of his crop.

Between Qum and Isfahan we were skirting the edge of the Dasht-i-Kavir, one of the most fearsome wastes in the world. After the infrequent rains it is a quagmire. For most of the year, when the temperatures rise to over 125° in the shade, it is a treacherous skin of hard crystalline salt with the sucking mud waiting below to engulf man or animal that sinks through the skin.

Reza Shah had, at one stage, forbidden the camel in Persia, as being symbolic of the old conservative East. He decreed that it had to be replaced by train, taxi, bus and lorry. Up to then I had therefore seen very few camels in Persia as they had mostly taken to travelling by night. This is in any case often done in hot countries to avoid the heat of the day. It also enabled the police to close their eyes to the long furtive strings of muffled camels that padded by at night. I had seen such ghost-like caravans occasionally elsewhere silhouetted against the night sky. Here the pretence was given up. The desert beat the diesel and only the trusted camel and the hardy camel-drivers could cross the salt pans of the Dasht-i-Kavir. At Qum lorries which had brought goods from Tehran, Hamadan and Isfahan transferred them to camels. Caravans were assembling and setting out for the small oasis towns scattered through the desert. Some were destined eventually for Meshed over 500 dangerous miles away along tracks lined by many a carcass bleached white by scouring sand and sun.

The edge of a *kavir* or giant salt pan carries a fringe of camel thorn and wiry tussock grass from which hardy sheep and camels can find a living when there is any water for them after the infrequent rains. After this comes a barren gravel glacis rising gradually at first, and then more steeply until it runs into a tangled ridge of bare, eroded rock and boulders, sand and gravel conglomerated together in fantastic shapes. In places there are dunes of fine blown sand rising up to 600 feet. Occasionally a small river or stream issuing from a mountain or rock feeds an oasis of varying size. The carpet of vegetation spreads out like a fan from the foot of the hill as far as the irrigation reaches.

The next place of call after Qum was fabulous Isfahan, the most beautiful city in Persia and surely one of the most beautiful in the

167

whole world. The history of Isfahan goes back about 2,700 years since when, strangely enough, a Jewish colony has always maintained itself there as in so many other place in the East. Shah Abbas made Isfahan his capital at the beginning of the 17th century. This great ruler was also a great town planner and unhampered by the regulations of modern town planners but armed with dictatorial powers and unlimited labour and wealth he laid out the centre of Isfahan as a model city.

The city is essentially an oasis and is watered by the Zaindeh Rud which flows through its centre where it was canalised and lined on both sides with avenues of lovely trees and graceful streets. These streets are lined with the shops and studios of craftsmen of all kinds and those Persian artists who specialise in painting miniatures on camel bone and ivory and who use a few cat's whiskers as a brush. Queen Mary used to patronise one of them.

The river and avenues lead like a spoke to the hub of the city, the Maidan-i-Shah or the Shah's Square. The layout of this lovely rectangular *place* would be the envy of many modern cities. It is so spacious that it served originally as the first recorded polo field, in the time of Shah Abbas, and a pair of stone columns at each end mark the original goal posts. This *maidan* runs almost due north to south and is overlooked on three sides by palaces and mosques. At the north end is the opening of the impressive vaulted *suks* or bazaars said to have extended originally for 17 miles and to have been the finest Oriental bazaar in the world. At the opposite end is the Masjid-i-Shah or the Shah's Mosque. The gateway to the mosque is in the middle of one end of the vast rectangular *maidan* but the axis of the mosque cannot be at right angles to the side of the *maidan* as the *mihrab* has to face Mecca. The angled junction between gateway and courtyard is effected with grace and ingenuity. The grandeur and exquisite colouring of the tiled arabesques and black kufic inscriptions create a wonderful impression. The mosque is beautiful, within and without, by daylight but the vista seen from the flat roof of a house bordering the *maidan* of its minarets and gold-leafed dome floating above the wall of the courtyard in a bright moonlit sky is a never-to-be-forgotten poetic dream.

Another fine mosque bordering the *maidan* is that of the Sheikh

Lutfullah, the inside of whose dome is covered with the tiled representation of a peacock's tail of exquisitely life-like design and colour.

The third great mosque of Isfahan is the Madresseh-i-Shah Hussain. The main courtyard of this mosque or theological college contains pools of water, lined with flower beds and overhung with cypress trees reflected in the water which also reflects the graceful marble pillars of the veranda.

The arched cells for the students surround the courtyard and the beauty and tranquillity of the place form an ideal setting for religious meditation. These three mosques form a magnificent trio which would be hard to equal anywhere in the world.

There are in Isfahan many other beautiful testaments to the building genius of Shah Abbas including the Ali Kapi, a marble pavilion from which he used to watch the polo on the Maidan-i-Shah.

The city is embraced by a wide girdle of irrigated walled gardens and orchards, giving way to more open fields surrounded by hedges and ornamented with circular brick towers which are dovecotes. As the irrigation fails the fields gradually give way to desert and mountain.

Bridges across the river lead to Julfa-i-Isfahan or Julfa of Isfahan, the colony where Shah Abbas settled Armenian craftsmen, artists and traders from Julfa on the Armenian border. They helped to bring beauty and prosperity to the city that he made the glorious capital of his empire.

There is, or was, a Persian saying: 'Isfahan – Nisf-i-Janan' which means 'Isfahan is half the world' and in the days of the great Shah when it was a trade centre for a wide area and the capital of a world power, there was a good basis for this saying.

The inhabitants of Isfahan were foolish enough to riot in the time of Tamburlaine. He had 70,000 of its inhabitants massacred and, according to his habit, made a pyramid of their skulls. However, it grew again to a city of over 200,000 and its old commercial reputation is maintained in the still extensive covered bazaars. These were unique in my experience as they were cool, clean, free of flies, quiet and well-conducted – a tribute to the power of tradition.

169

The American missionaries in Persia had passed me from one of their stations to the next and I received wonderful hospitality from them all. Isfahan was the last place where I stayed with them.

From Isfahan the road towards Shiraz went along the plateau between the foothills and the desert until we got to Persepolis about 40 miles north-east of Shiraz. The mean height was about 8,000 feet and it was so cold after dark in the bus that I was very glad to share a blanket offered me by the man sitting next to me.

Persepolis is known to Persians as Takt-i-Jamshid or Jamshid's Throne and to the Arabs as 'The Thousand Pillars'. Its construction was begun by the great Emperor Darius who extended the Persian Empire to India in the east and whose westward progress was checked by the Greeks at Marathon. He was one of the greatest of the numerous great figures in Persian history and was a fervent worshipper of Ahura Mazda and probably made Zoroastrianism the state religion of Persia. Only about 14,000 Zoroastrians survive in Iran today although they are more strongly represented by the Parsis of India.

Darius completed the organization of the Persian Empire and the system of communications begun by Cyrus the Great. As befitting a great king he began the construction of a new capital to mark the glories of his reign.

He chose Persepolis, in a fertile area clear of the desert and a site which had been inhabited from the stone age. The essence of the plan was the levelling and making symmetrical of a rocky spur projecting from a gently sloping hill. Part of the rock was cut out, side walls were constructed and the space between the rock and walls filled up to form three great terraces. Wide diverging and converging staircases decorated with sculpture led from one level to another. One staircase consisted of 106 steps with so gradual an ascent that a horse could go up them. Doubtless this was the intention.

The terraces were covered with vast halls of audience, and intervening courtyards, private palaces and harems, treasuries and offices made of stone and brick. There is an abundance of figures of men and animals in relief on the walls and an often repeated figure of a bull with a man's head guarding many of the entrances. The most striking decorative feature is a row of processional

170

figures of subject races, bearing tribute. Their wide range of nationality — Assyrian, Pathan, Indian, Arab, Turkoman, Mongol and others, is depicted by their dress and the gifts they are bearing.

Persepolis was begun about 500 B.C. by Darius and continued by his son and grandson Xerxes and Artaxerxes. Minor building apparently went on until it was sacked and burnt by Alexander the Great. This must have been one of the most notoriously wanton acts of destruction in history, the only reason apparently being to symbolise his might and conquest of Persia.

No attempt was made to restore it until the 1930s. Indeed the Persians looted the stone for building material and the iron clamps which held the stone together for spear heads. When I saw it, partial excavation and restoration had been carried out by a resident archaeological mission from the University of Chicago who were kind enough to give me lunch and show me round.

Enough had been done to enable one to picture its original sublimeness and to agree with the words that Marlowe made Tamburlaine say:

> And ride in triumph through Persepolis! —
> Is it not brave to be a king, Techelles! —
> Usumcasane and Theridamas,
> Is it not passing brave to be a king,
> And ride in triumph through Persepolis?

I got a lift from Persepolis to Shiraz on a lorry. Shiraz, provincial capital of 129,000, should be a poetical and inspiring city as it was the home in the 12th and 14th centuries respectively of Saadi and Hafiz, two of the greatest poets in a country of great poets. I found it a sad, dusty and uninspiring town. It is the metropolis and market place in winter of a large number of the nomad tribesmen of the south of Persia.

I arrived at Shiraz late in the evening and had run out of cash. The banks were closed and no one else seemed disposed to cash a traveller's cheque and so I went to the British Consul's house for help. I got none. I stayed with some English missionaries to whom I had been introduced. They were most kind to me and I met the British Consul-General for the Persian Gulf at their place.

171

I hired a big American car with a Hindustani-speaking Persian driver to take me to Bushire the day that the ship was due to sail from Bushire. I told the driver the time the ship was due to sail and that I had to be there in good time. The road from Shiraz to Bushire must be one of the most remarkable mountain roads in the world and the driver did the journey of 180 miles in what was then the record time of $9\frac{1}{2}$ hours.

The road was made out of mule tracks by British engineers in the First World War. Starting from a height of about 5,000 feet it climbed over a mountain range at a height of 9,500 feet, dropped several thousand feet into a valley, repeated the performance three more times and then dropped down to sea-level – a remarkable achievement in the relatively short distance of 180 miles.

Some of the river gorges between the mountains are over a mile deep. At one place we passed what was claimed to be the longest span of telegraph wire in the world, erected by British engineers and stretching from one crag to another over a mile away. At some corners on the road a lorry or a bus had to reverse, so sharp were the bends and so narrow the road. The views were naturally superb.

The country was wild, cold and inhospitable and there seemed nowhere where we could get any food. By the time we reached the last stage to Bushire over the flats and evil-smelling sulphurous streams I was quite hungry. As we passed over the sandy coastal plain the road was completely undefined and the driver followed any track of his choosing.

We reached Bushire in good time before the British India steamer was due to sail. To my dismay I saw that she was sailing right past the port without stopping. On inquiry I learnt that during the date season in Iraq alternate steamers made a direct, express journey to Karachi and Bombay to get the dates on the market as soon as possible. The agents in Tehran had omitted to mention this.

I thus had to spend a week in Bushire. The town was more Arab than Persian in character and I soon found its heat, dust, glare and evil smells most unattractive.

I looked around for somewhere to stay and found a small hotel kept by an Armenian. It seemed to me the only place where one could stay and so I made arrangements accordingly. The natural water at Bushire is so sulphuric that only the locals can drink it without unpleasant results. Others drink soda-water which was then four annas a bottle. This does not sound much but it was twice the current cost of soda water in India where four annas represented a quarter of the cost of a day's food at a decent standard of living. The temperature was so great that one had to drink a lot and apart from not being very nice it became quite expensive. Every meal that I had at that hotel consisted of a leathery omelette and a leathery chapatti and a little salt. The rooms were hot and unprotected from the dust and glare of the street and the beds were hard wooden platforms. I think that I can thus claim to have stayed in the worst hotel in the world.

I found even a day or two of this very trying and boring as I could find nothing of architecture, historical or human interest in the hot, dusty streets of Bushire. Luckily the manager of the Cable and Wireless Station about seven miles away heard of me and very kindly took me to stay with him at his cool, gracious house. It turned out that he lived fairly close to me in England.

In addition to the great wealth that she derived from oil, Persia used the four gallon petrol containers in a more diverse manner than I have ever seen anywhere else. This was very noticeable around Bushire. They were filled with earth and stone and lashed together to make piles for small bridges and causeways or similarly filled they were stacked up as children stack toy bricks to make huts and small dwelling houses. They were slung on a yoke to make universal carrying receptacles; used as pots, pans and cooking utensils of all kinds and also as ovens and racks and shelves. They were beaten out flat to line and strengthen walls and doors, or made up again into tin trunks. They were flattened out, rolled, punched and soldered to make jugs, cups, coffee pots, washing bowls, buckets, watering cans, dippers, panikins and vessels of all shapes and sizes. Finally, they were used as lavatory pans and seats.

The next week the ship called at Bushire but embarkation was not so easy. When I entered Persia and declared my traveller's cheques the currency control official had written down in Persian in my passport considerably more traveller's cheques than I possessed. I had changed them all at the State Banks, as required by law in view of the fact that the black market rate was so much higher, and retained all the receipts issued by the State Bank. When these were checked there was naturally a balance unaccounted for. This was illegal and I had my last and longest row with Persian officialdom. I was nearly two hours before I was allowed to board the ship and apparently only then through the good offices of the captain and first officer. It was very doubtful for some time as to whether I would be permitted to leave the country. My misdeeds were written down in Persian and covered several pages in my passport. The calligraphy was not the usual graceful flowing script but an angry and ugly scribble. I kept it for many years as a souvenir. I suppose it was only poetic justice as, although I had not committed the offences with which I was charged, I had broken the currency legislation by buying Persian currency at favourable black market rates in Baghdad and smuggling it across the frontier.

It was rather stormy and the ship rolled quite a bit. I felt very unwell and thought it was sea-sickness. After we had got to Karachi and I boarded the train for Lahore I went down with a very bad attack of malaria – the first – and – with one relapse – the last I ever had. I must have picked it up during my unwanted stay in Bushire.

I had found Persia a country full of interest and beautiful buildings and, although so much of it is waste, abounding in lovely and impressive scenery. I met inefficiency, corruption and obstructionism fairly frequently in official quarters but amongst all types of people I found friendliness and hospitality.

There was, as in many countries, a feeling, that was sometimes exploited for political ends, that they were superior to foreigners. This is not surprising and largely justified in a country which had an organized system of government a thousand years before Christ and which has persisted throughout the centuries, although with considerable variations, as one of the oldest national entities and probably the oldest monarchy in the world. It had, for example, a postal service in 500 BC. A Persian king has humbled a Roman emperor. The great Nadir Shah gave a sounder defeat to the great Afghan fighting tribe of the Ghilzai than the British ever did, and captured Herat, Kandahar and Kabul; Meshed and Tabriz; Bukhara and Khwarazm; beseiged Baghdad; forced the Russians to evacuate Gilan; defeated the Turks near Sulaimaniya and again near Erevan; occupied Tiflis and forced the Khan of Crimea to evacuate Daghestan; punished the Mir of Sind. The climax of the Persian ruler's glory and conquests, still talked about in India when I was there, was his conquest and massacre of Delhi in 1739. He replaced the crown on the head of Mohammed Shah and retired to Tehran with immense booty including the fabulous gem-studded Peacock Throne which graces the Gulistan Palace to this day.

The language of Persia is still the classical language of Muslims as far off as Kabul and Calcutta, Lahore and Hyderabad and not long ago Bukhara and Samarkand. Its literature is an oft mined treasury. Its camel driver and muleteers have the classical poets by heart. It is said that its flowers and the perfumes distilled from them have no equal in the world. Its wine has a widespread but covert reputation in parts of the Islamic world. The influence of Persia grafted on to the proselytising zeal of the Arabs caused the spread of Islam to be that of a polished, urbane culture in addition to a religious belief.

Iran now arouses thoughts of oil but for centuries it was noted for the beauty of its poetry, women and gardens and it is these attributes that linger in the memory of the ordinary traveller.

7

Burma

The following year, Khan Anwar Sikander Khan, head of the Urdu and Persian Department at Aitchison College and later principal of the Sadiq Public School, Bahawalpur, and I, escorted the boys on a trip to Burma.

As the previous year I had visited India's neighbour to the west – Persia – I was very pleased to have a chance to visit her neighbour to the east. One contrast between the two countries immediately sprang to mind. Persia lacks water – she has in many places cultivable soil but an insufficient rainfall turns large areas into desert. There is no lack of water in Burma and with the water come luxuriant jungles and great rivers. If Egypt is the gift of the Nile, Burma must be the gift of the Irrawaddy, the Salween and the Chindwin. The Burmese appreciate the rainfall which enables them to grow their rice and forms their great rivers on whose broad waters so much of the trade of the country is carried.

It was agreed to do the journey as cheaply as possible – partly to save money but mainly to show the boys how those less fortunate than themselves lived and travelled. Third-class travel in India was normally intolerable to those not inured to the heat, dust, overcrowding and stench of mass humanity, which it involved. It was arranged that we should hire a complete third-class compartment for our party of about 20 and the three servants who were accompanying us. This was less than half the number who would normally occupy it. The compartment was thoroughly washed out and disinfected and one evening we set out on the 48-hour journey to Calcutta where we were to catch a British India ship to

Rangoon. The long journey was not very comfortable on the hard wooden seats, which were too narrow to lie down or to sleep on with any comfort or security.

I found one feature of the journey very interesting. It was the time of the Kumbh Mela, a great Hindu religious festival, which is held annually at Hardwar in what was then the United Provinces and is now Uttar Pradesh, where the Ganges emerges from the mountains onto the great plains of northern India. Every twelfth year this festival is particularly important, sacred and desirable for any devout Hindu to attend. This was a twelfth year and it was estimated that over two million pilgrims would visit Hardwar within the few weeks of the festival.

The junction for Hardwar was situated on the main trunk line from Lahore to Calcutta, on which we were travelling, and on this junction hundreds of thousands of pilgrims were converging. Most of these seemed to want to get into our carriage, which was more or less fully occupied with ourselves and our baggage, which was on a more generous scale than that of the ordinary third-class passenger, for whom there was no special luggage department, and which we had therefore to stack in the compartment. At the same time it was obviously the primary objective on the train as all other third-class compartments had reached saturation point even by the standard of Indian pilgrims. That meant that they contained about three times the number for which they were designed and that it was physically impossible to get a single additional body in the compartment, even if half the body was out of the window. Although this made conditions acutely arduous even to a point that the weaker not infrequently died in such moving Black Holes of Calcutta, it had the great advantage that no ticket inspector could possibly enter. Conversely no passenger could leave to perform natural functions and hope to regain his or her place. The result can be left to the imagination.

Our servants were two brawny, broad-shouldered, deep-chested Sikhs and a tall, tough Punjabi Muslim; all armed with stout sticks. At every stopping place in the Punjab they manned the doors and fought off the invading crowd which, even if they could read, completely ignored the reserved notices stuck all over our compartment in the three commonest Indian scripts in that region.

177

It was a very real battle and there were several bloody exchanges. There is a special corps of Railway Police on all the major railways in India who were on most stations and escorting the trains. However, half a dozen police were powerless to control thousands of pilgrims who had been camping for days on every platform through which the trains to Hardwar ran and fighting for a chance to board each train as it arrived.

The boys at Aitchison College never lost an opportunity of pointing out how much tougher the Punjabis were than other Indians. It was almost automatic for anyone in the Punjab to add 'the sword arm of India' after a reference to the province in any public utterance. I had been a little sceptical of this insistence but its truth was illustrated in a small way on this journey. As I mentioned above, in the Punjab there was a fierce pitched battle to safeguard our compartment at every station. As we got into the United Provinces the battles became less fierce. By the time we reached Bihar and Bengal all that was necessary was for our servants to stand in the door and roar at the crowd for a very respectable space to be cleared for us. The other races of India evidently believed in the tradition of the martial races.

It had been arranged for us to travel on deck from Calcutta to Rangoon. As a result of all the confusion on the railways we arrived about six hours late in Calcutta, which made it Saturday afternoon instead of Saturday morning. The ship was due to sail early on Sunday morning but we were not allowed to embark before then because the quarantine officers would only be in attendance then. As all the shipping offices were closed I could get no information. However, I contacted an old schoolfriend, whom I had told I was coming. He helped me to find out exactly where the ship was berthed. I went down to the ship and took a boat out to fix up the arrangements. When I got near the ship an officer informed me that I had contravened the quarantine regulations, which surprised me. However, he showed me the space on the deck allocated for us and arranged to rope it off. We boarded the ship early next morning and found we were again beset by crowds — mostly pilgrims. This time they were Muslims, nearly all Indians, returning to Rangoon from the pilgrimage to Mecca.

The journey in the ship was even more uncomfortable than on

the train, as there was no clearly marked boundary to our domain and no privacy at all although our servants stood guard on us, turn by turn, day and night.

Our fellow passengers, especially the Hindus who made up in noise what they lacked in number, considered it a social and religious duty to cleanse and clear all the sacred orifices of the body first thing in the morning. This included a ritual bringing up of phlegm in incredible quantities from depths of the body inaccessible to those who had not put in years of Yogic endeavour. The dawn chorus still lingers in my memory.

We ate in the second-class saloon but unanimously decided that on the return journey we would travel in second-class cabins. We raised the balance in cash amongst us and made the necessary arrangements. This involved me in what I considered was an unreasonable reprimand from the Principal when I returned.

We passed through the vast estuary of the Irrawaddy and docked at Rangoon which is not on the main stream of the river. On the wharf was an immensely fat man dressed all in white, with tie and *topi* and carrying a furled umbrella. Apparently an Anglo-Burmese and coolie master, he did not hesitate to belabour the coolies with his umbrella if they did not carry out his orders quickly enough. In my years of residence in the East, before and since that event, it has been the only occasion on which I have seen physical force used on labour.

We saw a launch go out to a flying boat anchored in the river. One Burmese lost his footing in stepping from the launch to the plane and fell overboard. He was immediately sucked under the thick chocolate water and never seen again. The current was obviously moving at a tremendous rate but it struck me as being the epitome of fatalism that no one even attempted to search for him.

It was an example of the tremendous death-dealing, as well as life-giving, power of this great artery of Burma, which is 1,300 miles long. The monsoon in Burma lasts from May to October and during this season the Irrawaddy carries more water than any other river in the world with a comparable catchment area. It also has a terrific silt load – not only was the water of the river discoloured but the discolouration was visible a hundred miles out to sea. Consequently, once anyone is caught in an undertow and carried

179

below the surface of the water the chance of rescue is remote, as the victim cannot be seen.

Rangoon is the natural focus of communications in Burma, being the junction of the river, metre-gauge railway and roads leading to all parts of the country. Before it became such a centre it was famous as the site of the Shwe Dagon or Golden Pagoda. This pagoda, the height of St Paul's Cathedral, is the largest and most famous pagoda in the world. From a hill north of the town it dominates Rangoon physically and spiritually. According to tradition pagodas were originally modelled on the most beautiful thing known to man – a woman's breast – but the shape gradually became elongated and almost spire-like.

The first sight to catch our eye on coming up the Rangoon river was the Shwe Dagon – majestic in its simplicity – serene above the morning mist and the last sight as we left was its golden spire reflecting the rays of the setting sun with added splendour. Many delightful views could be obtained of the Shwe Dagon from different quarters of the city but probably the most enchanting aspect was to see it across the Royal Lakes against the bright blue of the sky and with the beautiful trees forming a worthy framework.

There are four gates to the great pagoda but the most impressive is where the long flight of broad steps is flanked by teak pillars covered with gold leaf. All the approaches are lined with stalls, selling vegetables, curios, articles of craftsmanship and other produce but chiefly a wide range of lovely flowers which are placed on the shrines by the worshippers.

These gave rise to a smell peculiar to all pagodas in Burma, an odour of sanctity compounded by the perfume of fresh flowers and slightly tinged by the smell of other flowers past their prime. The perfume was ideally suited to lead the mind to thoughts of the change and decay of physical objects and of the immutability of the eternal truths. The atmosphere of peaceful meditation and heavenly aspiration was almost palpable at the Shwe Dagon, which was a veritable citadel of the spirit.

Clustering round the main spire were countless satellite spires and golden Buddhas, some of the former were heavily carved and ornamented, others smooth but adorned with gold leaf. Each had its group of pious attendants who scrupulously cleaned it every morning.

I found it very difficult to get around to see all these features as they were mostly set in marble or tiled courtyards; we were expected to go barefooted and the temperature of the surface was terrific.

I was somehow disappointed in the general effect of the ensemble at close range as one was too close to the base of the main spire to see it properly and it lost its effect. It seemed to me like what I could understand of the Buddhist religion – diffuse, lacking a central focus and unity. It certainly did not give the impression of a beautifully designed and integrated whole like, for example, the Taj Mahal, but rather of excessive and repetitive ornamentation added as pious afterthoughts with no thought for artistic unity.

An interesting ceremony takes place at the Shwe Dagon on the evening before the Buddhist New Year. Women in procession wearing bright silk clothes and with flowers in their hair, carry pots of water on their heads to invoke the blessing of rain and plenty in the coming year; men bring up the rear, some playing musical instruments, others dancing, following either a set ritual or improvising with genius and energy.

In spite of its numerous pagodas I found Rangoon a well-planned modern city, with fine public buildings and wide clean streets well served with motor buses and trolley buses. The better class residential area contained a large number of fine houses and really beautiful gardens with a far wider range of flowers than was possible in the north of India. The University consisted of a series of well-planned buildings set in its own garden estate. The next time I saw Rangoon, after having been recovered from a Japanese PoW camp, the damage and disorder were widespread and the streets were littered with useless Japanese occupation currency.

Rangoon was very cosmopolitan. The carefree nature of the Burmese did not lead them to take kindly to storekeeping. We found that most of the shops were owned by Indians. Indeed, much of the most valuable rice land had passed into the hands of Indian *banias*, or storekeeper/moneylenders, owing to the improvident nature of the Burmese. Apart from Indian storekeepers, we found that every little town had its Punjabi policemen, Madrassi

181

rickshaw coolies, Chinese shoemakers and Japanese dentists, watchmakers and photographers. I wondered at the time how some of the places we saw on the Irrawaddy, really only villages, could support a Japanese dentist and photographer. During the war it became obvious that many of these had been spies and map-makers.

On the whole, as I found later in Thailand, the men disdain business. The women show a much keener business sense than the men and most of the Burmese shopkeepers, traders and brokers were women. They also seemed to do most of the work in the fields.

There are many different races in Burma. In addition to the Burmans proper there are Shans, Karens, Chins, Kachins and numerous other minority races. Most were Buddhists but some of the Karens had turned Christian. On the whole they all had the round Mongoloid type of face and their complexion varied from dark to very light brown. The traditional dress of the men was the *lungyi*, which is like a sarong, and the *aingyi* or jacket. On their heads they usually wore the *gaungbaung* or silk kerchief. This was not tied like a turban but merely drawn unfolded over the head and tied in a knot on the back or side. The men were stocky and muscular, good-natured and laughing on the whole but said to give way to sudden impulses of temper, which made them treacherous. The women were pretty, dainty creatures dressed in a differently tied *lungyi* and the *tamein*, or double-breasted jacket of coloured silk. They wore their hair in elaborate coils usually with brilliant flowers on them and never wore any headdress.

There is no purdah system in Burma – the women have a great deal more freedom than most women in Asia. Their courtship and marriage customs are more akin to those of European democracies than Asiatic societies. With their tubular figures, doll-like size, and faces thickly covered with heavy white powder giving them a ghostly complexion they seemed asexual and unlifelike to me.

We arrived in Rangoon just before the Water Festival, when, to mark their appreciation of the lifegiving rain and to propitiate the deities who control its fall, there are celebrations every year. These last for three days and take place in mid-April just before the hoped-for monsoon. This festival is celebrated with even more abandon than the carnivals of Mediterranean lands. We saw work dislocated, buses, trams and other public services stopped, and the entire Burmese population of Rangoon lived in bathing costumes or other suitable attire. They passed the three days in an orgy of throwing, splashing and playing with water. Luckily all non-Burmese are spared, except for an occasional playful sprinkling. The locals armed themselves with specially-made syringes, hoses (fire and otherwise), buckets and every form of container, commanded every point of vantage and drenched each other to the skin. Lorries, grossly overloaded with people clinging to every possible place and clanging gongs and hurling water, rushed ceaselessly up and down the streets at breakneck speed. Here and there a religious effigy was escorted with decorum at a more sedate pace. The whole festival showed the Burman's love of fun but it also showed the eagerness with which he seizes an excuse for a prolonged holiday – a characteristic, as mentioned above, which has led to the influx of more industrious races – chiefly Indians of all types.

A bountiful nature and charitable organisations inspired by Buddhist teachings prevent extreme want, and life is, in general, a merry, carefree existence to the average Burman. There is no caste system and everyone mixes in full and equal social intercourse. The people are truly democratic, sturdily maintaining their rights. They have always been difficult to govern and that is why, perhaps, they have the terrible type of government they now have.

Many Burmese become more serious in later life and don the yellow robes of the *poongyi* or monk to spend the rest of their days in meditation and meritorious acts. This is a mode of life which all men, including Buddhist royalty, are supposed to follow at one period of their lives.

Just as, when passing through towns and villages we found that the passers-by nearly always included a *poongyi*, so as we journeyed through Burma we found we were rarely out of sight of a pagoda of some kind. They were found on most prominent hills or points of vantage. We had heard about a celebrated pagoda at Pegu – a town not far from Rangoon – with the largest reclining Buddha in the world, 180 feet in length and 46 feet in height at the shoulder. We made a trip out to see it but to my mind its size was its only outstanding feature.

We saw the sights of Rangoon, including the oil refinery at Syriam on the south side of the Pegu river. My two recollections of this are going into a large freezing chamber, which was part of the process for making paraffin wax, and watching the Burmese women packing different coloured candles at amazing speed, grabbing the right number of each colour from different heaps without looking at the heaps and packing them into boxes with equal speed. Doubtless the process is now done more quickly and cheaply but less gracefully by machinery.

No visit to Burma would have been complete without seeing Mandalay, and the most interesting way of reaching it was by one of the Irrawaddy Flotilla Company's shallow-draft paddle steamers. I thought that we would also see a great deal of the country from the steamer. I had overlooked the tremendous seasonal variation of the river and as the monsoon had not started the level was very low and for a large part of the journey our view was mostly obscured by the banks of the river. This was very disappointing but nonetheless the journey was interesting.

We started off in the steamer *Indaw* of about 1,000 tons, which very soon picked up on either side of it two huge roofed barges of its own size. The three vessels together carried an enormous varied cargo of rice, silk, cotton, maize, groundnuts, oilcake, tobacco, timber, lacquer work, woodwork, cattle and a baby elephant.

As the Burmese are Buddhists they are not supposed to take life but like people of other religions they get round prohibitions by sophistry. A fish when taken out of the water dies but no one may be said to have taken its life. Fish therefore is the chief source of protein for many Burmese and they are skilled and ardent fishermen. The fish is largely eaten in the form of *ngapi*. It is placed in a trench with salt and reduced to a partially decomposed jelly by men working it with wooden mixers attached to their feet. Needless to say its smell is pungent and pervasive. The Malays make a similar product called *blachang*. It does not seem quite as noisome as *ngapi* — when I was a PoW we used small quantities of *blachang* to flavour our rice. Mingled with the nauseating smell of fresh Burmese lacquer work, cochineal beetles, and the monstrous rank green cheroots which Burmese of both sexes from the age of about five upwards constantly smoke, it gave a unique smell to our vessel. *Ngapi* was a major article of trade and we were constantly loading or unloading it. The places where it was made in any quantity could be smelt a mile or more away.

I noticed that there was a much greater appreciation of cleanliness in Burma than in India. Nearly all the cheroot smokers, when travelling, carried an enamel pot in which they deposited the ash.

It was soon obvious that the navigation of the Irrawaddy was very difficult. Although the water was low, the current was still very powerful, the river was constantly changing its channel and was very shallow in places. We found the channel marked nearly all the way by bamboo buoys. I was told that at this time of the year the channel and silt beds sometimes changed from day to day and at many places we took on pilots with up-to-the-minute local knowledge.

Coming alongside with such unwieldy craft in such a strong current was a tricky business. The usual technique was to go a little distance upstream of the landing stage, creep in fairly close to the bank, cut the engines and let the current swing us round onto the required position. We did some stages by night and it was very interesting to see landmarks being picked up and silhouetted in the beams of the powerful searchlights. The Burmese boatmen believe that by crossing the bows of another vessel as close as possible they cut off its luck for themselves. They did this constantly and recklessly, ignoring all warnings from our siren, and they had some narrow shaves. The ship and its attendant barges had almost flat roofs and straight sides all made of corrugated iron and were certainly not things of beauty. However, they were fairly comfortable and cool inside.

Meals were of a strange order. Very early in the morning we had a *chota hazri* of a little fruit and a cup of tea. The next sustenance came between 9 and 10 a.m. and consisted of an enormous meal comprising everything normally served at breakfast such as cereals, porridge, fruit, toast and marmalade and egg and bacon, buttressed if one wanted it with curry, grilled chops and similar dishes. The next food was about 6 p.m. and consisted of a normal evening meal; a light snack was available if required, before turning in for the night. It was, I suppose, a fairly sensible way of eating in a hot climate.

The first place of any importance that we came to after Rangoon was Yandoon, which seemed to be a great centre for making *ngapi*. After that we came to Donabyu which we were told was famous for its cheroots. The next interest was Gandama Hill. This was really a rocky cliff rising from the side of the river with numerous carvings of Buddha cut out of the living rock inside alcoves also cut from the rock.

We reached Prome after three days. This was said to have the largest seated Buddha in the world. By this time we were rather sated with Buddhas standing, seated or reclining and in any case we had no time to see it.

Between Prome and Pagan the river passed through the oil-fields. At times sampans, paddy-gigs, huge teak rafts, pagoda-crowned hills and tree-lined cliffs lent some interest to the voyage. Quite often, unfortunately, the river passed through dull, bare banks and the perpetual, unintelligible droning chant of the leads-man merely emphasised the monotony.

Pagan was the capital of Burma in the second century A.D. and for almost a millennium it was a great centre of Buddhist religion and culture. Its importance has long since declined although it still retains a respected place in Burmese tradition and many pagodas in varying degrees of preservation are found there. The craftsmen in that area were renowned for their beautiful lacquer work. I bought a little lacquer occasional table there for a few rupees. It was beautifully made and decorated and the legs were fixed on by lacquered wooden screws so that it could be packed flat. I still have it.

Although Mandalay is only 400 miles from Rangoon by the metre gauge railway, which follows the valley of the Sitang, it is about 700 miles by the Irrawaddy, which makes a great loop. We got to Mandalay on the sixth day from Rangoon. Here we changed on to a smaller vessel and went straight on to Bhamo. Past Mandalay the Irrawaddy flowed through majestic gorges with grim cliffs towering 600 feet above the river. We had some magnificent views in places.

Bhamo is right on the Chinese border and has been in Chinese occupation on several occasions in the past. It seemed to me to show many signs of Chinese influence such as in its architecture and the dress of the people. It had a delightful Chinese style temple. The only regular and reliable method of travel between Bhamo and Mandalay was by river and so we returned the same way.

Mandalay, the second city of Burma, is in the dry belt. We had arranged to return to Rangoon by train, engaging a whole coach. The railway had kindly agreed to make the coach available to us, free of charge, for a night or two on a siding so that it could be a cheap headquarters for us until we moved on. We found the heat and dust of Mandalay very oppressive, especially as the roads were tar-sealed only in the centre of the town and the coach an uncomfortable sleeping place. I became very hot and irritable and, unfortunately, lost my temper with one of the boys who teased me a bit. I regretted this as he was a reliable, basically very pleasant Punjabi Muslim. Our difference did not last very long. I was very pleased after the war to meet him and some of the other boys who were all majors with very good war service in the (British) Indian Army. I was still a captain, my rank when captured in Singapore.

Mandalay was the capital of Thibaw, the last king of Burma, and it seemed to me that it had never recovered from his departure. Thibaw was a son of King Mindon. He was born in 1878 and came to the throne as a result of a palace intrigue, which involved the murder of 80 members of the royal family, possible rivals or enemies. This was only rather more than usual in Burma. Those who gained the throne normally had all possible rivals publicly murdered, usually by strangulation, to reduce the risk of future attempts to seize the throne. I do not see how this was reconciled with the principles of Buddhism.

Thibaw married Supayalat, the daughter of a court noble, who kept him enthralled by her beauty and her insistence that he was the centre of the universe and that France and Britain, at that time rivals for power in Burma, were petty provincial principalities. He lived in a make-believe world for a few years surrounded by sycophantic courtiers and flower-bedecked maids of honour until his

187

intrigues with France and his extortions from the British timber companies led to war with Britain in 1885.

In spite of the reluctance of the British to intervene and gloomy prophecies by some of the difficulties of campaigning in Upper Burma – subsequently proved to be true in the Second World War – this war of 1885 did not last long although there were difficulties and setbacks at first. On the 1st January, 1886, Burma was annexed by the British and administered as the largest province of the Indian Empire, to which territory Thibaw and his queen were exiled. It was not until 1937 that a Burma Office separate from the India Office was set up in England to deal with Burmese affairs. A few years after this Burma was plunged into war. The various retreating armies left large quantities of arms behind them. There had always been a tradition of banditry in Burma and the country was very disturbed for some years after the war.

I thought that Thibaw's Palace was the only place of interest in Mandalay. It was something of the same nature as the Forbidden City in Peking – really a city within a city. The walls formed a square, each being about a mile long. The core of the wall was an earthen dyke, formed from the spoil from excavating a moat, and faced with bricks of a mellow red tone. Each wall was pierced in the middle by a great gateway surmounted by elaborate porches with graceful wooden carvings. The gateways were approached by picturesque bridges across the moat.

The royal palace stood in the centre of the great enclosure. The great halls of audience were bare and deserted. The Lion, the Deer, the Lily and the Bee Thrones looked tawdry. King Thibaw's great watchtower was unsafe. An air of melancholy pervaded the pavilions in which Thibaw and Supayalat once played out their game of being all-powerful potentates. In one of the throne rooms the magnificent pillars of teak were still standing and the remains of their gold leaf decorations and delicate carvings made it possible to imagine their former glory.

Mandalay Hill was well worth climbing in spite of the heat and the fact that there are over a thousand steps to the top. The steps are such that each is an easy height above the other and they are completely covered by a roof supported on posts through which can be seen delightful views of the city. From the top on one side, the whole of Mandalay presented a delightful spectacle.

On the other side of the hill, the lovely line of the more distant hills appeared in the misty distance whilst at the foot of the hills on which we stood was the Temple of the Thousand Buddhas — actually a group of 729 white pagodas, each containing a figure of Buddha and a marble tablet inscribed with the Buddhist Law.

We found the summit of the hill an ideal place for yet another pagoda and a monastery. The priests seemed to wear an air of even greater detachment than usual but a gift of alms, not verbally solicited but importuned by the very atmosphere of the place, evoked the usual response — a clanging on the great bronze gongs which echoed round the hill top and a droned prayer which ended as abruptly and informally as it began.

We went down to Inle Lake in the southern Shan state of Yawnghwe. The people lived in houses raised from the water on bamboo piles and the animals lived on similar platforms. The only agriculture was on floating islands as on the Dal Lake in Kashmir. The chief point of interest about this lake is the leg-rowers. The boatmen balance themselves in what would be to other people an extremely precarious position on the extreme edge of the boat facing the direction in which they want to go. Sometimes they have a bar on which they support themselves with one hand. They twist one leg around the oar, which is supported by the outside of the thigh, the back of the calf muscles and the big toe which is curled up also to grip or support the oar. Sometimes they put one or two hands on the oar to strengthen the grip. It is very logical as there is little doubt that the thigh muscle is one of the strongest in the body and that the legs are stronger than the arms. The boat is swiftly propelled through the water by quick but unhurried, powerful strokes. At the end of each stroke the body lunges forward and the oar is returned for another stroke by an outward and forward swing of the leg. I did not learn whether they could use each leg. It was a strange sight to see a long boat being shot through the water by leg-rowers, moving backwards and forwards with a strange rhythm but perfect timing. Presumably it would be even more disastrous than usual to catch a crab.

189

We saw, but did not visit, several *kyaungs* on the lake. These were Buddhist monasteries and wildlife sanctuaries where all the wild fowl were very tame as they soon learn that Buddhist law forbids killing.

We found the village bazaars a very interesting sidelight on life and conditions away from the towns. The crowds were usually very mixed. In addition to the Burmese proper and immigrants from overseas, we saw Shans, Chins and Karens in places. Some had their hair tied up like Sikhs but with no turban; some wore large hats made of thin strips of wood or palm leaves woven together. The goods were as varied as the people but *ngapi* and dried fish of many kinds and venerable antiquity always seemed to have pride of place. Burmese vermicelli was also very common and a great range of fruit, flowers and vegetables, some kinds never seen before.

We visited the pleasant hill station of Maymyo with its green hills and fields, formerly a notable polo centre.

At Pekkon we saw the celebrated giraffe-necked Padang women. Their necks are stretched to a great length by the periodic addition of brass rings. They seemed to have a constantly pained expression, which was not surprising, and as they had metal bands around their legs as well life must have been a real burden to them.

We returned straight down the railway to Rangoon and had a more comfortable return journey on the ship and train than our outward journey.

The chief impressions left on me by this visit to Burma were the smell of *ngapi* and cheroots; the frequency with which pagodas dominated hills and points of vantage; the brightness of the silk *lunggyis* and *tameins* worn by nearly all men and every woman and the pride which the women took in their hair. This was usually coiled in a knot on top of the head and decorated with flowers or more formally incorporated with a cylinder of cut hair. There was a third curious and to my mind ugly style. A ring is shaved bare round the middle of the head, above and below this the hair is short and combed downwards except for a tuft on the crown which is allowed to grow long and combed upwards.

I recall vividly the carefree, unsophisticated nature of the

Burman, which contrasted with the struggle to live or the pre-occupation with making money in India, his kindliness and his readiness to laugh and joke.

8

Domestic, Princely and Sporting Life

I was the first European on the staff of the College who had not been allocated his own bungalow. In addition to the very impressive bungalow for the principal there were three similar somewhat smaller bungalows for the original complement of European masters. Gwynn lived with his wife in one of these. One was occupied by two of the sons of the Nawab of Bahawalpur, the premier Muslim prince of the Punjab (descended from Caliph Haroon-ur-Rashid of Baghdad) and his European guardian and family. The third was rented to a European 'box-wallah' and his family. This was the bungalow that precedent would have given to me.

With my suite in my boarding house consisting of sitting room, dining room, bedroom, bathroom and a small room for the thunderbox I was quite comfortable. However, three factors influenced me in my decision to ask for this bungalow.

The first was that I realised that I would have more privacy in a separate bungalow some distance from the boarding house. The second was that I would have extra accommodation for guests, temporary or permanent. With regard to the latter there were a number of well-paid commercial types in Lahore who did not get a house with their job and would be only too pleased to pay me for some rooms in the desirable setting of the college. The third factor was uniquely Indian in its importance – my *izzat*, which I have explained earlier. It was subtly suggested to me by Indian masters and the boys of my house that my *izzat* would be greater if I lived in a bungalow and that their *izzat* also would be greater if their housemaster lived in his own bungalow. (They also probably thought that they would have a bit more freedom if I was further off.) I therefore asked Barry if I could have the bungalow when it could be made available. After a half-hearted attempt to dissuade me he agreed.

As soon as the bungalow became vacant I moved in. I had become friendly with Mike Durell who worked for Western Electric and we agreed to share it.

I did not ask him for any direct rent. We pooled all the household expenses and in lieu of rent he paid a greater share than I did. This was a good arrangement for both of us. One minor advantage was that he had a southern Indian Christian bearer and so we could have bacon for breakfast if we wanted it. The brick bungalow stood in its own garden with an in and out drive from one of the roads in the college compound. There was a large *porte-cochère* in front giving onto a passage that ran right through the house dividing it into two symmetrical halves. This was three or four yards wide and long enough for us to play chair polo in it. There was a sitting room on one side at the front and a dining room on the other; then two bedrooms on each side, each with its own dressing room, bathroom and lavatory. The latter two were quite primitive as nearly everywhere in Lahore. There was no plumbing – just a large zinc bath and dipper. The bath was filled with hot water by the *bhisti* when the *ghusul* was ordered through our bearers. He heated the water in four-gallon petrol tins and brought them in on a primitive bamboo yoke. He gained access to the bathroom through the lavatory, which had an outside door. In the lavatory the mahogany thunderbox stood four-square. This, as I have said, was presided over by the *mehtar* with oriental occultism. Never to be seen, rarely to be heard, he brooded somewhere in the background but always removed the contents of the commode when it was necessary and disposed of them in an equally mysterious way.

Indian commodes had a aura of majesty about them as they were so large and impressive. It made the phrase 'on the throne' seem more realistic. I saw one once at a *dakh* bungalow in the Simla Hills which had a brass plate on which was inscribed 'This commode was used by Sir Arthur Wellesley (later Duke of Wellington) when Commander-in-Chief in India'. A caretaker had

had this done and it had been handed down as an heirloom from father to son.

The ceilings in the bungalow were very high to reduce the heat a little. The roof was flat and had 5–6 feet of earth over it as an insulating layer. All walls except the back were surrounded with a deep veranda pierced with wide Indo-Saracenic arches. On the outside of the arches a mat or *chik* made of bamboo about finger thickness was hung; over the outside of the windows there was a reed mat or *chatai* and on the inside of the windows there were thickish curtains. This was to keep out the heat. The floor inside the house was either some kind of hard, smooth plaster or brick. Any carpets or rugs were taken up in the hot weather. About three times a day the *bhisti* came with his *mashak*, or goatskin full of water, and splashed the floors of the veranda and occupied rooms liberally with water. He also sprinkled the *chatai*. The electric ceiling fans with wooden blades about a yard long were then turned on and, with the evaporation of the water, provided some sort of air-conditioning. The Indians had been well aware of the cooling effects of evaporation for centuries. When travelling they often had canvas water bottles called *chaghal* in the traditional goatskin shape, which poured from the neck. These were also standard equipment in the Indian Army. The water slowly percolated through the canvas and gave a refreshingly cool drink even on a blisteringly hot day. Another way of utilising this principle was a porous earthenware water-bottle or *sarhai*. In the old days there was an *abdar* whose job was to cool bottles by putting them in wet straw and whirling them around his head at the end of a cord. I never saw a refrigerator or any other domestic electric appliance in Lahore. They were still very rare and expensive. Everyone had ice-boxes – wooden coffers lined with zinc. A large block of ice was delivered daily and this kept drinks cool until the next day. Bottles full of beer, water, soft drinks and soda-water were placed on the block of ice and covered with a sack or heavy cloth. For hygienic reasons it was inadvisable to put the ice in a drink.

There has been a tendency in the post-Empire epoch to refer to the princely pay and conditions of the British in India. This impression is exaggerated. My pay was the equivalent of £1 a day.

I remember how elated I was to think that I was earning a whole pound in a day. Income tax was very low. This was adequate for one starting a career but far from princely. I could just get by without saving anything and for my first two years I could not afford a car. I then bought an old, unreliable second-hand model.

My post was not pensionable. It did not worry me at the time. I was young and had little thought for the future. However, I went straight on to seven years' war service before I got a pensionable post. When I retired I realised what a disadvantage it was to lose 12 years off one's basis of pensionable service.

Our houses were large but of a standard of finish and decoration that would, even then, have been below that of the average manual worker in Britain. Spring mattresses, let alone inner spring, were unknown. I slept on a plain wooden frame with no head or foot rest with a blanket and sheet over a webbing network. This was on a concrete floor. The furniture in the bedroom was a very plain wardrobe, a chest of drawers and one upright chair. The legs of most articles of furniture were placed in tins of water to prevent white ants climbing up and attacking the furniture. At the foot of the bed was a tin trunk to take anything that would not go in the wardrobe or chest of drawers. A bamboo framework was tied to the legs of the bed to take a *machchar-dan* or mosquito net. In the sitting room was a settee, two or three armchairs, a desk and two upright chairs, one for myself and the other for my language teacher or *mulaqati*. This was the term given to someone who came for a *mulaqat* or interview. The latter was a favourite Indian occupation, usually to request some privilege for the person himself or his protégé; sometimes to complain against or subtly sow seeds of doubt against a rival; sometimes just to give or try to obtain information; sometimes merely a sincere courtesy call carried out with exquisite grace and aplomb. The room was bare of pictures, ornaments, trinkets or embellishments of any kind – as was the bedroom. This was the pattern repeated almost universally for bachelor officers. When Europeans were married the *memsahib* would introduce a few more homely touches and a little more comfort.

Any princely touches were provided by Maula Baksh. When I came back to the house after having been out for any time he would appear at the door with a pair of slippers and try to unlace my shoes and take my socks off before I could. He would manage to convey an impression of slighted but dignified disapproval if I did this myself. Then he proceeded to squeeze and massage my feet in a skillful way, which relieved the discomfort and swelling caused by walking for any length of time in very hot shoes. I was rather taken aback when he first did this but soon grew to appreciate his attention. It had rather biblical overtones. He never washed my feet but I once had a petition from a junior Indian clerk at the college (who thought quite wrongly that I was in a position to get him some privilege) which ended 'In the name of J. Christ, Esquire, a gentleman whom Your Lordship so greatly resembles'. This was rather more grandiloquent than the standard peroration which was 'Ever praying for Your Honour's long life, prosperity and numerous progeny'.

When I was going out to dinner, Maula Baksh would brush my evening clothes and lay them out on the bed before I had my bath. He hovered in the background whilst I was dressing and insisted on holding the legs of my trousers when I put them on so as to retain the immaculate creases he had pressed into them. When I had finished dressing he would give me an unneeded brush and eye me all over to see if I came up to his standard. When I was not going out to dinner he thought that I was capable of dressing myself. Sometimes I would not tell him when I was going out just to test his intelligence network. He nearly always knew.

Once, after a very hot and trying day, Maula Baksh did something that annoyed me. I lost my temper and sacked him. I instantly regretted my words but did not recall them – I would have lost *izzat*. He also said nothing but turned up with my *chota hazri* in the morning and carried on as if nothing had happened, to our mutual satisfaction.

The *chaukidars* or nightwatchmen were a great Indian institution. They did not do anything but, if you did not employ one, their confederacy arranged for you to be robbed. In the Punjab they were usually aging Sikhs who had often had military service. All *chaukidars* had string beds or *charpai* on which they sat or lay all night drowsing or sleeping with an occasional pull at a hookah if they were not Sikhs. Sikhs did not smoke as it was strictly forbidden by their religion and I have never seen one contravene this rule. They compensated by being prodigious drinkers.

At the college the three boarding houses which were along a straight road and about 100 yards apart had a *chaukidar* each. As night fell the *chaukidar* would take up his position on his *charpai* in front of each house. At night as one came into view of the one awake he would break into a paroxysm of loud coughing until the one next to him was awake. This one would then follow suit and so every *chaukidar* was awake as he was passed. When I went to live in the bungalow I inherited the only Gurkha *chaukidar* in the college whom I retained. I went to a fancy dress ball one night in the costume of a Pathan tribesman. As I was fumbling with the door handle on my return I felt the blade of the *chaukidar*'s *kukri* against my throat as he challenged me. I thought he was probably pulling my leg but decided it was best to identify myself.

I went to Patiala in charge of the school cricket team, for which I played, for the annual fixture against the Patiala Old Boys. We again stayed in the delightful Baradari Palace, formerly the residence of the Maharaja, and played on the ground attached to the palace where many matches had made Indian cricket history. I was amused before the match to see the heavy roller being pulled over the wicket by a ponderously dignified elephant with thick leather boots over his feet which he put down at each step with meticulous care so as not to cause any damage to the sacred turf. I noticed that one of the many strange communal monopolies of types of work in India held true. All the *mahouts* in Patiala were Muslims as they were throughout the north of India – even in Sikh and Hindu states.

As the Old Boys had two Indian test players in their team it was not surprising that they were victorious. One was my old friend Joginder Singh who had toured England with the 1932 team captained by the Maharaja of Porbandar. The other was Yadavendra Singh, the Yuvraj, or heir apparent, of Patiala. The latter was a fine cricketer whose natural talent had been moulded into a complete batsman by coaching from test players from England and elsewhere. He had played many a fine innings in big matches. He was the most spectacularly handsome and striking man I have ever seen. Quite well built, his height of well over six feet made him seem slim. He had regular features and large luminous eyes fringed with lashes like tiger's whiskers; an imposing finish was given by his beard and moustache.

After the match, boys, Old Boys, nobles and notabilities of the state dined in the magnificent state dining room of the old palace. The Maharaja did not join us; he rarely ate in public. The table was brilliant with silver. A gravely attentive waiter stood behind each guest. It was a tradition in Patiala that Plat Patiala was available at every meal. This was whole chickens (uncommon in Indian cuisine where they are usually jointed before cooking) roasted in a special tandoori oven and glazed and curried to a special recipe. They were superb. In addition to this there was a wide choice of European and other Indian dishes for each course. Among the sweets, *khir* was served. This was a sweet made of ground rice, milk and sugar. In Patiala, it was always served with thinly beaten out silver leaf on top of individual portions.

It was customary for one or two masters to play in the teams with the boys. I took my turn in the cricket team but was barely worth my place. I also played on occasions for the Gymkhana Club which represented the Europeans in Lahore. Here, again, I did not get into the team if all the best players were available. When I did I batted seven or eight and did some change bowling. I was very surprised on one occasion when I was chosen to open the batting. So was the senior member of the Indian ground staff who had often bamboozled me in the nets. When I went in to take first strike I found out that the bowler was Emir Elahi who was an Indian test bowler with every imaginable variety of spin of bewildering oriental subtlety.

The derision of the ground staff had produced a reaction of determination in me. I did not attempt any forcing strokes but defended as stubbornly as I could and painfully amassed 27 runs. Admittedly it was slow going but I had a certain satisfaction until the captain sent out a message with the drinks, 'Get on or get out'. Of course I did the latter.

We had one or two very good Indian bats in the Gymkhana Club team. One of the Europeans was very fat and his footwork was non-existent. He used to stand at the crease and hit a large number of sixes. Such was his reputation that, when he was in, the unfenced road round the cricket field became choked with Indians waiting to see him perform.

One example of determined defence remains in my mind from the Gymkhana cricket ground. The North of India were playing an England XI. Gover, the England fast bowler, was slinging down some fierce balls at the Indian number seven or eight who was a dour Sikh and mainly a slow bowler. He was a left-handed bat and was stopping each ball with an absolutely straight dead bat. As one ball left Gover's hand there was a violent earth tremor. The batsman swayed to and fro but never took his eye off the ball. He managed to keep his bat if not his body absolutely vertical and once more stopped the ball dead.

I gave up playing cricket for the Club team as it became too expensive. We played Indian teams from Lahore but all the European teams were visiting teams from other towns. It was customary for each member of the home team to put up a visiting player for the weekend. Many were accompanied by their wives and, even in India, it became somewhat of a financial burden.

Ironically, it cost less to play the type of polo that we played. We nearly all used our Punjab Light Horse mounts. Thus everyone could keep one pony on the official allowance. There were always some who were not interested in polo but made their ponies available. We played only four *chakkars* a game in our grade of polo, instead of the proper seven. Thus two ponies each were sufficient – more than two *chakkars* in one game is too much of a strain for any pony. There was not the expense of entertaining the visiting teams for the weekend as they all came from Lahore.

I started up a college magazine, which I edited, for general interest and to encourage the boys to write articles in English. After a slowish start I received a steady flow of reasonable articles from the boys. Eventually I found that one of the Indian clerks in the college office could take shorthand and I dictated anything I wanted to put in the magazine myself for him to type for the printers. Before that I had a strange experience. The proof of some written copy that I had sent came back with some completely irrelevant word in it. After going into the reason for the strange word I found that the Indian compositors had very little

199

knowledge of English and just set up the type letter by letter as it were. By taking the loops in my bad writing in the wrong combinations they had made this word.

After three years I went home on leave to England. Trains, fields and vistas all seemed on a miniature scale compared with India. I little thought that a war and eight years would intervene before I saw England again.

I shared a cabin with a namesake who was a Deputy Commissioner in the old Central Provinces, now Madhya Pradesh. He was a learned, witty and delightful companion and he became one of my best friends. Later he invited me to spend holidays with him, one at Buldana and the other at Chhindwara when he was stationed at these places.

I found conditions there very different from the Punjab. The majority there were Hindus; the language was Hindi but sufficiently similar to Urdu for me to get along.

For the clarification of those who are not familiar with the position, I think that the following is the best explanation. Hindi and Urdu have exactly the same grammar. Urdu developed as a *lingua franca* among the Muslim Moghul invaders of India. Hindi developed from Sanskrit and is essentially a Hindu language. A great deal of the everyday vocabulary is common to both languages but, even in the same region, for some common terms influenced by religion, the days of the week for example, Muslims tend to use one set of words and Hindus another. For less commonplace terms Urdu has borrowed from Persian and, as Persian had previously borrowed them from Arabic, there are many Arabic words in Urdu. Hindi has made parallel borrowings from Sanskrit. Educated speakers of both languages tend to use many English words for expressions connected with modern life. Urdu has its own script, a slightly modified form of the Persian script which itself is a modified form of the Arabic script. (The British Indian Army used Urdu as a *lingua franca*. It was written in a transliteration into the Latin alphabet, reading from left to right, in which form it was known as Roman Urdu.) Urdu proper is written from right to left at an angle of 45° to the horizontal usually on unlined paper. As some of the letters are long, if it is written on lined paper the line tends to bisect the letters. Hindi is written in the Devanagari script, or, as it is more usually called, Nagari script. This is written from left to right, vertically under the line. Some people use Urdu, Hindi and Hindustani as synonyms. I think that the best usage is to keep the distinction between Hindi and Urdu and regard the term Hindustani as covering the two.

In Madhya Pradesh there were not the limitless vistas of the vast Indo-Gangetic plain as in the Punjab. There were some flat fertile areas. Indeed, the area known as Berar consists largely of immensely fertile black volcanic soil which grows rich crops of cotton. (The soil is so soft and friable that it is very difficult to make roads on it.) There was also a lot of rugged, thickly-wooded jungle split up by rivers running in deep rocky gorges and strewn with boulders the size of houses. (In the Punjab the term *jangal* (jungle) was applied to any uncultivated land.)

The irrigation is quite different from the immense network of canals in the north of India. The rivers and streams are not fed by the snow and ice melt in the Himalayas but by the monsoon rains. When they are in spate they are led into 'tanks' or reservoirs of varying size which impound the water until it is released in the dry weather. Each 'tank' feeds its own separate area whose size varies greatly depending on the volume of water available and the area which can be fed by gravity.

The jungles of Central India were inhabited by the aboriginal Gonds and by game of every kind including a large number of tigers in places. Some of the Gonds had left the jungle and were working in coal mines in the province. Like most coal miners they had a strong union. It struck me as most incongruous that they should go straight from a very primitive existence deep in thick jungle to a routine, arduous industrial occupation. Those who remained in the jungle had the most marvellous tracking abilities. They made wonderful *shikaris* or huntsmen. One of their skills was to be able to imitate the call of a tiger or tigress as required to attract a beast of the opposite sex. Presumably they had to stop at the right time or be in great danger from a frustrated feline.

My host had shot 17 tigers, about half of which were man-eaters. If there was not a Forestry Officer or anyone else who was an expert shot, it was considered that the Deputy Commissioner should shoot a tiger that had killed a villager or too many cattle.

Reg Hill had decided that 17 tigers were enough except when duty called. (This was long before tigers became scarce. At the time I could not understand the desire to preserve tigers in view of the death and terror they could cause.)

One day a villager came in and complained that a tiger had killed and partly eaten one of his buffalo. The kill had not been dragged very far by the tiger before it had partly eaten it. The tiger had then gone off to sleep away the heat of the day, probably not far away. Reg decided to sit up over the remains of the kill and arranged for a string bed to be tied up very quietly in a tree commanding a view of the kill. He assumed that I would like to go with him with another rifle to see if I could get my first tiger. It did not really interest me very much. I was quite content to leave the great cats alone if they had the same attitude to me.

Tigers normally return to their kill between 4 and 6 p.m. and we arrived at the *machan* in good time. Nothing had arrived by sunset and Reg, who had brought two powerful torches, decided to sit through the night. I spent an acutely uncomfortable night on our unsteady *machan,* bitten to death by mosquitoes, suffering from cramp and not daring to move for fear of startling the great beast. Finally dawn came but no tiger as far as our knowledge went. They can move in an astonishingly noiseless way. Perhaps it had approached silently in the shadows and something had aroused its suspicions.

Some time earlier it had been announced that the Viceroy was coming on tour to the district. It always seemed to be assumed that His Excellency would like to shoot a tiger wherever he went. A suitable tiger was located in the district and kept under observation by a *shikari*. Alas, somehow the tiger broke one of its forelegs and no other tiger had been spotted within a reasonable distance. After a council of war the intrepid Indian Veterinary Officer approached the tiger in its lay-up and anaesthetised it with chloroform on cloth at the end of a very long bamboo pole. He then set the tiger's leg. Until it recovered enough to hunt again the tiger was fed with dead goats and calves left within easy distance. In the fullness of time it went out into the jungle and was duly shot by the Viceroy. That seemed to be the end of an incident, which would be highly improbable anywhere outside of India. The final essentially

Indian touch came when the audit *babu* queried the expenditure on the meat, which the tiger had eaten. Reg had to think up some acceptable explanation.

We had some very exciting runs after the wild boars in the jungle with the special type of lance for that purpose. A great deal depends on the horse in country like that. My host lent me one of his two horses, which were well used to the country. We managed to stick one hog each.

The houses in Madhya Pradesh did not have flat roofs covered with earth as in the Punjab but were steeply pitched and covered with tiles. This was because of the greater rainfall which was also rather more spread out through the year. The Deputy Commissioner's bungalows were more or less hexagonal in shape and quite attractive in appearance. They had self-contained guest accommodation at a little distance from the house but I slept in the main house which had pleasant, spacious airy rooms with through ventilation from opposing windows.

One morning I was sitting quietly reading in the sitting room when Reg was in court. It gradually dawned on me that there was a commotion in the dining room. I went there and saw the Muslim cook with a huge butcher's knife in his hand, chasing the Hindu house boy round the table. I managed to stop them and a summary enquiry revealed that the cook was accusing the house boy of getting at his daughter. I called Reg back as soon as possible. The cook produced his daughter, unveiled, in front of us, a most unusual procedure. She was a very beautiful and voluptuous young woman and looked at us in a way that did not suggest she was given to repelling advances. Reg sent her immediately for a medical examination. She was declared *virgo intacta*. Reg's wife was away at Pachmarhi, the hill station for Madhya Pradesh, and we were alone in the house. We had suspicions that the whole event might have been rigged or utilised to try to compromise one or both of us. Later events supported this theory as there was an ineffectual effort on the part of some Indian politicians, with the aid of the cook, to smear Reg's name in connection with this affair.

The nearest railway station to Buldana was Malkapur, 26 miles away. I had to catch a night train on the way back to Lahore. When

I woke up in the morning I was rather embarrassed to find the other three occupants of the carriage were women. Such situations were always avoided when the long distance trains started but it was not possible at small intermediate stations.

The next year when I was about to go on holiday again to Madhya Pradesh I went to the section of the General Post Office at Lahore which arranged the forwarding of letters. It was run by two elderly *babus*. I went up to them and said, 'I'm going on holiday again to Central India'. One of them immediately said 'To R.J.J. Hill Sahib, Deputy Commissioner, Buldana.' I was quite surprised; Lahore had a population approaching half a million. He had either just been looking through the records or had one of those remarkable Indian memories. The intra- and inter-departmental messengers' intelligence network would probably have been adequate to inform him of the posting of any Deputy Commissioner within the Punjab but he did not know that Reg had been posted to Chhindwara.

At Chhindwara we were reduced to playing one-a-side polo and going 79 miles to see *Gone With The Wind* at Nagpur. I ate and drank so much for dinner that I slept through the film.

9

Motor Trip to South India

The principal of the Maharaja's College in Cochin, an important princely state in the south of India, was seconded to Aitchison College for a period and whilst he was with us he decided to buy an ancient Fiat. When his time with us was finished he invited me to stay with him and asked me if I would like to drive his car down to Ernakulam in Cochin State.

I had previously learnt something of the roads in Central and South India through which I would have to pass and I would not willingly have driven my own car all the way down from the Punjab, but as he was quite keen for me to get his car down for him I agreed. As I was about to start I noticed a starting handle in the car. I tried to fit it but after several attempts was unsuccessful and therefore foolishly threw it away.

I had commenced the holidays in question in the Murree Hills in the north of the Punjab whence I started the journey, which turned out to be 2,934 miles by the route I followed. Everything went well on the straight flat concrete roads of the north of India. I passed through the great wheat-growing plains of the Punjab down the Grand Trunk Road, which had been the route of so many invaders through the centuries. The towns on the route were still important strategic centres, garrisoned by British and Indian regiments. Most had been the scenes of historic battles between invaders and defenders of India from earliest recorded history to the British conquest of India. The only limit on one's speed was the performance of the car, although there were traffic hazards in the form of massive carts drawn by pairs of bullocks or buffalo, horses, cattle, camels and other animals, either ridden or driven. There were no hills and apart from these checks the only reason to slacken speed was the periodic crossing at right angles of an irrigation canal, either major or minor, whose bridge the road often approached on a sweeping curve, making it necessary to drop down to 50 or 45 miles per hour.

Rawalpindi, Lahore, Amritsar, Jullundur, Ludhiana and Ambala were all told off in the first day like beads on the rosary of history. Every mile brought me closer to Delhi, the capital of India, the ninth city to rise on the same site. Moghul and pre-Moghul remains became more frequent.

The two cities of Old Delhi and New Delhi epitomise the bipolarity of India – the mixture and to a large extent the successful blending of old and new. Two of the most famous buildings in Old Delhi are the Jami Masjid and the Lal Qila. The first, the Great Mosque, is in the traditional Moghul style for a mosque and must vie with the Jami Masjid at Lahore as being one of the biggest mosques in the world. It is said that, on Id, 100,000 Muslims throng the great courtyard. It impresses largely by its size as it is somewhat austere and not particularly graceful in proportions.

The Lal Qila, or Red Fort, was in Moghul times the Indian equivalent of the Kremlin in that it was a great complex of palaces, places of worship and administrative buildings all within the setting of a large fort.

As I wandered through its lawns and courtyards, I was very impressed by the beauty of many of its buildings such as the Diwan-i-Am, or Hall of Public Audience, and the Diwan-i-Khas, or Hall of Private Audience. The first was a white marble pavilion with openings in its walls raised on pillars. The Moghul emperors sat there at stated times and, in theory and probably in practice, any subject, no matter how lowly, could come and put his *darkhwast* (petition) or *shikayat* (complaint) concerning any maladministration or injustice to his emperor. The Hall of Private Audience was where the emperor met his chief officers of state.

Some of the marble arabesques in the Lal Qila are the most graceful that I have seen. On one building is the inscription in graceful Persian characters which may be transliterated:

Agar firdaus ba ruh-i-zamin ast;
Hamen ast, hamen ast, hamen ast.

If there be Paradise on earth,
This is it, this is it, this is it.

At the height of the Moghul glory this was the nerve centre of an empire which embraced Turkistan, Persia, Afghanistan and almost all of India from Karachi to Calcutta and from Kashmir to Hyderabad in the Deccan. From the corners of this empire, caravans arrived daily with silks, rugs, gold, jewels, exquisite examples of craftsmanship and objets d'art (and even snow and ice from the Himalayas to cool the sherbet). The hyperbole of the poet can thus be understood and accepted.

New Delhi is a great architectural memorial to Lutyens and Baker. What was then the Viceroy's Palace dominated the other great buildings. The residential areas were laid out in graceful symmetry and the perfect circle of Connaught Circus formed a shopping and business centre which could stand comparison with any in the world.

In the countryside not far from Delhi stands the Qutab Minar, that amazing column raised by Qutab-ud-Din Aibak, 'The Polestar of the Faith', who was a Turkoman slave of Mohammed Ghori. The latter was one of the great raiders from Afghanistan who renewed the Muslim attacks on India in the twelfth century. His first attack was repulsed by the combined Hindu princes of the north of India under the Rajput, Prithvi Raj Rahtor, on the plains outside Delhi where the fate of India has so often been decided. Smarting under defeat, Ghori returned the following year to defeat an Indian army weakened, as so often happened, by the quarrels of the Rajput princes. His slave-viceroy raised the 238-foot column of seven fluted tiers to be his enduring monument. From the top one gets a superb view of the nearby ancient monuments and of miles of the surrounding countryside.

After I left Delhi I could feel subtly and imperceptibly the influence of Moghul civilisation laying a veneer of polish and culture over the toughness and possibly even crudeness of the Punjabi character. I approached Agra; Agra which rivalled Delhi as a Moghul centre in many ways such as Urdu learning and

Persian poetry, and Agra which treasured and gloried in the incomparable jewel of Moghul architecture – the Taj Mahal.

The countryside also appeared to become somewhat softer. The vast expanses of plains were broken up by more frequent trees through which flew or strutted multitudes of peacocks, all secure in the knowledge that they would not be molested as they were protected by the strongest of all sanctions in India – religion. As they spread their gorgeous tails in the sunshine I wondered whether their beauty had inspired old Moghul craftsmen. It had certainly inspired the decoration of the Sheikh Lutfullah Mosque in Isfahan, the inside of the dome of which reproduces in faïence and azulejo tiles the natural glory of a peacock's tail. As Moghul art owes so much to Persian tradition perhaps my fancy was not too far-fetched.

I saw the Taj Mahal by moonlight with its great but graceful dome sailing like a proud galleon on a sea of clouds. I saw the Taj Mahal by daylight and marvelled alike at the graceful but powerful symmetry of the whole and the delicacy of the patterns inlaid on its walls in semi-precious stones. The Pearl Mosque at Agra is also a building of exquisite beauty and would probably be more famous but for the proximity of the Taj Mahal.

At Agra I struck south from the Grand Trunk Road which continued, in name at least, to Calcutta. Actually there were gaps between Delhi and Agra in the concrete construction and at Agra there was no more concrete whichever direction one took. The road became pretty bad, unsealed and full of potholes.

After leaving Agra the Chambal river had to be crossed on a ferry. This is not one of India's major rivers but nevertheless it was a river of a very considerable width and the current was flowing strongly. The ferry was a sturdy locally-constructed craft with no engine or sail. The approaches to the ferry were not very good and the vessel was moving somewhat as I drove the car onto it. Once the car was on board half a dozen sturdy coolies hitched themselves to ropes and pulled the vessel a short distance upstream. They then released the ropes and the ferry was propelled across the river by the strength of the current and the efforts of one muscular fellow leaning on a huge steering oar. I thought that we would be swept quite a way down stream but somehow he steered the clumsy craft across the river into the quiet water of the opposite bank fairly near the landing stage and a little more pulling on ropes got us alongside. The deep, intricate system of gullies caused by erosion in the countryside around the Chambal had long been and still is the stronghold of ferocious bandits fighting pitched battles with armed police.

The next town of importance was Gwalior. I skirted along the massive flat-topped hill crowned by a huge, frowning fort. This was captured by the British, under Lake, through the help of an Indian sepoy who scaled the vertical cliff face carrying a rope ladder. He was helped in his climb by a large iguana whose claws could find holds in small crevices. This ruse is still used by criminals in India to help them scale the mud walls of buildings and courtyards.

India is a huge country and apparently a large proportion of the population both indigenous and European is constantly on the move. This leads to a most colourful collection of travelling companions of all kinds. Pilgrims, sadhus, faqirs, professional beggars, seasonally migrating tribes, individuals seeking work, farmers going to market, moneylenders from near and far, professional criminals, prostitutes and pimps, jugglers, musicians, conjurers, snakecharmers, confidence men, bandits, cut-throats, religious mendicants, soldiers going on leave, Government servants on tour, *shikaris* or professional hunters, horse-copers, travelling masters of a multitude of crafts, wedding parties and *dhobis*, or washermen, out on drunken sprees, could all be seen on a day's journey. It was such a constant and multifarious collection of travellers to and from all corners of the vast subcontinent that made it possible for thugs to infiltrate travelling parties without being suspected. At appropriate times and places they then robbed their chosen victims. It was months before their non-arrival and disappearance was noted. This made it almost impossible to apprehend their murderers, before the brilliant and dedicated work of Sleeman which, for about 20 years from 1830, eliminated the bloodthirsty and ruthless associations of robbers who were estimated to have killed about 40,000 Indians a year for centuries.

Any place of any size had facilities of some kind for travellers. Hotels in India were good and very reasonably priced. However,

209

after Gwalior and Jhansi I had left a route of any importance. Not only did the roads deteriorate still further but at most night stops there were no hotels but merely rest houses. Rest houses were buildings erected and maintained by the province or state in which they were found. They were on the whole gaunt, cheerless buildings with a minimum of essential furniture such as beds, tables, chairs, cupboards and lamps. Europeans always travelled with a bedding roll in India and usually a mosquito net and wash basin or *chilamchi*. The latter was an article of faith with every true pukka sahib who considered that to wash in anything except one's own *chilamchi* was to court some terrible disease. These bowls were usually made out of aluminium and were fitted with a leather cover and so served to carry one's toilet gear.

A cook was attached to every rest house and with a few blessed exceptions these cooks considered that the Vedas had laid down that the menu for dinner should be invariably tomato soup, some kind of fried fish, tough roast chicken and caramel custard.

Soon after leaving Jhansi the route came to the Betwa river. There was a pontoon bridge over this river in the dry season but during the monsoon it ran too swiftly to anchor the bridge and was crossed by a ferry. There were intermediate periods when the current was still too swift for the pontoon bridge to be safe but when the water was not deep enough to operate the ferry with ease. I arrived at one of these times. I drove unconcernedly down the concrete ramp to the ferry only to find the car sinking down in several feet of silt on the bottom of the ramp. Maula Baksh had accompanied me and the further we went from the predominantly Muslim areas of the north, the more carefully he starched the *shamla*, which is part of the turban left sticking out above the *kula* or skull cap in the northern Indian Muslim manner of tying a turban. It now stood up proud and erect some nine inches above his own formidable height. With his blazing eyes, hawk nose, drooping moustache and thin beard he was an impressive figure. By now we had got to an area where we began to run into linguistic difficulties, but it needed no words, only a few imperious gestures from Maula Baksh to gather together a group of local villagers who soon unloaded the car and then manhandled it out of the silt. I certainly wanted to cross the river there as if I could not it appeared that I would have to make a detour of some 300 miles.

I did not have a road map and never heard of anyone using one in India. The network of motorable roads was so exiguous that one could go thousands of miles with only a few places where there could be any possible alternative route. I soon learnt that in the case of any possible doubt a rigorous cross-examination of an informant was necessary. The first answer to any question seeking direction was that the desired destination was '*Ek kos bilkul age, sahib*', 'Two miles straight ahead, sahib.'

After a certain amount of discussion amongst the locals it was decided that it was possible to bring the ferry alongside a high bank of the river a few hundred yards from the proper ramp. A track was hacked through the jungle and somehow the car was got along it. The loading flaps were let down from the ferry onto the bank. By this time it was dark and I had the ticklish job of driving the car on to the ferry solely by means of its headlamps. There was very little room for a mistake either sideways or lengthways and I was very relieved when it was safely on board.

For some distance either side of Jhansi I passed over the Central Indian earth roads. These are exactly as described and are nothing but the natural, usually lateritic, earth levelled off to make a road – with some attempt at drains. In the dry weather when they have received attention they can be just like billiard tables but after rain the sticky soil usually becomes impassable and one has to wait for the road to dry out.

After a day or two the earth roads were left behind. The character of the country had by now completely changed from the broad fertile expanses of Northern India. The route passed over the Vindhya and Satpura ranges which divide the Indo-Gangetic plain of the north of India, largely peopled by races of an Aryan origin, from peninsular India, which consists firstly of Central India and gradually merges into Southern India, populated by Dravidian races which had been there for millennia before the Aryans entered the north about 1500 B.C.

The rough, rocky road ran through thick, wild jungle strewn with enormous boulders with little cultivation and villages few and far between. Some of it was famous tiger-shooting country and one evening going past a pool I saw a tigress drinking with two cubs not far off the road. I did not stop to observe them.

Although India suffers so much from drought she is a land of great rivers. In the northern plains the rivers are at their highest in the hot, dry summers as they are fed by melting snows from the Himalayas but in Central and Southern India the rivers vary greatly shortly after storms. Some of them have very big rocky or otherwise impervious catchment areas with a quick run-off and comparatively narrow but deep rocky beds. After a storm a wall of water 30 or more feet high rushes down the gorge-like beds. I came to one such river, which was just beginning to flood as I approached. In 20 minutes the bridge was covered by a raging torrent about 30 feet high, sweeping debris and drowned animals before it. It only needed a wait of a little over an hour for the bridge to be motorable again. I crossed the mighty Narbada (now called Narmada) just as the water was beginning to trickle over the bridge. The Tapti and Godavari also lay across the route but were crossed without incident.

By this time the bad roads had put the self-starter out of action and I regretted the impetuous action which had led me to throw away the starting handle, which I later learnt was indeed the correct handle for the car but had to be fitted by turning it first anti-clockwise and then clockwise – a continental subtlety that I had never come across before. For the rest of my journey the car could only be started by running it down a hill or getting it pushed. The former was not easy to arrange but the latter comparatively simple in India as wherever one stopped, even apparently in the middle of an uninhabited jungle, it was only a few minutes before people began to creep out from between the trees. The day's run through Ahmadnagar into Poona was uneventful but the road deteriorated so badly that for long stretches I left it completely and ran along the verge, which was smoother. I had a number of punctures.

A taste of the fleshpots of Poona and I set off south through Satara to Kolhapur, the capital of an important Indian state of the same name. The roads here again were simply cut out of the red lateritic soil, and running along the eastern flanks of the Western Ghats were fairly good.

I was now in Mahratta country, the home of the tough 'hill-rats' who supplied a fine regiment to the old Indian Army – the Royal Mahratta Light Infantry. Ploughing on down south, sometimes becoming absolutely smothered and choked with the fine red dust, I passed through Belgaum, which became widely known later to many in India as the site of one of the two Cadet Colleges during the war. At Dharwar the route turned somewhat inland towards Bangalore. My recollections of this small town are a sign stating that it had the last petrol pump for 300 miles. This was a good example of Indian salesmanship. It was true, but it was possible to buy petrol in tins at little towns along the route. Not long after leaving Dharwar we came to the Tungabhadra river. This is a tributary of the Krishna (Kistna) river and, although not a major river by Indian standards, it was a wide and formidable obstacle, especially as there was no road bridge. The only way to get a car across was on the railway.

I loaded the car on a flat top truck by means of the ramp. I had previously arranged for the flat top to be available. I then went to sit down in a carriage for the long wait for the train to start which seemed to be essential for operating the railways in India. I knew that there was no refreshment room or refreshment car and so I had brought some sandwiches. I opened them and started to eat. Suddenly a sacred monkey from a nearby temple darted in one window and out of the other, snatching as it did so not only the sandwich in my hand but the whole packet. It had obviously acquired the skill from long practice.

I noticed a very interesting linguistic phenomenon. The regional language was the Dravidian tongue of Telegu although most of the Muslims, who were mainly descended from the Moghul conquerors who entered India thousands of years after the Dravidians were established there, could speak Dekkani north of the river. This was a modified form of Urdu and I could get along with them. South of the river no non-English-speaking person, either Hindu or the few Muslims we met, could speak a word of anything except Telegu. Communication became difficult. The Tungabhadra river formed the boundary of the Nizam of Hyderabad's dominions and the southern limit of any long-term Muslim sovereignty in India. This must have been the reason for such a clear-cut linguistic frontier.

The country again became wild and sparsely inhabited and the road was so bad that one day I drove steadily for 13 hours and covered only 259 miles. Man, beast and jungle seemed somehow to be closely bound together. One had lost altogether the influence of the two monotheistic religions of the north – Islam and the Sikh religion. The spirit of animism seemed to brood palpably thick and malignant over jungle thicket, village and primitive wayside temple, each of which (unlike in the north where they are much less common) had its phallic *lingam* liberally smeared with red dye and ghi.

Maula Baksh became more and more disapproving and disdainful. He told me that he did not like the people in those parts and when I asked him why he said, 'They are black, they eat pigs and the women do not wear enough clothes.'

By this time the car had taken such punishment from the execrable roads that it needed considerable repairs. Also, I was running somewhat short of money because of the longer time taken by the journey than estimated and because of the money already spent on repairs. The welcome I got at Lavender's Hotel in Bangalore will always place it in my mind as one of the world's best – a bright lounge full of lovely flowers, good rooms, wonderful food and a manager who instantly agreed to cash a cheque for me and had his own driver/mechanic work all night on the car so that it was ready for an early start in the morning.

Bangalore is the capital of the great state of Mysore which had two long regencies under British Residents, who effected the reforms and development that any reasonably intelligent administrator can carry out provided that he has sufficient authority, continuity of tenure of office and adequate funds. Dams for irrigation schemes had been built which impounded considerable bodies of water, some large enough to support flourishing yacht clubs. Railways and reasonable roads had been constructed. Mining, agriculture, forestry and industries had been developed. Mysore had a major sandalwood industry using the wood and oil in many ways, of which one is to produce delightful soap. There was a thriving weaving and handicraft industry. The silk industry flourished, based on local silkworms, and Mysore saris were noted for exquisite beauty of design and delicacy of weaving. The big

214

afforestation programme gave rise to large forests of graceful casuarinas. It was very pleasant to drive through these and a welcome change from the somewhat treeless nature of parts of the journey.

Although on a plain, Bangalore is at an altitude of 2000 feet and therefore has a moderate climate for India. The summers are not overwhelmingly hot and the cool weather is delightful. It is a big railway centre and wherever there were big railway centres in India there was a large Anglo-Indian population. Anglo-Indians used to dominate two departments in India — Posts and Telegraphs, and Railways. There was also a good number of retired Anglo-Indians in the Kiplingese sense of the word.

After Bangalore the road ran across a wide, open, rocky plateau towards Mettur where we passed a huge dam under construction. We also passed long strings of women walking alongside the road naked from the waist up. Maula Baksh's disapproval knew no bounds. Mine was far less all-condemning. It was indeed a strange sight to someone from the prurient purdah-bound north, where almost all a doctor was allowed to examine of a woman patient was a hand shyly pushed through a curtain. Customs vary strangely throughout India indeed and in many circles in the south it was considered incorrect for a woman to appear before a Brahman with her breasts covered. The deeply entrenched marriage customs of some castes in southern India would normally be regarded as incest.

The next place of any importance was Coimbatore, a large cotton-milling centre. To me it was strange to see the crowds of Indian mill operatives thronging the streets at the end of a shift. We had now reached the final stage of the journey, the crossing of the Western Ghats and the drop down to the coast. There are not many gaps through the mountain range that flanks the west coast of peninsular India and the road took the opportunity of the gap at Palghat. It was a steep and rocky route with many tortuous bends through narrow ravines in places. When we reached the coastal region the blue sea, golden beaches, waving coconut palms, rice swamps and general greenery made it seem quite a different world from the arid north with its sandy plains baking in the fierce heat.

The way of life was very different too. The north of India is the home of the more virile type of Hindu races, truculent Sikhs and warlike Muslims. There were continuous bloody clashes made more bitter and lasting by the fact that neither community had an overwhelming strength, which led to the development of what must have been some of the bloodiest and bitterest religious fanaticism that the world has ever seen.

In parts of the Malabar coast, the first part of India touched by Europeans, Christians were in a majority – the only part of India where this was so. There was also the highest percentage of literacy in India and especially the highest percentage of literacy amongst women. There was also the highest proportion of Communists. It seemed to me that there was a causal relationship between these three statistics. A tolerance and a happy-go-lucky air were noticeable compared with the struggle for existence in the north. This did not mean that the standard of living was higher – it was probably lower, or at least the cost of living was lower.

There were marked differences in the housing and diet also. In the north houses were square and flat-roofed, made of brick or sunburnt mud. They also usually opened on one side only onto a walled courtyard. This was the only side with doors or windows on the ground floor. Often the lower storey was a shelter for the animals and the family lived on top. The whole building was highly defensible, as was often necessary. The flat roofs were covered with 4–5 feet of earth as a protection against the sun, which was as ever-present and fierce an enemy as feuding neighbours.

In the south, some houses were made of brick or timber with steeply pitched tiled roofs because of the more constant rain. More modest houses were made of timber with grass or bamboo walls and thatched with leaves. All were more open to the cooling wind. In the north in the hot weather the heat is so fierce that the houses are shut up to keep it out.

The diet in the Punjab was mostly pulses, wheat and other grain, a great deal of milk and milk products and meat. On the Malabar coast the diet was chiefly fish, coconuts, rice, bananas and other fruit. I met here for the first time the way of cooking fish in the milk made by squeezing the grated flesh of coconuts. This was a delicious way of cooking and one which I later found to be common in the Pacific Islands. In general, life on the Malabar coast was much more like life on a Pacific island than it was like life in the north of India.

The most outstanding difference in the way of life was the much more important position of women. In fact, I found that I was in a matriarchal, matrilineal, polyandrous society. This was the exact opposite of the north where polygamy was fairly common. The married woman was head of the house which she set up on marriage and was visited in turns by her various husbands, usually not more than two or three and often brothers. I never discovered how the roster was arranged or where the husbands lived when they were not living with their wives.

A matrilineal society was an obvious result of such a system if there was to be any attempt at preserving a lineage at all. I did not find out the details of this system either but the eldest son of the oldest surviving sister was often the heir. Some such matrilineal system was followed in deciding the succession to the maharaja-ships of Cochin and Travancore. In the former case it seemed to result in maharajas often being about 70 years old when they assumed power.

I delivered what was left of his car to Mills and spent a few carefree weeks with him and his family. I went fishing miles out to sea with the local fishermen in their shallow-draft boats and explored a little of the long system of lagoons that run for many miles parallel to the sea but are cut off from it by sand dunes and coconut groves which are sometimes several miles wide.

Apart from the importance of the coconut in the local cuisine and of copra as a cash crop, there was an important industry based on the sinnet made from the husk of the coconut, which surrounds its shell. The husk was plaited into long lengths of sinnet which were themselves made up into ropes, mats and other articles. I found later that the Pacific islanders do not trouble to do this on a commercial scale with their coconut husks.

I made my first acquaintance with basketball at Ernakulam and although I was at least a head taller than nearly all the students at the Maharaja's College, so high did they jump that I seldom touched the ball. I was impressed into the local European hockey team and we went north by train to Calicut for the annual match against the Europeans of Calicut. Vasco da Gama, after rounding the Cape of Good Hope, was the first European to reach India by sea. His landfall was near Calicut, which gave its name to calico, in which stuff a huge trade soon grew up. A statue of Vasco da Gama still stands near the beach at Calicut.

Not only the Portuguese, but also the Dutch, visited and settled the Malabar coast and both races, intermarrying with local women, gave rise to the burghers who still persist and retain such names as Da Souza, Da Costa, Vandenberg and Verghese, but are otherwise indistinguishable from ordinary Malayalis.

I made a trip or two to Madras on the South India Railway. There was no restaurant car on the train and the only food available at the stations appeared to be small curried onions and rice served on banana leaves. Banana leaves were used sometimes in the south of India for plates even on the most formal occasions such as a banquet in the palace of the Maharaja of Cochin or Travancore. Again, very different from the gold or silver plate of princely banquets in the north.

Madras had an air-conditioned hotel, which was very unusual in those days and my first acquaintance with air-conditioning. I thought Madras was a sprawling, formless city and that it seemed to lack the innate sense of personality and unity of the northern Indian cities. Fort St George, the first British stronghold in India, seemed unimpressive. I visited a glorious beach but the towering surf, memorials to those who had been drowned and reports of voracious sharks put any thoughts of bathing out of my head.

I was in Madras when the Second World War broke out. I returned to Ernakulam to pack, sent a telegram as a true trooper of the Punjab Light Horse reporting my address and volunteering for any service considered appropriate. The days passed and to my disappointment and chagrin I heard nothing. I remember thinking what a great military opportunity had been lost by not utilising my services.

There was a Naval Control Station with a smallish patrol vessel and minesweeper on Cochin Island just off Ernakulam and I offered my services there. I was accepted as a coding clerk, unpaid and supernumerary. One of the first long telegrams I decoded was directions on how to black-out lighthouses which had a follow-up to say that if certain dyes could not be obtained lamp-black could be used.

Shortly after this I started to decode a cable which opened with the words 'German cruiser...' I finished it in a fever of excitement to read 'operating off Manora Light, Karachi'. I rushed in, waving it with terrific excitement to the Naval Captain in Charge who merely told me to decode it again. I checked everything again and it came out just the same. Still the Captain was unimpressed but when an amendment arrived shortly afterwards saying 'For German cruiser read British minesweeper' it was my turn to be impressed by the phlegm and perspicacity of the silent service.

Shortly afterwards it was time to return to Aitchison College for the opening of another term and I found that my military service had been deferred on the directions of the Governor of the Punjab as my work was considered to be of national importance.

10

An Old Koi-hai

The significance of the title of this chapter is that a common summons to a servant in India was '*Koi hai?*' The literal meaning of this is, 'Is anyone there?' This in itself indicates the number of servants that abounded in India. It was a catchphrase given to anyone who had served long enough in India to learn the customs and acquire some knowledge of the language.

I found after a few years that there were very few Europeans who had a better knowledge of Urdu than I had. This does not mean that I was a brilliant linguist – just reasonably good, interested and moderately industrious. The general standard was rather poor. Most of those who were better than I were missionaries and members of the Indian Civil Service. Some 'box-wallahs', such as Mike Durell, had the knack of communicating with Indians using a very small vocabulary without being inhibited by any knowledge of the grammar of Urdu. I used to find this somewhat irritating in comparison with the work that I had put in.

As in many areas in India, the linguistic position in the Punjab was complex. The regional language was Punjabi. I found that a harsh, guttural and difficult language and hardly learnt any of it. Urdu was spoken by all educated Indians in the province as well as Punjabi. I considered Urdu a mellifluous and expressive tongue although it had many phonetic pitfalls for those trying to learn it.

Two of the commonest of these were that certain consonants were sometimes aspirated and sometimes doubled. To the European the differences caused thereby were difficult to detect at first but could completely alter the meaning of a word. The boys would

220

give me Indian tongue-twisters, some involving these traps, and roll about in helpless laughter at my efforts.

Nearly all Muslims wrote Urdu in its own script. Many Hindus used the Urdu script, some used the Nagari, some knew both. Some Sikhs used Urdu script, some used Hindi. In addition the Sikhs had a script of their own, Gurumukhi, in which they wrote Punjabi. Their holy book, the *Guru Granth Sahib*, was written in this. Some Sikhs were literate in this script only. Gurumukhi is sometimes referred to as a language but it is really a script for writing Punjabi and its use is confined to Sikhs, with rare exceptions.

The position in the Punjab was thus the reverse of China. In the Punjab some people, literate in their own script only, could, of course, talk to fellow Punjabis but not necessarily write to them.

Indians, knowing English, often incorporated it in Urdu and only cumbersome equivalents could be found for some English scientific phrases. Two hybrid sentences stick in my memory. At a garden party I heard someone say '*Is* ice-cream *ka* flavour *achcha hai lekin* consistency *thik naihin*.' 'The flavour of this ice-cream is good but its consistency is not correct.'

In a physics lecture supposed to be in Urdu I heard, '*Jab hawa* upward pressure exert *karti hai*.' 'When the air is exerting upward pressure.'

Earlier, after I had been in Lahore only a few months, and could pass a few simple remarks in Urdu with educated Indians, I found myself out in the country near an old Sikh. I made some remark to him in what I proudly considered to be Urdu. He replied, '*Are sahib, ham angrezi naihin jante hain*.' 'Oh sahib, I do not understand English.'

This was very mortifying and nonplussing but I recovered and said, 'Listen brother, I am trying to speak your language. You try to get on my wavelength.'

Enlightenment dawned and we could then understand each other a little.

One of the numerous criticisms of the British administration of India made by the Indian National Congress was that provincial boundaries sometimes split an area of the same language so that one part of it formed a section of another province. They seemed to suggest that this was done on the principle of divide and rule but this was not so. It was sometimes the result of a historic development and sometimes based upon old boundaries established by former Indian rulers. Once the Government of independent India started to redefine the boundaries of provinces, which are now called states, they found they had opened Pandora's box, as the linguistic position in India is infinitely complex. No doubt, some of the new states are more logical and homogeneous but where does the breakdown into languages stop, where is the boundary line between a language and a dialect in India? The Sikhs claimed that Gurumukhi was a separate language. Made more ardent by the connection of Gurumukhi with their religion and their considerable fanaticism, they persistently agitated for their own linguistic state. This was eventually granted in the form of splitting the Punjab once again and carving up the state of the East Punjab. (Incidentally there should be 'the' in front of Punjab, just as in 'The Five Rivers' in English, as it means 'The Five Rivers' from the Persian words *panj*: five and *ab*: water, river.)

Even when the Sikhs got their own state they were not satisfied. Disaffection and religious fanaticism smouldered until finally they led to the storming of the Golden Temple at Amritsar, all the consequences of which have not yet been played out.

Feeling over language also led to the bloody rioting in Bombay where the Gujarati- and Mahratti-speaking areas meet.

I never received an invitation to the home of any of the Indian masters as their wives were in purdah. Although they were far more modernised and westernised than the vast majority of Indians, I suppose that some of the Muslim wives wore the *burqa* when they went out. This really was a hideous hardship. It was not just a light veil over the head and face like the version of the yashmak as understood in Europe. The best way to describe the *burqa* is that it was like a small bell-tent suspended on the crown of the head. Made of heavy white calico it reached right down to the ankles. There was a small lattice in front of the eyes so that the wearer could see where she was going. The effect of a garment like this on comfort and hygiene when worn in a shade temperature of 120°F (50°C) can be imagined. It was difficult to understand how the Punjabi Muslims had such good physique in general as their mothers always had to wear such clothes when they went out. They were not worn in the home unless strangers were present.

Hindu and Sikh women did not wear the *burqa* but they remained in seclusion as much as possible and when approaching men in public usually drew a corner of their sari over their face. Women of all communities who worked in the fields could not observe purdah very strictly and so to a large extent it became a status symbol to have a wife or wives in purdah. This was one factor which kept it going.

In some Hindu princely states a strange phenomenon could be observed. Some of the ruling families were quite Europeanised. The princesses had gone to England quite often with their parents. A few had even gone to school in England or out into general society in Calcutta, Bombay or other large cities. They could play tennis, ride well, drive cars and shoot. Then, when they married, they formally went into purdah. Whether they ever emerged again depended very largely upon the enlightenment or otherwise of their princely husband and to a lesser degree on their own attitude and strength of character. The princely husband's attitude was significantly influenced by his caste, race, tradition, type of education and the general public feeling in his state. Although Patiala was amongst the most westernised of states as far as the men were concerned, the princesses were all in purdah and I never caught a glimpse of any of them.

All India Radio were running a series of talks on the countries near to India and they got me to give talks on Persia and Burma. From that beginning they asked me if I could give some talks on different sports. I got further and further away from subjects on which I had any real knowledge but they paid me quite well by contemporary standards. Then I did some sports commentaries including, with friends, commentaries on the All India Badminton Tournament. Luckily there was no television in those days and no listener could tell when a mistake had been made.

One evening, a young Sikh from Patiala who was a lieutenant in an Indian Army cavalry regiment was driven up by his driver to see me. The regiment was, of course, mechanised but they still retained their tradition of playing regimental polo. He was a fine player and had some good ponies, one of which he asked me if I would buy as he said that he was short of money. I knew the pony to be much better than any I had been able to ride and the price mentioned was very reasonable. However, it was more than I could afford. I did not like to say so as I was pretty sure that he would think that I was just haggling with him and I did not want to create this impression. The only solution that I could think of was to get him drunk. This would have been impossible if he had been like some of the older, hardened Patiala drinkers and I would have succumbed before him. However, I had drunk nothing and he had had a start. By exercising a certain low cunning I succeeded in my object and his driver carried him out to his car.

I received my second generous invitation to a holiday in Patiala from the Maharaja through Major Joginder Singh, the Sikh in the Guardian's Department who helped to look after the Patiala princelings at the College. I was taken to Patiala in the old Rolls Royce that brought the boys in to school daily from Patiala House in Lahore. It was always driven by Baba Singh, an old and trusted retainer of the state. He alone knew exactly when and how to work the handpump to keep the petrol supply going. (I do not know why the Maharaja allocated this car for such a purpose. He had 26 other more modern Rolls Royces and about 100 other cars. He retained a highly competent Rolls Royce-trained engineer with the improbable name of Tweenie. He was the only teetotaller that I came across in Patiala and drank large quantities of tea all day.)

I stayed once more in the old palace which had been turned into a guest house. I arrived in the evening and was told that next morning we were going shooting once more. This time to the famous *jhil*, or lake, called Bhupindersagar. Bhupinder was the Maharaja's name (this sounded rather comic to me) and sagar meant sea or ocean. It was famous for its vast number of duck. I was told also that the Maharaja was coming and thought it best to confine myself to the role of spectator in such renowned shooting company. It was just as well that I did. I saw the most incredible feats of marksmanship. On several occasions the Maharaja, using three guns and two well-trained loaders, shot six birds from one flight. Two as they approached, two overhead and two as they flew away. Later on, in the evening, as geese started coming in he shot some with rifles. What made this even more remarkable was that the light did not seem very good to me.

After the shooting was over we drove back to Patiala at a great rate. The Maharaja went to the new palace in which he lived. The rest of us went to the club. We sat down, at the bar right in front of a clock, to have some 'Patiala pegs', or huge whiskeys, before dinner. Everyone but myself had 20 drinks in an hour – just about as fast as the steward could pour them out and seemed completely unaffected as they set off to prepare themselves for dinner. I had refused one round and did not feel fit enough to go into dinner but excused myself and went straight to bed.

Two of those taking part in that drinking, which they seemed to regard as nothing out of the ordinary, were the Sikh major and Laurence Tarrant (son of Frank Tarrant, the noted cricketer, who had been retained by the Maharaja a long time but was not himself a cricketer) in the Guardian's Department for the Maharaja's sons. I thus constantly met them at the College. On occasions I suggested that they might be overdoing it although they had such heads that they never got drunk. They laughed it off and said it kept the mosquitoes away. Certainly they never got malaria but when I returned after the war, having managed to survive Japanese PoW camps, I was sorry to find that they were both dead. I drew my own conclusions. The Maharaja himself died at the age of 48, his magnificent strength and vitality weakened by excessive drinking and concupiscence.

Not surprisingly I had a hangover in the morning after the evening's drinking session. I mentioned this to Captain Muir, a First World War fighter pilot who looked after the Patiala aircraft. He said, 'I've got just the cure for that – a champagne flip.' I was a bit puzzled. He produced a pint of nicely chilled champagne and said, 'Here's the champagne. Get that down you and I'll give you a flip in the plane.' He then took me up in a light aeroplane to what seemed to me to be a great height, screamed down in a hair-raising dive and then performed aerobatics at a pretty low altitude. It certainly cured my hangover. I was so terrified that I forgot all about it.

One of the events of that holiday was a gun dog trial of which two features stand out in my mind. The first was a mobile bar, which consisted of an elephant with a large leather contraption thrown over its back containing glasses and drinks of every description. This continually wandered around so that people could help themselves. There were also *sowars* or troopers of the Patiala cavalry in attendance to carry messages, including a request for the elephant if it was considered that his route was too circuitous.

There were a few European sportsmen present but most were Indians, including the Maharaja of Jind who was rather hard of hearing. This led him to think that everyone else had a similar weakness. He spoke, in English, in a very loud voice criticising other people's handling of their dogs in what he thought was *sotto voce* but which was clearly audible to anyone in the neighbourhood, often including the target of his scorn.

The highlight of this visit to Patiala and the basic reason for my invitation, was so that I could see one of the *durbars* which the Maharaja held several times a year. I suppose that it was basically similar to the ceremony at the court of a European feudal monarch at which the liegemen expressed their fealty. At the same time it had greater overtones of mysticism and religious bonds than, I suppose, were ever present in European feudalism. Indian princes who had been invited to the coronation of George V noticed how familiar some features of the ceremony, the anointing and sword of justice, for example, were to the ceremony when an Indian prince ascended the *gaddi*. Their theory was that they had originated in India, where there were well-organised states long before the Christian era, and had passed to Europe in the time of the Roman Empire.

As the day approached, the excitement increased in the countryside even amongst the lowliest peasants. There was a strange paradox in the Indian states. Some were enlightened and well run. Some suffered a degree of oppression, corruption and efficiency that would be unthinkable in British India. The British were loath to interfere until the misrule was really intolerable. The chief reason for this was because it was a very tricky and difficult action and usually always caused nearly as much unrest as it sought to overcome. For example, the British found it much more difficult to suppress *satti* (the burning of a widow on her husband's funeral pyre) and *thaggi* (ritual murder and robbery, from which our word thug is derived) in the Indian states than they did in British India.

Most Indian princes believed the dictum, '*L'état, c'est moi*' and regarded the entire tax yield as basically their privy purse. What they remitted for any of the essential services of the state was a concession. The more the state raised in taxes the higher the ruler's personal income in general. Thus in Indian states the peasants tended to be oppressed. The Viceroy, Residents and Political Agents had very limited power to influence the internal affairs of a state although they tried to ameliorate abuses and suggested economic and other reforms. In very bad cases the Viceroy would intervene and depose the prince. Some rulers were very enlightened and altruistic, working long hours every day in the administration of their estate, keeping closely in touch with their subjects and providing a type of personalised administration which was the best type of government for India.

The standard of administration, justice, economic, social and political development in an Indian state depended primarily on the character, education and enlightenment of the ruler. Hence the importance of the Chiefs' Colleges. The next most important factor was the character and ability of the Resident in important states or the Political Agent in less important states and how they got on with the rulers. A great deal could be achieved informally on the basis of good personal relations.

The Government of India was always pressing the princes to set a formal limit to their privy purses and to write this into the constitution of the state. The ideal was set at 10% of the tax revenue as the maximum for the privy purse. There were not many states in which this was even formally accepted. Even in these the boundaries between the two were often blurred, sometimes wilfully, at others because of genuine difficulty. For example, should the expenses of a *durbar* be fully or partly paid from the privy purse?

The peasant complained of oppression in some states (and also in British India under some landlords). In some states the peasant was contented. Even when the peasant complained he had a vast respect and considerable affection for his ruler compounded of admiration of his prestige, wealth and power and a strange bond of religious, cultural and communal unity. This type of relationship

227

could not be achieved by British Commissioners although they were almost universally admired and respected for their integrity and efficiency.

The attitude of the unsophisticated Indian to his superiors was exemplified by a common form of address to both ruler and British official – *Mabaap* (Mother and Father). It struck me as strange that this was the only case in which Indian usage did not give precedence to males.

Through the pomp and pageantry of ceremonies, often with religious connotations, the prestige of the prince was enhanced. He had a communion with divinity. The people felt that they had one form of access to the gods through him. This applied chiefly to Hindu princes and people. However, I felt that some of the same feelings were present in Patiala on the day of the *durbar* as we drove through the crowds to where the ceremony was to be held.

The income of a state was not, of course, in direct proportion to its size as fertility, rainfall and other factors affected it. Patiala, with an area of 5,900 square miles mostly of rich, well-irrigated soil tended by sturdy farmers following relatively advanced methods, had an annual revenue the equivalent of £1,250,000 at pre-war rates. It was considered that at least half of this went into the privy purse. There was at times discontent and unrest in some villages in Patiala. This was caused more by grasping rack-renters of huge estates than by the exactions of state revenue.

However, the Maharaja was free to indulge his fancy on a grand scale. Apart from the old palace there was the new Moti Bagh Palace of pink sandstone, which covered eleven acres and was said to have bathrooms as large as ballrooms, and six other royal residences in the plains or the Simla Hills. The Patiala tradition was to buy en masse. A European tailor used to motor out from Lahore to receive orders for suits by the dozen and shirts by the hundred. The *durbar* was an opportunity in which the Maharaja and his subjects delighted to display pomp, ceremony and flamboyance on a grand scale.

The *Durbar* Hall was a large, finely proportioned room with a lofty ceiling from which were hanging huge crystal chandeliers placed as closely as possible over the whole surface. The

Maharaja had been inspecting some chandeliers in a shop in Calcutta. He voiced a desire to buy some and the assistant seemed to cast doubt on his creditworthiness. The Maharaja thereupon bought up the whole stock and had it sent to Patiala.

With my Sikh friend, Joginder Singh, who was a noble in the state, I took up my place in a corner of the hall to watch the ceremony. All the senior officials, army officers, nobles and landowners of the state arrived to take up their allotted places. The civilians were in white silk *achkans* with gold buttons and gauze turbans of pastel shades of pink, blue, turquoise and yellow. Some had strings of pearls wound once or more round their necks; most of them had rings with large diamonds, emeralds or rubies in them. The civilians, entitled to do so, wore swords with hilts encrusted with jewels and decorated with chased silver. Some wore European-type shoes but most had the oriental boat-like slipper (the same shape for each foot) embroidered with gold and scarlet thread and with back-curling toes.

Naturally, most of those present were Sikhs. For nether garments they wore what in India is know as the *pajama* – that is a type of white trousers close fitting at the knee and below, very much like what is called a jodhpur in England. (The literal meaning of *pajama* is clothing that comes down to the foot, from the Persian words *pai* meaning foot and *jama* meaning clothing.) Hindus wore a similar garment. The few Muslims wore the Muslim *shalwar* or white trousers, drawn in at the waist by a cord, very full round the behind, tapering down to the ankle opening which was still very wide. The military officers were on the opposite side from the civilians. They were all in scarlet and gold braid full dress uniform, their turbans tied in the regulation Patiala style – that is crossed from either side of the head very symmetrically in such a way that they came to a peak at the top of the middle of the forehead. This left a neat triangle of the *pagri* or inner turban in the middle of the forehead below the peak of the turban. (Many racial groups and castes had their own specific way of tying their turbans in India. This style originated in Patiala but became very widespread among Sikhs.) All in all the *Durbar* Hall was a scene of multicoloured, scintillating splendour, but the climax was yet to come.

In India, and the orient in general, it is considered fitting that a magnate should keep his audience waiting in direct proportion to his importance. The Maharaja of Patiala was noted for his unpunctuality. However, after a little while I felt a frisson of expectancy run through the assembly. Shortly afterwards one of the Marharaja's stable of Rolls Royces drew up at the door. (Some of the more conservative princes always made state entrances on elephants, specially painted, made up, caparisoned in scarlet and cloth of gold and surmounted by a silver howdah. On an earlier occasion I had seen the Maharaja ride through Patiala City on such an elephant but that was a religious festival. I suspected that it was the same elephant which, on less glamorous occasions, pulled the heavy roller over the cricket pitch. This was one of the slightly less ornate *durbars*.)

There was a brazen blare of great oriental horns. A *chobdar*, or herald, announced the arrival of the Maharaja giving him a selection of his manifold titles, one of which was the Persian for 'Faithful Ally of the English'. His Highness entered the hall. Everyone bowed deeply from the waist and joined their palms together in the respectful obeisance and greeting of *namaskar* and at the same time a sonorous murmur of '*Huzur*' (Your Majesty) ran round the hall. The Maharaja, a man of immensely broad shoulders but only medium height, was a truly princely figure. His face was fleshy but handsome, with magnificent curling moustaches, large rather deep-set luminous but smouldering eyes, set in long, thick lashes and full, sensuous lips. There was a suggestion of a slightly evil, dissolute scowl in his expression and it was not difficult to imagine that he could be an oriental voluptuary and despot. He was dressed in the same general style as his nobles but with even more magnificent jewels on his fingers, sword and scabbard.

His silk turban was wound round with several strings of pearls worth a king's ransom. Fixed to the front peak of the turban was a *kalgi* or branching aigrette of plumes and great jewels. Round his neck was a collar of diamonds set in platinum and several necklaces of massive diamonds and emeralds. His cummerbund or waistband was decorated with diamonds with a pearl the shape and size of a small pear hanging from the middle. He had several diamond bracelets round each wrist and the buttons of his *achkan* were also made of diamonds. Around his waist, under the cummerbund, he had a broad piece of the gold lamé so liked by Indian princes. To this was fastened the famous Patiala emerald, supposed to be one of the biggest in the world and about four inches by two and a half.

It must not be thought that all this regalia was the personal property of the Maharaja. Most, if not all of it, had a status like the Crown Jewels in Britain. They were kept in the *toshakhana* or state treasury by hereditary guardians and issued only on the occasion of important functions and against the signature of all into whose hands they came. When the people saw their Maharaja bedecked in such splendour many of them took a certain proprietary interest in it as a symbol of the state in which they were a part. Some even referred to '*hamara jawahirat*' or 'our jewellery'.

His Highness mounted the dais and sat down cross-legged on the *gaddi* or throne like a large cushion or divan, set in a large gold-plated armchair and surmounted by an elaborately embroidered silk baldachin. By some feat of oriental telepathy, simultaneously with the princely posterior touching the *gaddi* the guns started firing a salute. The princes were very jealous of their precedence and a concrete and recognisable sign of this was the number of guns to which they were entitled. This was settled by agreement with the Indian Government and usually incorporated in a treaty signed with nearly all important princes. The number of guns was often the subject of petty squabbles among the princes and of intrigues and petitions to influence the Viceroy, representing the paramount power, to increase them. Five States were entitled to 21 guns, six were granted 19 guns. They were followed by 13 with 17 guns. Most of the rest went down by odd numbers to nine guns. Some were non-salute States. In all there were 118 salute States. The princes with eleven and nine gun salutes were known as rajas, those with 13 and above as maharajas or 'great kings'. Patiala was entitled to 17. These duly rang out.

When this had finished a few senior heads of department read aloud reports and plans. After this the essential business of the *durbar* began which was really an affirmation of feudal loyalty and a strengthening of the bond between the ruler and his nobles and through them with the people. First of all the Yuvraj came up

231

to signify fealty and allegiance to his father. His apparel was almost as resplendent as his father's. Then all the nobles came up to the *gaddi*, having discarded their footwear, knelt down and presented *nazar* to the Maharaja. This was a number of gold and silver coins wrapped up in a *rumal* or silk square. It was a combination of symbolic tribute, a public manifestation of loyalty and a token rent for estates probably originally granted by the Maharaja or his predecessors. Everyone approached and made his obeisance in strict order of seniority. Joginder Singh took his place. The amount of the *nazar* also varied with seniority. Some of those presenting *nazar* accompanied it with the gestures made by certain types of Indian as signs of great respect. This was a type of fluid circling of the right hand and forearm from the region of the ground clockwise until the hand reached the neighbourhood of the head. (I believe that it was meant to symbolise pouring dust on one's head in the presence of a great superior as a sign of humility. Some Indians did it to Europeans.) Others presenting *nazar* contented themselves with a bow or *namaskar*. It was customary for the princes to touch the *nazar* as a sign of acceptance and almost simultaneously wave it to one side with a slight movement of the hand as a sign of remittance. This the Maharaja did. All the time this was going on two of the *chobdar* in scarlet, gold-braided uniforms were standing behind the *gaddi* and gently waving fans made of ostrich feathers, so large that it took both hands to manipulate them.

The only prince who was known to accept *nazar* was the Nizam of Hyderabad, the first in precedence, the richest and the meanest of them. He kept two boxes by the *gaddi* at a *durbar*; one for gold and other for silver coins.

When all the civilians had paid their respects it was the turn of the army officers. They also went up in order of seniority, made a smart salute, presented the hilt of their sword towards the Maharaja and drew the sword out of the scabbard a little way. This was to signify their loyalty to the Maharaja, which he accepted by touching the hilt of the sword.

The relationship between a prince and his great nobles was very complex and fluid. At some times and in some states the prince had almost absolute power to promote and demote and did so.

232

There were constant intrigues and changes as one courtier succeeded another. This occurred in Patiala. Often the prince could not rule without the support of his nobles and many had as much trouble with them as King John had with his nobles. It would be difficult to say what role the *durbar* had in Patiala in cementing and manifesting the loyalty of the nobles.

When the *durbar* was over most of the audience, myself included, went to the palace where drinks were served and numerous servants brought in on huge silver trays a large variety of *mithai* or Indian sweets all covered with gold or silver leaf which was meant to be eaten with them. This was fairly common amongst rich Indians who considered that gold and silver had great health-giving qualities. They sometimes ate them with honey as a tonic. I was told that crushed pearls were sometimes eaten in the same way although I have no direct knowledge of this.

Afterwards, when some of the Maharaja's sons at the College came to my sitting room for an occasional tutorial I wondered what they thought of its relative drabness and austerity compared with the splendid ambience of their own home.

As I have previously stated, one of the besetting sins of most Indian princes was unbridled extravagance. In some it was so outrageous that the state's income would be largely squandered on whims, hobbies or vices indulged in with no thought of their cost. Sometimes it led to increased taxation, amounting to oppression; sometimes to the collapse of the fiscal system of the state leading to some sort of British intervention. At the College we tried to inculcate some ideas of economy into the boys. One of the ways that this was done was by officially limiting their pocket money. They were supposed to hand over their money at the beginning of each term and they were given a modest weekly pocket money according to the form that they were in. They were not supposed to accept money from visitors of any kind or get access to it through their servants. I do not think that the system was very effective. Even if the boys did not retain hidden treasure I am sure that they got generous gifts from visitors. However, it did at least make them give a little thought to the principles of budgeting and realise that others had severely limited incomes.

On these same general principles we tried to instil into the boys

233

the principles of good administration, civic responsibility and equitable treatment of their subjects or tenants. Unfortunately, it was not uncommon for these qualities to be lacking in Indian princes or great landlords. An Indian state with a bad ruler must have been one of the worst possible types of government as it could be a medieval type of oriental tyranny enforced by a modern relatively efficient state machinery. The best, of which I hope our boys formed examples, were a type of relatively enlightened paternal autocracy which suited the Indian peasant.

It was obvious that as regards curbing extravagances of all kinds, we had not succeeded with the then ruling Maharaja of Patiala. I think that the odds were stacked against us as far as the major princes were concerned. Any influence that we and their European guardians could exert was very largely offset by the hordes of servitors, self-seeking sycophants and intriguers, superstitious women relatives and tradition-bound and power-hungry priests with whom they were surrounded when they went home. Some were purposely protected by their parents from such influences by being placed from an early age almost exclusively in the care of European nannies and later guardians.

I think that our best results were with the less important princes and the great landowners who generally turned out to be relatively enlightened, well-balanced and responsible citizens and administrators.

11

End of an Epoch

In the Christmas holidays of 1939 I went to Kashmir for the skiing with Mike Durell. We drove up by the same route as I had followed in the summer of 1936. The desperate poverty of the Kashmiris at Tangmarg where we again had to leave our car, and drain out the water to prevent freezing, was even more striking than in the summer. An even fiercer battle was waged by an under-nourished group of about 40 men, under-clad in the bitter cold, to earn a few annas by carrying our baggage the three or four miles to one of the hotels or boarding-houses that had been opened at Gulmarg for the skiing season.

We were quite comfortable in bedrooms in a separate wooden hut as an annexe to one of the hotels. We had our baths in the usual big zinc tubs with hot water carried in from outside.

There were no ski-hoists or similar mechanical aids but the scenery was just as magnificent as in summer. We rode up to the higher slopes on ponies along tracks that had been opened up through the snow which was 12–16 feet deep in many places. Kashmiris carried up our skis on their backs and went back on the ponies. Sometimes we went up lower slopes on our skis with furred skins attached to them to stop them slipping back. There were two pistes of varying difficulty from Khillanmarg down to Gulmarg. The trees were blazed and daubed blue and red to show the different tracks.

I had never been on skis before. We hired equipment from the Ski Club of India at Gulmarg and went out to have a go the first evening. I saw some slope and decided to try to get down it. I got to the bottom with a few falls. The next morning, we went out with the beginners' class under the Austrian instructor. I wanted to try the slope again but he said, 'You try that, you break your neck.' I have indelibly printed in my memory the monotonous refrain of the instructor to me, 'Try a Christiana, captain.' Then after my effort, 'Dat is not a Christiana, captain. Dat is not a Telemark, captain. Dat is noddings. Try again captain'. (He called most people captain.)

The vast expanses of snow on the mountain slopes around and above Khillanmarg were very even and for beginners these huge uniform snowfields unimpeded by trees or boulders were easier and more enjoyable than I found conditions later in Switzerland. One could take them at any angle or speed according to one's skill.

We had a happy holiday there before motoring back to Lahore to start work again. On the way back we met a landslide across the road. There was at that time no mechanical earth-moving equipment of any type in Kashmir. A gang of coolies were clearing the tons of earth, mud and rocks by pick, crowbar and two-man shovel, one pushing the handle and one pulling on a rope tied just above the blade. The last was a common sight in India. We were wearing thick European winter clothes surmounted by *poshteens*, the long ear to ankle coat of the Pathan tribesmen of the North-West Frontier made of goat or sheep skin with the wool inside. We could barely keep warm. When we got out of the car we were horrified to find that the Kashmiris were wearing thin cotton clothing with just a woollen pullover on top. None had really good footwear and some had merely something like a sandal made of woven grass. They had almost cleared the road when we arrived and when they had finished we gave them a few rupees *bakhshish* for which they seemed very grateful.

In May, 1940, my pony fell in a polo match and I smashed up my right shoulder. I had to have an operation. This was performed in the Lahore Hospital by an Indian surgeon with an international reputation. He told me before the operation that the chief danger was that in the conditions of the Indian hot weather the wound might go septic. He was going to take some sinew out of one leg to tie up my shoulder.

I therefore went into hospital three days before the operation and had my right leg and injured shoulder disinfected several times a day. When I recovered from the operation I was surprised to find that the sinew had been taken from my left leg. The surgeon gave me some medical reason for his change of mind at the operating table but it seemed strange to me. One of the stitches did turn septic and it was about four months before it healed. This was very unpleasant in the heat and the sweat.

I enlivened my post-operative stay in the hospital by giving a drinks party in my room with the aid of Maula Baksh and the connivance of the nurse but not of the matron.

I never went to church but to my surprise the Bishop of Lahore seemed to think that it was his duty to visit me. Unfortunately, I was on the bedpan when he arrived and he never came again. However, I had several jolly evenings with the Roman Catholic father, our conversation enlivened with liquor.

I found what seemed to me a very reasonable and equitable system in the hospital. Below a certain income, which applied to most Indians, all medical treatment was free. Above this level, incomes were divided into various brackets and charges were made for the different types of operation and treatment according to one's income bracket. As far as civil servants were concerned this was public knowledge as it was all set out in the Civil List. Notices setting out the charges were displayed at various places in the hospital.

When I came out of hospital my right arm and shoulder were powerless. I could only raise my right arm with my left arm. I gradually strengthened it by exercises up the wall with the weight supported by the wall. It really was necessary then for Maula Baksh to help me dress and do my hair.

I had long wanted to go to Afghanistan. It so happened that Mike Durell was making arrangements to fit a cinema in the British Embassy in Kabul as a counter to all the propaganda that the Germans were turning out in Afghanistan. It had taken him a long time to get a visa but just before the hot weather holidays began he had gone to Kabul to start the work. I decided to go to Peshawar, try to get a visa, and join him. After staying in Dean's Hotel for about three weeks nothing had come through. (I learnt, too late, that instead of going through official channels, a Parsi merchant in Peshawar who did a lot of business in Kabul had his own channels through which he could have got me a visa in a day or two.) It was very hot and my shoulder was giving me trouble. I decided to leave the heat and dust of Peshawar and go to the peace, cool and quiet of the Simla Hills where some Anglo-Indian friends had kindly invited me to recuperate with them at the house they owned in Dagshai, a small hill station in the Simla Hills. The invitation was made even more attractive by the presence of their very beautiful and sexy daughter. We went for long walks and climbs, visiting some of the old Gurkha forts. Once we watched a battle between two armies of langurs, the long-tailed sacred monkey of India associated with the god Hanuman, the same type that had stolen my lunch in the railway carriage on my journey to Southern India. It appeared as if each side had a General Staff directing the battle and organising flanking attacks whilst the females of the species were urging on their men folk and passing them ammunition to throw at the enemy.

I had quite a scare once when going along a narrow path with a great drop on one side and a steep cliff on the other. A giant iguana as large as a good-sized pig came charging down the track. I thought that it was going to attack me but as soon as it saw me it was as scared as I was. It wheeled round in a flash and rapidly scaled the precipitous face above the track, clinging on with its long sharp claws.

Dagshai was an idyllic spot set amid stupendous mountains with the snow-capped peaks of the Himalayas in the far distance. The nearer, lower slopes were covered with beautiful forests of deodars and pines. The deodar is a type of cedar and the word means divine tree in Sanskrit. Its beauty made it easy to understand how it got its name and religious associations and why Indian poets praised it. In addition to the lovely forest mantle of the hills there were huge clumps of rhododendrons and colourful flowers.

It was interesting after dark to sit on the veranda and watch the headlights of cars many miles away across the deep valley making the long zigzag climb up the mountains to Simla. They looked like tiny glow-worms creeping along.

Sometimes we motored down to Barogh to have dinner in the

238

railway refreshment room, another establishment, like that at Kalka, noted for the excellence of its food. This was because it was where the up and down trains on the narrow gauge single line railway from Kalka to Simla crossed. V.I.P.s sometimes ate there and it maintained a high standard. This was the line on which we had travelled to Chail for our cricket match against Patiala.

When I thought I was fit I managed to get released for military service. I did not mention my operation. The doctor who examined me noticed the scar only just before I was putting on my shirt. My arm seemed to have regained its normal strength but there was one test that I had not given it – flopping down on the ground as quickly as possible. This is necessary at times in military life. I found that I could not take the weight of my body on my right arm. However, my easy life in the civil branch of the establishment had ended. In October, 1940, I went to the Cadets' College in Bangalore, one of two establishments in India that ran pressure-cooker courses for turning such as me into temporary officers and gentlemen. In February, 1941, I was commissioned into the 2/12 Frontier Force Regiment. I was proud to get into the regiment of my first choice which had a fine reputation and was composed equally of four renowned Indian martial races – Punjabi Muslims, Pathans (the tribesmen of the North-West Frontier) Sikhs and Dogras (Hindus from the Simla Hills).

It was not until five years and many vicissitudes later that I returned to the College. All great wars effect momentous social changes and nowhere more than in some aspects of life in India. The two world wars had greatly aided the emancipation of women in Britain. The second did so in India. Women who had been in purdah when I left were now serving in the Women's Auxiliary Corps, India. Grace Jivanandhan, the shy and retiring Indian Christian who taught the junior boys, was now giving parties at the Gymkhana Club, to which she invited me, and dancing with British officers.

I was pleased to meet my old colleagues. I also traced Maula Baksh who seemed to be doing quite well running a small Indian eating house. I gave him some *bakhshish* in recognition of his faithful service.

A talk to the boys on my experiences as a PoW seemed to

239

arouse interest but I remember one question which suggested that the Japanese guards ate the same as us and that it was only because we were Europeans used to eating much more that we suffered from malnutrition. This was quite incorrect. Prejudice and propaganda had been at work.

I found when I reached the Regimental Depot at Sialkot that I was the only officer whose civilian clothes had survived the war. The others had just left their kit in tin trunks in the depot and the clothes had all been eaten by fish insects, moths and other insects prevalent in India. A Sikh officer in the regiment had offered to have mine looked after by his wife. With the pious devotion and industry of an Indian woman she had aired them regularly and packed them with strong-smelling *nim* leaves which the Indians use as insect repellents.

By law, in India the posts of all who served in the forces had to be reserved for them. For various reasons, including the obvious forthcoming independence of India, I decided not to try to exercise this right. In due course I joined the Colonial Administrative Service. About 18 years later, after I had retired from the Colonial Service, I came home via Lahore, then in Pakistan, to meet some of my old friends and colleagues again. This time only Muslim staff and boys were there. I had a very happy reunion with Zulfiqar Ali and Mohamed Akram in Lahore. The College now had an intake from a wider social range. I met the Muslim principal and was offered my old job again at ten times the old salary (not much ahead of inflation) and my old quarters, now with air-conditioning and modern plumbing. Babur Ali, whom I remembered as a roly-poly little boy in the third form, was the owner and manager of a huge modern air-conditioned packaging plant. He lived in a marble palace to which he invited me and tried to persuade me to rejoin the staff of the College. I went to Bahawalpur where, with money provided by the Nawab of Bahawalpur, the premier Muslim prince of the Punjab, whose sons I had taught, Khan Anwar Sikander Khan, my friend and former colleague at Aitchison College, had founded a school and was its principal. It was on broadly similar lines to Aitchison College but its intake covered a wider social spectrum like the modernised Aitchison College. It had fine buildings and equipment and spacious playing fields. Grace Jivanandhan had joined the staff. He wanted me to do so also. These offers were very flattering but the only reason I had left the service in Fiji was to be in England whilst my sons were at school.

By then I realised how lucky I had been to see one of the most colourful cross-sections of the last days of the pre-war British raj in India – surely one of the most interesting phases of the most picturesque and fascinating country in the Empire.

GLOSSARY

Anglo-Indian	a. Of mixed Indian and English blood. b. Kipling's usage – an Englishman who, or whose family, has settled in India and/or was born there and retired there.
Babu	An English-speaking Indian clerk with a good but stereotyped use of English vocabulary in a somewhat incorrect way and an Indian accent.
Bakhshish	A tip or small present.
Baraf	Ice, snow.
Bhisti	A water carrier (Kipling's Gunga Din).
Biri	A type of roughly rolled Indian cigarette.
Bund	An embankment.
Cha(i)	Tea.
Chapatti	A common type of Indian bread made by wholemeal flour mixed with water between the hands; from *Chapat*, the palm of the hands with fingers extended.
Chota hazri	('a little thing brought into the presence') Toast and/or fruit and a cup of tea brought to someone when they are woken up.
Coolie	A labourer who does any kind of hard manual work.
Chaddar	A sheet.
Cummerbund	A waistband, sash.
Dafadar	An Indian officer in a cavalry regiment.
Dakh	Post, mail, staging place.

Faqir	A Muslim holy man living on begging.
Gaddi	A type of chair adorned with gold and with an elaborate silk cushion, equivalent of throne.
Garm	Warm.
Ghi	Clarified butter.
Guru	A religious teacher.
Hammal	Someone who carries a load, a labourer.
Huzur	Your majesty.
Jami masjid	Friday mosque.
Jube	A small channel carrying a steam of clear water on each side of a street for drinking or washing.
Khiabin	A street.
Kukri	A short, curved Gurkha sword.
Lekin	But.
Mahout	An elephant driver.
Maulvi	Literally a man learned in Persian and Arabic, who claims to have a standing in Islam.
Mohur	An Indian gold coin.
Mujtahid	A Muslim spiritual director, a great theologian, a purist.
Munshi	A teacher, a man who does work requiring literacy.
Namaskar	A respectful salutation made by putting the hands together in front of your face and bowing.
Pakka/Pukka	Cooked, boiled; referring to bricks it means made in a kiln not just sun dried; it also means just as about perfect as anything can be or applied to first-class, senior, well bred people.
Pan	Betel nut.
Pani	Water.
Peepul	Bo tree or holy tree, a type of fig.
Sadhu	A holy Hindu beggar
Syce	A groom.
Suk	A bazaar.
Tandoor	A clay-lined originally underground oven on which bread, meat etc. is cooked by applying to the sides.
Tiffin	Lunch.

Wal(l)a(h)	A person (owning or doing what is mentioned before this word).
Yogi	A Hindu religious person usually inspired or possessed in some way.
Zamindar	Landowner.
Zenana	Women's quarters, harem.